Dream in Shakespeare

Dream in Shakespeare

From Metaphor to Metamorphosis

Marjorie Garber

With a New Prologue by the Author

Yale UNIVERSITY PRESS

New Haven & London

Yale University Press books may be purchased in
quantity for educational, business, or promotional
use. For information, please e-mail
sales.press@yale.edu (U.S. office) or
sales@yaleup.co.uk (U.K. office).

Designed by Sally Sullivan
and set in Baskerville type.
Printed in the United States of America.

Library of Congress Control Number: 2013932810
ISBN 978-0-300-19543-9 (pbk.)
A catalogue record for this book is available
from the British Library.

10 9 8 7 6 5 4 3 2 1

To Allen and Rhoda Garber

Contents

Prologue:
In a Nutshell

"I could be bounded in a nutshell," declares Hamlet to Rosencrantz and Guildenstern, "and count myself a king of infinite space — were it not that I have bad dreams" (II.ii.254–56). The "bad dreams," a fair enough description of his actual experience in the Danish court, are also a Renaissance symptom of melancholy. But what of the nutshell?

Nutshells were small, worthless, and fragile, proverbially the opposite of something of value (later sources often mention it hyperbolically in wagers — "a Noble to a nutshell," "the World to a nutshell," "don't stake your life against a nutshell" — though it's always possible that some of these references are actually back-formations from *Hamlet*).[1] Yet if we recall that Rosencrantz and Guildenstern are Hamlet's "schoolfellows" (III.iv.204) and that he is almost manically on the qui vive when he meets with them, we might also suspect a second meaning to the nutshell in the form of a learned joke, whether the joke is intended to be shared with them, to go over their heads, or to be Shakespeare's joke on, or with, Hamlet.

The passage in question is from Pliny's *Natural History,* as rendered into English by the Elizabethan translator Philemon Holland in 1601:

> We find in Histories, almost incredible Examples of Sharpness of the Eyes. Cicero hath recorded, that the Poem of

1. "A Noble to a nutshell": Henry Parrot, *Mastive* (1615); "the World to a Nutshell: Sir Roger L'Estrange, An Answer to . . . a Dissenter (1687); "don't stake your life against a nutshell": Jeremy Collier, *Essays upon Several Moral Subjects* (1702–3). All cited in *OED,* nutshell, 2a.

Homer called the Iliad, written on Parchment, was enclosed
within a Nutshell.[2]

The parchment epic described here is a mise en abyme, an object
receding into the distance, seen by someone, sometime, somewhere, but not by the current chronicler (Pliny) or the reader.
Nonetheless, it had what we might call shelf life. If no one could
verify it, still many quoted the story, and quoted it, indeed, in a
shorthand that seemed to suggest a common reference point.
Stephen Gosson, dedicating his slender antitheatrical pamphlet
The School of Abuse (1579) to Sir Philip Sidney, used the nutshell
Iliad as an example of value in small things: "The whole worlde is
drawen in a mappe; Homers Iliades in a nutte shell: a kinges
picture in a pennye."[3] By Jonathan Swift's time the story was so
familiar that Swift could use it to ridicule the habits of modern
readers: "I have sometimes heard of an *Iliad* in a nutshell; but it
hath been my fortune to have much oftener seen a nutshell in an
Iliad," he wrote in *A Tale of a Tub*.[4] But what is it doing in *Hamlet*—
if, indeed, it is there?

Bear in mind that Homer's *Iliad*, or certain events from it, are
very much on Hamlet's mind at this point in the play. The "Pyr-
rhus" speech he urges the First Player to perform (lines 446–94
in the same scene) and his lines on "Hecuba" in the "rogue and
peasant slave" soliloquy (lines 552–56 at the end of the same
scene) are reflections on events in the *Iliad* in which a son properly avenges a murdered father and a wife properly laments the
death of a husband. Hamlet castigates himself for being, instead
of a man of action, a "John-a-dreams" (563). To be "bounded in
a nutshell" (or "enclosed within a Nutshell") is not, in other
words, merely to have a small, cramped place in the world rather

2. Pliny, *Natural History in Thirty-Seven Books,* trans. Philemon Holland (London: George Barclay, 1847–48), printed for the Wernerian Club, p. 305 (Pliny,
Natural History 7.85). The Latin reads "Oculorum acies vel maxime fidem exce-
dentia invenit exempla. in nuce inclusam Iliadem Homeri carmen in membrana
scriptum tradit Cicero."

3. Stephen Gosson, *The School of Abuse, Containing a Pleasant Invective Against Poets,
Pipers, Players, Jesters, etc.* (1579; reprint, London: Shakespeare Society, 1841).

4. Jonathan Swift, *A Tale of a Tub* (1704), in Swift, *Gulliver's Travels and Other
Writings,* ed. Louis A. Landa (Boston: Houghton Mifflin, 1960), p. 317.

than to be "king of infinite space," but also to be encapsulated in the dream-theater of the *Iliad*.

If this seems fanciful — and why should it not? — consider that other dream-merchant-in-a-nutshell, Mercutio's Queen Mab. Mab's chariot is "an empty hazelnut," and in it she gallops

> Through lovers' brains, and then they dream of love;
> O'er courtiers' knees, that dream on curtsies straight;
> O'er lawyers' fingers, who straight dream on fees;
> O'er ladies' lips, who straight on kisses dream,
>
> [*Romeo and Juliet* I.iv.59, 71–74]

and over the noses of parsons and the necks of soldiers, who dream, in consequence, about benefices and battles. Mab, like the *Iliad* of Pliny (or perhaps we should say the *Iliad* of Cicero), is so tiny that to see her would require "incredible . . . Sharpness of the Eyes." But she is the spirit of dream and wish fulfillment, with the mischievousness of a Puck, the instincts of a psychoanalyst, and the creativity of a theater director.

When *Dream in Shakespeare* was first published, in 1974, I had no premonition of how much its themes and ideas would inform the rest of my career. But now it seems as if dreams, ghosts, fantasies, conflated images, and notions of wish fulfillment have haunted almost everything I've written, whether the topic is ghosts and ghost writers in Shakespeare, cross-dressing and cultural anxiety, dog love, or sex and real estate. Dreams, dreamers, and dream worlds have caught my attention and my imagination not only in literary texts but also in cultural performances, politics, and public affairs — and in the lecture hall and the classroom. As I wrote in a recent essay on the future of the humanities, "I began my own scholarly and theoretical work on Shakespeare with a book on dreams and then a book on ghosts. The logic behind both of these books was the logic of the 'after/before,' the untimely appearance, or reappearance, of something that never seems to be fully present, but always returns. The humanities is such a dream, and such a ghost."[5]

5. Marjorie Garber, "After the Humanities," in *Loaded Words* (New York: Fordham University Press, 2012).

In the years since the book's initial publication there has been a good deal of attention to sleep and dream in the early modern period from a variety of critical perspectives, including literary theory, material culture, studies of affect and emotion, cognition, and theater history. "Sleep and waking" constituted one of the six "non-naturals" of Galenic medicine (the others are food, air, motion and rest, evacuation and repletion, and the passions of the soul), and healthy — or unhealthful — dreams were therefore a matter of common interest in the early modern period. An exhibition at the Folger Shakespeare Library in 2009, entitled "To Sleep, Perchance to Dream," offered evidence about the belief, rituals, and habits of sleepers and the role of dream interpreters and interpretations in public life through a display of printed, handwritten, and visual materials from Renaissance England. In effect a whole field of inquiry has developed around questions of sleep, dream, cognition, imagination, fantasy specters, and phantasms. Neuroscientists, psychologists, and literary scholars are asking questions that not only are uncannily similar but also draw upon a common vocabulary and sometimes upon shared research. I have been intrigued by these developments, and by the ways in which such disparate fields in the humanities, the sciences, and the social sciences have converged to address the riddle of the unconscious and its ties to the creative imagination. But I am even more energized by what a focus on dreams and ghosts has done for our understanding of theater.

That the theater might itself be a dream-space, "the other scene" of what is sometimes taken for reality, has been enormously generative for modern directors, actors, and scholars, from Edward Gordon Craig, Konstantin Stanislavski, and Antonin Artaud to the present day. Craig and Stanislavski, collaborating on the Moscow Arts Theater production of *Hamlet* in 1912, imagined the play as Hamlet's dream, the protagonist recumbent at the front of the stage.[6] The staging of ghosts and spirits in the tragedies was for Craig the key to meaning and

6. Christopher Innes, *Edward Gordon Craig,* Directors in Perspective (Cambridge: Cambridge University Press, 1983), p. 152.

interpretation: "The fact of their presence precludes a realistic treatment of the tragedies in which they appear. Shakespeare has made them the centre of his vast dreams, and the central point of a dream, as of a circular geometric figure, controls and conditions every hair's breadth of the circumference." The Ghost in *Hamlet* and the visions in *Macbeth* were for Craig the touchstones of a truer reality: "The imaginative, that is the real in art," he contended, "and in no modern play do we see the truth of this so tremendously revealed as in *Macbeth*."[7]

For Antonin Artaud, another strong proponent of what we might call dream theater, Shakespeare was, likewise, a precursor of modernity. Convinced of "the profound poetic bearing of both dreams and theater," Artaud wanted to make the theater of the future "a kind of total creation in which man must reassume his place between dream and events."[8] Like Craig, he saw the wish-fulfillment aspect of the dream as crucial to the revival of an art form, though for him the wish was often a version of nightmare.

Although Artaud has had his greatest influence on modern theater as a theorist, he was able — as Susan Sontag notes — to produce "the two great 'dream plays' by Calderón and Strindberg (*Life Is a Dream* and *A Dream Play*)."[9] He also hoped to direct productions of Euripides's *The Bacchae,* Seneca's *Thyestes,* and Shakespeare's *Macbeth, Richard II,* and *Titus Andronicus.* The selection of Shakespeare plays is instructive: all three are plays in which the protagonist becomes estranged from himself, and in which a phantasmagoric world opens up on the stage as the visual and dramatic counterpart of an inner psychological and emotional condition.

"The theater, like dreams, is bloody and inhuman," Artaud

7. Edward Gordon Craig, "On the Ghosts in the Tragedies of Shakespeare" (1908), in *Craig on Theatre,* ed. J. Michael Walton (London: Methuen, 1983), pp. 169, 176.

8. Antonin Artaud, "The Theater of Cruelty" (First Manifesto), in *The Theater and Its Double,* trans. Mary Caroline Richards (New York: Grove Press, 1958), p. 93.

9. Susan Sontag, "Artaud," in *Antonin Artaud: Selected Writings,* ed. Susan Sontag (Berkeley: University of California Press, 1976), xliii.

wrote in his First Manifesto, "The Theater of Cruelty" (1932): "The theater will never find itself again, except by furnishing the spectator with the truthful precipitates of dreams, in which his taste for crime, his erotic obsessions, his savagery, his chimeras, his utopian sense of life and matter, even his cannibalism, pour out, on a level not counterfeit or illusory, but interior."[10] Artaud's list of topics for a future theater (crime, erotic obsessions, savagery, chimeras, cannibalism) matches eerily well with the language and action of Shakespearean tragedy, from *Titus Andronicus* through *King Lear, Timon of Athens,* and *Coriolanus.*

Almost a century later, this vision of theater (and, indeed, of film) has become so familiar we sometimes take it for granted. Present-day Shakespeare productions are very likely to include dream sequences, fantasies, moments when the action seems to take place not only *in* the audience but also, increasingly, *by* the audience, breaching the boundaries of actor and action. In this context the arguments of *Dream in Shakespeare* seem pertinent to a contemporary understanding of theatricality and practice — and also, crucially, to an understanding of the functioning of the imagination.

The interpretation of dreams goes very far back in human history. Ideas about the centrality and importance of dreams persisted through to the Renaissance and the time of Shakespeare. Dreams could be omens or portents; they could be caused by bodily sensations (heat, cold, an upset stomach), or they could be divinely inspired. Dreams could reflect the present or the past, or they could predict the future. They could be signs of guilt or of a guilty conscience, or they could be caused by demons or bewitchment. It's notable that every one of these types of dreams and dream interpretations shows up somewhere in Shakespeare's plays.

Some dream symbols were thought to have specific meanings: if a man dreams that he is big with child, his dream signifies wealth, gain, and profit. If an unmarried woman dreams she has a beard, it means she will be "speedily matched to her content."

10. Antonin Artaud, "The Theater of Cruelty" (First Manifesto), p. 92.

To dream you see apple trees or eat apples is a sign of joy and pleasure; to dream of seeing or eating oranges signifies wounds, grief, and vexation (talk about comparing apples and oranges!). On the other hand, some Renaissance dream theorists insisted that "the Rules of Dreaming are not general"—rather, "they admit of various interpretations," depending upon the person and the circumstances.[11] And here, of course, is where Shakespeare comes in, together with his onstage and offstage audiences, then and now. Dreams in Shakespeare show us something about the dreamer, and something about the audience, and something about the larger meaning and patterns of the play.

The unconscious, wrote Sigmund Freud, was *ein andere Schauplatz*, another locale, showplace, stage, or theater—or, as the phrase was translated and adapted by Jacques Lacan, "another" —or sometimes "*the* other"—"scene."[12] The dream-space *is* a theater space, as many later directors, playwrights, and philosophers have suggested: an alternative world of imagination, possibility, fantasy, threat, and desire.

As he developed his own theory about the interpretation of

11. "If a Man Dreams he is big with child," "If a Mayd Dreams shes hath a Beard," "To dream. You . . . eat sweet Apples," "To dream that one sees or eats Oranges," and "The Rules of dreaming are not general," from Marc de Vulson, *The Court of Curiosities*, cited in *To Sleep, Perchance to Dream: A Commonplace Book,* ed. Carole Levin and Garrett Sullivan (Washington: Folger Shakespeare Library, 2009), pp. 63, 66, 69.

12. Jacques Lacan, "On a Question Preliminary to Any Possible Treatment of Psychosis," in *Écrits: A Selection,* trans. Alan Sheridan (New York: Norton, 1977), p. 193; "The Direction of the Treatment and the Principles of Its Power," in *Écrits,* p. 264; "The Signification of the Phallus," in *Écrits,* p. 285. The reference in the "Signification" essay is the most frequently cited: " . . . that other scene (*ein andere Schauplatz*), that Freud, on the subject of dreams, designates as being that of the unconscious. . . ." Lacan's uses of the definite and indefinite article vary: in the first of these essays, "On a Question . . . of Psychosis," he says "ein andere Schauplatz, another scene" (p. 193); in "The Direction of Treatment," he says "the other scene, ein andere Schauplatz" (p. 193), and in "The Signification of the Phallus," he says "cette autre scène," that is, "that" other scene to which Freud refers (p. 285). According to Lacan the phrase *ein andere Schauplatz* appears some twenty times in Freud's works. My thanks to Jane Gallop for her help in tracking down these variants in the French edition.

dreams, Freud returned repeatedly to Shakespeare. In his land-
mark work of 1900 and its subsequent updated editions Freud
mentions not only *Hamlet,* as we might expect, but also *Henry IV,
Part 1; Henry VI, Part 3; Julius Caesar; A Midsummer Night's Dream;
Othello;* and *Timon of Athens.* Elsewhere in his writing he will comment with great insight on *Richard III* and *Macbeth,* both of them
also Shakespearean "dream plays." To give some sense of how in-
strumental Shakespeare was to Freud's thinking, here is a brief
example. Freud is analyzing a patient's dream about encountering lions in a desert, and the fact that in her dream the dreamer
did not fear the lions. After a long interpretation of the dream's
details, Freud closes with this observation: "So this lion was like
the lion in *A Midsummer Night's Dream* that concealed the figure
of Snug the joiner; and the same is true of all dream-lions of
which the dreamer is not afraid."[13] Shakespeare, and indeed, in
this case, a comically ineffectual play-within-a-play in Shakespeare, becomes the proof-text for psychic truth.

The unconscious in Freud's conception of it was also a "psychical locality,"[14] a phrase that closely resembles Theseus's description of the work of the poet:

> as imagination bodies forth
> The forms of things unknown, the poet's pen
> Turns them to shapes, and gives to airy nothing
> A local habitation and a name.
>
> [*MND* V.i.14–17]

To gauge the power of "airy nothing" here we might think not
only of the spirits in *A Midsummer Night's Dream* but also of Macbeth's "dagger of the mind" (II.1.33), later discounted by his

13. Sigmund Freud, *The Interpretation of Dreams,* in *The Standard Edition of the
Complete Psychological Works of Sigmund Freud* (London: The Hogarth Press and the
Institute of Psycho-Analysis, 1986), vol. 5, p. 462.

14. By "psychical locality," as he was careful to explain, Freud did not mean an
anatomical location in the brain, but rather something more like the focusing
mechanism on a microscope, a telescope, or a camera: "psychical locality will
correspond to a point inside the apparatus at which one of the preliminary stages
of an image comes into being." *Interpretation of Dreams,* vol. 5, p. 536.

wife as merely an "air-drawn dagger" (II.i.33, III.iv.61); or of the "unreal mock'ry" of the bloody ghost of Banquo (III.iv.106); or of Hamlet's conversation with Gertrude in her closet:

Queen:	Alas, how is't with you
	That you do bend your eye on vacancy,
	And with the incorporal air do hold discourse? ...
	To whom do you speak this?
Hamlet:	Do you see nothing there?
Queen:	Nothing at all: yet all that is I see.
Hamlet:	Nor did you nothing hear?
Queen:	No, nothing but ourselves.

[III.iv.116–18, 131–35]

When a stage direction in *The Tempest* says "Enter Ariel invisible," or when Oberon declares, "I am invisible, / And I will overhear their conference" (*MND* II.i.186–87), the audience may be reminded that visibility and invisibility, airy nothings and local habitations, are not so much in the eye of the beholder as they are in the provision of the playwright.

The subtitle of *Dream in Shakespeare* is "From Metaphor to Metamorphosis," and the trajectory from a dream as a kind of mental or dramatic figure of speech to a dream as the equivalent of the play itself is one of the things that makes dreams in Shakespeare so resonant and so moving. In plays like *A Midsummer Night's Dream,* which has "dream" in its title, or *Macbeth,* framed by witches and visions, or *The Winter's Tale,* with its emblematic "statue" scene in which a work of art comes alive, the relation of metaphor to metamorphosis becomes powerfully clear. Psychological insight and theatrical event combine to produce an effect we recognize as uniquely "Shakespearean." These are plays about fantasy and fear and desire and wish fulfillment. In them dream is sometimes adjacent to terror, as metaphors come to life and take over the stage. Theseus's dismissive line about imagination in *A Midsummer Night's Dream,* "Or in the night, imagining some fear, / How easy is a bush suppos'd a bear!" (V.i.21–22), is succeeded some years later by the nightmare appearance of the bear on the seacoast of Bohemia in *The Winter's Tale:*

> *Shepherd:* Name of mercy, when was this, boy?
>   *Clown:* Now, now: I have not winked since I saw these
>   sights: the men are not yet cold under water, nor
>   the bear half-dined on the gentleman: he's at it now.
>
>   [III.iii.102–5]

What Shakespeare achieves in his dream plays—which is to say, virtually *all* of his plays, from the early comedies and histories to the late romances—is nothing short of a profound reversal of categories. Dream, whether to Christopher Sly, to George, Duke of Clarence, to Bottom, to Brabantio, to Sebastian, to Lear, to Cleopatra, to Pericles, to Leontes, not only *portends* reality, it *becomes* reality. Not only did this perception change the plays and the characters—it changed drama and performance. It changed the history, and the theory, and the practice, of theater.

Today we often use the phrase "only a dream," as if a dream were minor or unattainable. But actors know the power of acting, and playwrights know the power of drama, and audiences, spellbound, know the intoxication that comes with performance. This is why we come to the theater; it is why we give ourselves over to the power of Shakespeare, his words, his scenes, his characters. Shakespeare scripts us, and he scripted, too, the actor's apologia, in the voice of Puck at the end of *A Midsummer Night's Dream:*

> If we shadows have offended
> Think but this and all is mended,
> That you have but slumbered here
> While these visions did appear.
> And this weak and idle theme,
> No more yielding than a dream.
>
>   [V.i.409–14]

Modern politicians are no match for Puck when it comes to the non-apology apology. If the play offended us, we need only think that we were sleeping and dreaming. The play we were watching was just a dream, he says. And winks at us, knowing that we know better.

Borrowed Robes:
An Introduction

Concepts of dream and the dream world in the English Renaissance derived from a number of significant sources: the literature and philosophy of classical Greece and Rome, the native heritage of English folklore, and the medieval tradition of the dream vision, which came to its culmination in England with the works of Chaucer. Shakespeare drew upon this extensive body of material selectively, transforming and refining structural devices to accord with his larger poetic purposes. It is difficult to say with assurance that he made use of the work of any particular author or school, because of the paucity of biographical information and the universal nature of the dream experience. What we can do, however, is to take note of the general context of belief within which he was working and to point out those similarities with previous theory and practice which seem most striking. For by briefly examining the materials of contemporary dream thought, we can better comprehend the singularity of Shakespeare's contribution; acknowledging those insights possessed by his predecessors, we may perhaps approach with a clearer understanding the remarkable nature of his own transfiguring use of dream.

Dreams in the works of early classical authors tended to be either objective and monitory or symbolic and allegorical, thus predicting by direct or indirect means the course of future action. Homeric dreams are largely of the former type and center about a dream figure in the form of a god, a ghost, a special heavenly messenger, or a human being, living or dead. In this way, for example, the ghost of Patroclus appears to Achilles and incites him to revenge (*Iliad* XXIII.62–107). Objective dreams of this sort appear with frequency not only in the epics [1] but also in the works of the Greek dramatists.[2] Their primary function is clearly that of plot development, and for that reason they are always direct in their instructions, never gnomic or metaphorical. Similar figures are present in several of Shakespeare's plays, from the accusatory apparitions of *Richard III* through the ghosts of Caesar, old Hamlet, and Banquo; all of these are in the revenge tradition and derive therefore not only from Patroclus, the first revenge figure of Greek literary tradition, but also from the intervening dramatic conventions of Senecan tragedy. The most frequent dream figure in Homer, the descended god, appears transmuted both in the ceremonial masque figure of Hymen at the close of *As You Like It* and in the Olympian deities of the four last plays, where the relative primitivism of the monitory device is well suited to the deliberately "artificial" or nonnaturalistic dramatic context. The *Macbeth* witches, though clearly prophetic figures, are variants of this tradition; they speak in purposeful ambiguities rather than in open warning or prediction, and their riddling prophecies, in part echoing Macbeth's self-delusive consciousness, are more closely related to symbolic than to direct or objective dream.

The tradition of symbolic dream, which likewise has its roots in Greek epic and dramatic practice, is part of a larger realm of gnomic prediction which also includes riddles and oracles. The stress placed upon ambiguity of language and image links this kind of dreaming, and its interpretation, to an abiding concept of poetry and dream as repositories of secret wisdom. There is only one symbolic dream in Homer, Penelope's dream of the geese and the eagle (*Odyssey* XIX.509–81), but symbolic dreams are found with even greater frequency than are direct dreams in the works of the Greek and Latin dramatists,[3] and

1. E.g. *Iliad* II.4ff.; *Odyssey* IV.787–841, VI.13–51.
2. E.g. Aeschylus *Persae* 176–99; Sophocles *Electra* 417–25; Euripides *Hecuba* 1–52.
3. John Barker Stearns, *Studies of the Dream as a Technical Device in Latin Epic and Drama* (Ph.D. diss., Princeton University, 1924; Lancaster Pa.: Lancaster Press, 1927), p. 36.

appear in great numbers in Herodotus's *Histories* [4] and in
Virgil and other Latin authors.[5] Shakespeare's use of this device places a primary emphasis on the potential ambiguity of
interpretation: the symbolic dreams of Clarence and Calpurnia, for example, contain true predictions which are misunderstood by their interpreters, in the first case through
error, and in the second, through guile. As in the case of the
witches in *Macbeth*, a proper understanding of the dream's
hidden meaning thus becomes an index of self-knowledge;
symbolic dreams in the plays are therefore closely related to
character development at the same time that they often contain
clusters of images which have an important bearing on language and action.

Shakespearean dreams are always "true," when properly interpreted, since they reflect a state of affairs which is as much
internal and psychological as it is external. The warning behind Homer's famous simile of the gates of horn and ivory, the
one gate issuing true dreams, the other, false (*Odyssey*
XIX.56off.),[6] thus becomes subjective in Shakespeare and has
reference to the subconscious state of mind of the dreamer
rather than to supernatural dream origins. The only false
dreams in his plays are not really dreams at all, but rather
inventions on the part of characters bent on manipulating
others, as in the case of the prophecy about "G" in *Richard III*,
or in Iago's narration of "Cassio's dream." These fictitious
dreams, likewise, have precedents in classical literature, both in
epic and in drama, where they are basically used to bring
about a certain course of action.[7] Shakespeare, in adapting
the device to his own purposes, extends and transforms it by relating the supposed dream to the psychological nature of both

4. E.g. VII.16, the dream of Xerxes.
5. E.g. *Aeneid* IV.465, Dido's dream; Valerius Flaccus *Argonautica*
VII.141–46; Silius Italicus *Punica* III.168–82; Statius *Thebaid* IX.570–84. Cf.
Stearns, *Studies of the Dream*, pp. 31–43.
6. Cf. also *Aeneid* VI.893–96; Plato *Charmides* 173a; Horace *Odes*
III.27, 41ff.; and other classical echoes of this popular figure.
7. E.g., *Aeneid* V.636–40; Plautus *Mostellaria* 486–505; *Miles gloriosus*
380–95.

its inventor and its hearer, so that it contains paradoxical "truths" of a wider significance for the play as a whole.

Perhaps more influential than any of these specific dream devices, however, is the interest shown by classical writers in the existence of a dream world, or at least a country and dewlling place of dreams. Descriptions of such places are included in the *Odyssey* (XXII.11–14), the *Aeneid* (VI.273), and the *Metamorphoses* of Ovid (XI.592–593) and are in each case directly connected with the idea of a journey. The journeys in both the *Odyssey* and the *Aeneid* are to the underworld, where the voyager converses with shades of the dead. Here the dreamer, reversing the pattern of the monitory apparition, has come to the dream figures, and enters for a moment the transforming world of dream, from which he will return greatly changed. The Ovidian instance is equally interesting: Iris enters the cave of Sleep to fetch a dream which will perform the metamorphosis of Alcyone. The Shakespearean pattern of the journey to the dream world follows the same triple movement, and its object, likewise, is regeneration. On balance it is this broader pattern which is for Shakespeare the most important heritage of classical literature: the intuition of the relation of dream to metamorphosis and transformation. The dream devices themselves tend in this direction, taking the dreamer momentarily out of time and leading him toward a moment of supernatural enlightenment, an accession of knowledge which is frequently self-knowledge. The pattern of the journey, so consistently related to the borderland of dream and the dream figure, is a larger structural form in which the same transformation occurs; the individual dream is transmuted by means of metaphor into an enduring dream state, the subjective condition of man in the world of dream. Increasingly, as Shakespeare's use of dream matures and develops with his art, this larger pattern is the one to which he most frequently returns.

Literary analogues to dream in the plays of Shakespeare are paralleled in importance by a developing line of psychological inquiry which had, by this time, anticipated a number of aspects of modern dream theory. The principal transmitter of these insights was the second-century (A.D.) dream theorist Artemidorus of Daldis; however, several earlier thinkers also displayed a surprising understanding of the processes of dream.

Plato's attitude toward dream is conditioned by the initial recognition, fundamental to Shakespeare's own dream world, of the antinomy of dream and reason. In the *Republic* (572) he cautions against "the wild beast within us," which may leave us "the sport of fantastic and lawless visions," and suggests as a remedy the retention of reason even in sleep. In thus significantly noting the power of the irrational over the subconscious mind, he describes a mode of dream activity which most closely resembles the anarchic designs of Caliban or the nightmare opening scene of *Othello*. Elsewhere, however, Plato acknowledges a positive element in dreaming, the potential acquisition of higher knowledge. The *Timaeus* (244–57, 265) speaks of the soul's accession of wisdom in a condition of divine madness allied to prophecy, and this was popularly taken by Neoplatonic dream commentators as evidence for the doctrine of higher knowledge conveyed through dream.[8] The conventional association of dream with madness is explicitly articulated in Shakespeare by Theseus (*MND* V.i.2ff.) and utilized with great dramatic relevance in a number of the plays, among them *Hamlet* and *King Lear*.

The concept of dream as an illuminative experience which leads to new knowledge, often divinely inspired, was countered in the classical period by a polar view attributing dreams to physiological and psychological causes. The effect of this skeptical view, as expressed by Aristotle in the essays *De Somniis* and *De Divinatione per Somnum*, was to depreciate the role of dream in the life of man. Yet in the course of his scientific exploration Aristotle makes the signal observation, basic to later

8. Francis X. Newman, *Somnium: Medieval Theories of Dreaming and the Form of Vision Poetry* (Ph.D. diss., Princeton University, 1963; Ann Arbor, Mich.: University Microfilms, 1963), pp. 6off.

Freudian analysis, that the hallucinations of the insane, the illusions of the waking, and the fantasies of dreams all share a common origin.[9] The world of dream was thus acknowledged to be considerably broader in scope than the nocturnal dream itself. This insight is of considerable importance to our investigation, because the part played by waking illusions in Shakespeare's plays is as great or greater than that played by literal dreams: it is the waking illusion, in fact, that provides the most salient test of the criteria of "reality"; and the exchange of the states of reality and illusion becomes in the plays the first transforming act of dream.

By far the most important single work in pre-Freudian dream analysis, however, was the *Oneirocritica* of Artemidorus of Daldis, a volume at once theoretical and practical and the model of the dream books which were to enjoy such popularity in sixteenth-century England. Artemidorus based his method upon the principle of association, a principle which dream interpretation shares with sympathetic magic and the occult. Association is also, manifestly, the fundamental principle of Freudian dream analysis, though with a critical difference noted by Freud himself: [10] Artemidorus concentrated his attention on the associations of the *interpreter,* whereas Freud was concerned with the associations in the mind of the *dreamer.* Shakespeare uses both methods in casting the symbolism of his dreams; the language of symbols in Clarence's dream or in Macbeth's vision of the dagger, for example, is particularly appropriate for the condition and state of mind of the dreamer and reflects the dreamer's own thoughts as elsewhere manifested in the play. In many cases, however, the dream possesses an extended metaphorical meaning in addition to a literal and specific one, and this extended meaning is often perceptible to the audience and not to the dreamer. Thus Hermia's dream of the serpent in *A Midsummer Night's*

9. *De Somniis* 458b 25–29; 460b 3–18.
10. Sigmund Freud, *The Interpretation of Dreams,* trans. and ed. James Strachey (Standard Edition, London: The Hogarth Press and the Institution of Psycho-analysis, 1953; rpt., New York, 1965), chap. 2, p. 130.

Dream functions locally in the plot as an intuition of bodily harm, but communicates at the same time a sense of the dark and irrational nature of dream vital to an understanding of the forest experience. This potential multiplicity in meaning is central to Shakespeare's use of dream in the plays and contributes to his enrichment and development of the dream form.

Artemidorus places particular stress on the ambiguity of individual dream symbols: they may mean one of a number of things, dependent upon the circumstances of the dream's occurence and the relation of its contents to the dreamer's life, occupation, and name. The dream itself thus could be given no objective interpretation, but was rather a subjective construct which took on specific significance when applied to the dreamer. This theory controverted earlier assumptions about inherently good or evil dreams: the moral content of the dream now became a function of interpretation. Perhaps the clearest example of a parallel insight in Shakespeare is the prophetic dream of Calpurnia, which predicts the assassination of Caesar; the deliberate misinterpretation given it by Decius Brutus reverses the apparent meaning and thus paradoxically contributes to its fulfillment.

Of the many contributions of Artemidorus, however, the most interesting from our point of view is the emphasis he placed on the relationship of puns and wordplay to dream interpretation. He records a dream experience of Alexander the Great which nicely exhibits the importance of language to dream. According to his account, Alexander became uneasy at his lack of success in the continuing seige of Tyre, and dreamt one night of a satyr dancing on his shield. The interpreter deciphered this dream by taking the Greek word for satyr, *satyros,* and dividing it into two parts, *sa Tyros,* "Tyre is thine." [11] Verbal ambiguity here becomes the point of transference between what Freud called the manifest dream content (*satyros*) and the latent dream thoughts (*sa Tyros*) which lie behind it. The pun is a kind of dream condensation, contain-

11. Ibid., chap. 2, p. 131*n*.

ing at once a literal and a metaphorical or hidden meaning. In Shakespearean dream utterances the same enriching ambiguity obtains: when Bottom says "Man is but an ass, if he go about to expound this dream" (*MND* IV.ii.207–08), the play on "ass" functions to remind the audience that the dream world brings together reality and illusion in language as well as in action. The language of dream in Shakespeare is the essential fabric of the dream state; it is the paradigm of all transformation, and transformation is at the heart of dream.

This conclusion was far beyond Artemidorus; he looked upon dreams as passive objects of scrutiny, capable of decipherment with the help of a chart of dream symbols. The idea of *creating* a dream, or of the Jungian association of dream and poetry, was completely outside the range of his thought. The importance of the *Oneirocritica,* as of the other examples of early dream theory, lies, once again, not in any conjectural influence it may have exerted upon Shakespeare, but rather in its availability to thinkers and writers of his age. Such ideas were in the air, and it is well to take note of them; they suggest an intellectual climate, but they do no more.

The remarkable degree to which dream lore and interpretation captured the popular mind in the sixteenth century is suggested by the great number of editions of Artemidorus which appeared throughout Europe in that period. A Greek edition was printed at Venice in 1518, a Latin edition at Basel in 1539, and a French edition at Lyons in 1546. The English version, which did not appear until 1644, had gone through a surprising twenty-four editions by 1740. Other dream books also enjoyed a considerable popularity: the anonymous Latin *Dream Book of Daniel,* for example, first appeared in Venice at the beginning of the century and was printed in English in 1542. Like others of its type it concentrated upon the distinction between divine and demonic dreams, for just as Hamlet doubts for a moment the origin of the ghost (*Ham.* II.ii.605–10), and Antigonus is reluctant to believe in the existence of walking spirits (*WT* III.iii.15–16), so Christian dream interpreters—and particularly those who espoused the Protestant view—were at this time preoccupied with the possibility of a devilish impersonation of the divine. The proliferation of dream lore was equally great among the less educated; coarsely printed chapbooks with such gaudy titles as *The Old Egyptian Fortune-Teller's Last Legacy, The Golden Dreamer,* and *A Groatsworth of Wit for a Penny* circulated widely throughout the period.[12]

The enthusiasm of English readers was in part an outgrowth of a great medieval interest in dream, which manifested itself in both popular and learned forms— in the evolution of native folk traditions and in the development of a poetry of dream. The folk calendar included a number of seasonal holidays whose central rite was the active seeking of prophetic dreams: Saint Agnes' Eve, Halloween, All Saints' Night, and particularly Midsummer Eve, which by Shakespeare's time had also become popularly associated with the delusive "midsummer madness." It is out of this native tradition that the singular figures of Puck, Queen Mab, and Ariel emerge as inhabitants of Shakespearean dream worlds. Significantly, both Puck and Mab have undergone a number of changes at Shakespeare's hand. Puck, under the name of Robin Goodfellow, was popularly imagined to be the national practical joker, responsible for domestic upsets and inexplicable pranks; only with *A Midsummer Night's Dream* does he begin to be considered a fairy and a resident of a special fairy world.[13] Likewise, Queen Mab, prior to her appearance in Mercutio's narrative, was associated with local superstition and such homely activities as the theft of dairy produce;[14] Mercutio himself acknowledges that for all her fanciful attributes she remains "that very Mab / That plats the manes of horses in the night" (*Rom.* I.iv.88–89). Ariel, who is a more complex figure, nonetheless has in him elements of Puck and, as Frank Kermode has observed, "often behaves

12. Norman MacKenzie, *Dreams and Dreaming* (New York: Vanguard Press, 1965), pp. 53, 75f.

13. Minor White Latham, *The Elizabethan Fairies* (New York: Columbia University Press, 1930), pp. 219–62.

14. Ibid., p. 117.

like an English fairy." [15] Neither Puck nor Mab is considered
diminutive in size until their appearance in Shakespeare, nor,
indeed, were many native English fairies so considered prior to
that time.[16]

The transformation of these folk fairies into their Shakespearean couterparts is of interest because it is related to a
motif we have already noted in Greek and Latin literature,
that of the journey to the dream world. The dream world for
Shakespeare is a place of metamorphosis, of transfiguration
and renewal; moreover, as is consonant with the usual idea of
dream, it functions below the level of consciousness, in the
realm of the imagination. When this concept is adumbrated
in *Romeo and Juliet,* the picture Shakespeare gives of Queen
Mab in action is one that skillfully combines invisibility, seemingly irrational phenomena, and a prankishness which is often
mischievous and occasionally sharpens toward the malign.
These same elements are present in the much more fully developed figure of Puck, whose world is expanded to fill an entire
drama, rather than a brief visionary monologue. When the
dreamers, following the Shakespearean pattern, pass into the
dream world of forest or island—in Mab's case, an early one,
simply the world of sleep—they encounter dream and transformation figures which have been sufficiently removed from
the human analogues of their folk originals to become themselves embodiments, as well as agents, of the transfiguring
world of dream. The raw materials of folk belief, like that of
classical dream thought, is here transformed by the poet so
that it reflects a state of mind.

But medieval experience provided Shakespeare with learned
as well as folk example. The development of superstitious
dream belief and fairy lore was paralleled in England by an extensive intellectual and literary tradition which absorbed the
ideas of the Neoplatonic dream theorists and culminated in the
dream poems of Chaucer, the most significant explorations of

15. *The Tempest,* Arden edition (Cambridge: Harvard University Press,
1964), p. 143.
16. Latham, *Elizabethan Fairies,* pp. 187–92.

dream in English literature before Shakespeare. The principal intellectual precursor of this literary development was the Neoplatonist Macrobius, author of the influential *Commentarius in Somnium Scipionis,* to which Chaucer refers in *The Book of the Duchess* (284), *The Parliament of Fowls* (31ff.), and the *Nun's Priest's Tale* (3123–24). Macrobius attempted to codify dreams and to place them in a hierarchy of values, giving the least emphasis to physiological dreams of the kind explained by Aristotle and the rationalists and reserving his most careful attention for those dreams which led to an access of higher knowledge, either directly or through a figurative and symbolic vision of the future. We may notice the extent to which this Neoplatonic tradition, later continued and expanded in the works of John of Salisbury and Alanus de Insulis, mirrors the speculations of classical writers and philosophers in confronting the question of truth and falsehood in dreams and in dividing fundamental dream forms into the direct and the symbolic. The contemporaneous investigations of the church fathers likewise concentrated upon the so-called higher dream, which conferred special insight; and the greatest religious dream poem of the period, the *Divina Commedia,* is structurally based upon the same threefold pattern of confusion, journey to the dream world, and harmonious regeneration which we noted in the great epics of the Greek and Roman classical period.[17]

The principal literary influence upon Chaucer's dream poetry, however, and the direct source of the vision form in English, is the French tradition of the dream or love vision, most clearly set forward in a poem which Chaucer tells us he had translated, the *Roman de la Rose* of Guillaume de Lorris. Many of the elements of the *Roman*—the god of love, the bemused and often sleepless narrator, the May morning, the garden with its allegorical or mythological inhabitants—recur in Chaucer's own dream poems—*The Book of the Duchess; the Prologue* to *The Legend of Good Women; The Parliament of Fowls;* and *The House of Fame,* which in part parodies and

17. Newman, *Somnium,* p. 74.

comments upon the vision form. Each of these poems presents a dreamer in a state of despair or confusion, who enters the world of dream, usually a garden or field, and is transformed by its agency, till he awakes or emerges from the dream to a renewed sense of harmony with his surroundings. To some extent this is once again the transcendent dream journey so central to the Shakespearean pattern. Similarly, the deliberate naïveté of the Chaucerian narrator is closely related to the condition of many Shakespearean characters in the dream state, a condition in which they undergo experiences without fully understanding them, and speak—like Bottom—wiser than they know. "Thou wost ful lytel what thou wenest" (743), says the Black Knight to the dreamer in *The Book of the Duchess,* but here as in Shakespeare it is precisely through the dreamer's confusion that a richer understanding of the dream experience is communicated to the audience. There are, as well, a few more specific resemblances between the works of the two poets. *The Book of the Duchess* concludes with the naïve narrator attempting to render his experience into rhyme, as Bottom will plan the genesis of "Bottom's Dream" with the help of Peter Quince. Both *The Book of the Duchess* and *The House of Fame* make reference to Ovid's *Metamorphoses,* and specifically to the journey to the cave of Sleep; metamorphosis, here and in the *Prologue* to *The Legend of Good Women,* is directly linked by Chaucer, as by Shakespeare, to the world of dream. *A Midsummer Night's Dream,* which borrows the framing story of Theseus and Hippolyta from Chaucer's *Knight's Tale,* is in its way both of the dream vision tradition and about it, making particular use of such standard elements as the seeking lovers, the May morning, and the mischievous god of love. And the special quality of dream logic, which compresses time and space and seems to make sense of the most improbable occurrences, is accurately and brilliantly portrayed by Chaucer as it is by Shakespeare.

Yet the Chaucerian dreams are each, by reason of their narrative nature, the record of a single consciousness, though an extraordinarily rich and humorous one, and in this they differ widely from the multiplicity of Shakespeare's dramatic technique. The poet whom Coleridge called "our *myriad-minded Shakespeare*" set for himself a different set of problems, and solved them differently, while borrowing with awareness and sensitivity from his predecessors. The "borrowed robes" of classical and native traditions alike sit lightly and gracefully upon him as he explores the rich world of dream and the irrational. Under his shaping hand the body of traditional material becomes itself transmuted and regenerated, as he explores the dream world and its relationship to the imagination, and finally achieves a synthesis of poetry and dream. In Shakespeare's most mature works the rudiments of traditional dream belief are barely discernible, so totally have they been transformed, the robes made "fresher than before." But the early plays are more dependent upon the received tradition, and by turning to them first we can observe the poet working through both dramatic conventions and conventions of belief to achieve his own vision of the world of dream.

I

Apparent Prodigies

Dream and Plot: *Richard III*

The great popularity of the dream as a dramatic device among the Elizabethans is surely due at least in part to its versatility as a mode of presentation. Both structurally and psychologically the prophetic dream was useful to the playwright; it foreshadowed events of plot, providing the audience with needed information, and at the same time it imparted to the world of the play a vivid atmosphere of mystery and foreboding. Thus the Senecan ghost stalked the boards to applause for decades, while the cryptic dumb show, itself a survival of earlier forms, remained as a ghostly harbinger of events to come.

Even in his earliest plays, Shakespeare began to extend and develop these prophetic glimpses, so that they became ways of presenting the process of the mind at work in memory, emotion, and imagination. What was essentially a predictive device of plot thus became, at the same time, a significant aspect of meaning. Dream episodes, in short, began to work within the plays as metaphors for the larger action, functioning at once as a form of presentation and as a concept presented. This is clearly the case with the dramatic action of *Richard III*. From Queen Margaret's curse to Clarence's monitory dream and the haunting nightmare of Bosworth Field, omen and apparition define and delimit the play's world.

The consciousness of dreaming which is to dominate the play throughout makes its first striking appearance in Richard's opening soliloquy:

> Plots have I laid, inductions dangerous,
> By drunken prophecies, libels and dreams,

> To set my brother Clarence and the king
> In deadly hate the one against the other.
>
> [I.i.32–35] *

Dreams here appear in what will become a familiar context for the early plays, clearly analogous to "plots," "prophecies," and "libels" as elements of the malign irrational. Richard has deftly contrived to manipulate circumstance by preying upon the vulnerability of the superstitious king. Encountering his brother Clarence on his way to the Tower, he is told what he already knows: the king, says Clarence,

> harkens after prophecies and dreams,
> And from the crossbow plucks the letter G,
> And says a wizard told him that by G
> His issue disinherited should be;
> And, for my name of George begins with G,
> It follows in his thought that I am he.
>
> [I.i.54–59]

The poetry here halts and stammers, a mirror of the simplicity and confusion which make Clarence such an easy target. He considers himself a reasonable man, and, confronted by unreason, he is both impotent and outraged. Yet such an absolute rejection of the irrational is a fatal misjudgment in the world of *Richard III,* and Clarence's skepticism becomes a means to his destruction, just as later his determined denial of the truth of his own dream will lead directly to his death.

Here, in the first scene of the play, a sharp contrast is already apparent between the poles of dream and reason. Significantly, Richard, the Machiavel, defines himself as a realist, in contrast to the foolish Clarence and the lascivious Edward; he intends to control his fate and the fate of others through an exercise of reason. Yet the very first evidence of his supposed control, the false prophecy of "G," is truer than he knows: not George but Gloucester will disinherit Edward's sons. Clarence's passive

*Citations from the plays are to *The Complete Signet Classic Shakespeare,* Sylvan Barnet, general editor (New York: Harcourt Brace Jovanovich, 1972).

skepticism about the irrational is but an image of Richard's more active scorn, and Richard's vulnerability to the powers of the imagination at Bosworth is prefigured by Clarence's prophetic dream of death.

The basic pattern of dream as prophecy is exemplified in simplest form by the dream of Lord Stanley as it is reported to Hastings in act III:

> He dreamt the boar had rased off his helm. . . .
>
> Therefore he sends to know youe lordship's pleasure,
> If you will presently take horse with him
> And with all speed post with him to the north
> To shun the danger that his soul divines.
>
> > [III.ii.11,15–18]

But Hastings, like Clarence, reacts with instinctive disbelief:

> Tell him his fears are shallow, without instance;
> And for his dreams, I wonder he's so simple
> To trust the mock'ry of unquiet slumbers.
>
> > [III.ii.25–27]

In the dream and its reception we have the fundamental design of early Shakespearean dream: the monitory dream which is true, but not believed. Stanley dreams that Richard—the boar—will cut off their heads, and Hastings rejects this suggestion absolutely. He reasons, further, that to react to it will have the undesirable effect of making the prophecy come true, since if it is known that they distrust him, Richard will give them reasons for distrust.

> To fly the boar before the boar pursues
> Were to incense the boar to follow us
> And make pursuit where he did mean no chase.
>
> > [III.ii.28–30]

This is a politic and sophisticated conclusion; it is also a false one, and it places Hastings in the revealing category of those who scoff at omens. He is in fact a prisoner of his own reason.

"A marvellous case it is," remarks Holinshed, with customary exactitude, "to hear either the warning that he should have voided or the tokens that he could not void." [1] It is only hours later, when he hears himself condemned, that he at last grasps the enormity of his mistake.

> For I, too fond, might have prevented this.
> Stanley did dream the boar did rase our helms,
> And I did scorn it and disdain to fly.
> Three times today my footcloth horse did stumble,
> And started when he looked upon the Tower,
> As loath to bear me to the slaughterhouse.
>
> [III.iv.80–85]

This belated account of an earlier omen, equally disregarded, establishes even more clearly Hastings's distrust of the entire realm of the irrational. It is only in the developing context of supernatural warnings that he, too late, can interpret the sign correctly.

For his part, Richard follows the same course with Hastings as he did with Clarence and Edward: he pretends to have discovered "devilish plots / Of damnèd witchcraft" (III.iv.59–60), ostensible reasons for his own deformity, and condemns Hastings to death for his cautious skepticism. Once again, he employs witchcraft as a device, something to be used rather than believed in. Apparently, then, he and Hastings occupy positions at opposite ends of the rationalist scale: Hastings the victim, warned by true omens he chooses to ignore; Richard the victor, creating false signs and prophecies through which he controls the superstitious and the skeptical alike. Yet they are more alike than they seem at first. When Richard himself becomes the dreamer, the recipient of omens and supernatural warnings, his rationalist posture is susceptible to the same immediate collapse; the terrifying world of dream overwhelms

---

1. Raphael Holinshed, *Chronicles of England, Scotlande, and Irelande* (1587), in *Shakespeare's Holinshed,* ed. Richard Hosley (New York: G. P. Putnam's Sons, 1968), p. 235.

him, as it has overwhelmed Clarence and Hastings, at the critical moment of his ill-starred defense on Bosworth Field.

The double dream at Bosworth is an apparition dream, related to the risen spirits in *2 Henry VI* and *Macbeth* as well as to the ghosts of *Hamlet* and *Julius Caesar*. Richard and Richmond, encamped at opposite ends of the field, are each in turn visited by a series of ghosts representing Richard's victims: Edward Prince of Wales, Henry VI, Clarence, Rivers, Gray and Vaughan, Hastings, the two young princes, Anne, and Buckingham. As each spirit pauses he speaks to Richard like a voice of conscience within the soul: "Dream on thy cousins smothered in the Tower" (V.iii.152); "Dream on, dream on, of bloody deeds and death" (172). And then, in a formal counterpoint, each turns to Richmond and wishes him well. The whole scene is symmetrically arranged, the contrast of sleeping and waking, despair and hopefulness, emphasized by the rigidity of the form. For Richard, "guiltily awake" (147), this is the fulfillment of the last term of Margaret's curse:

> The worm of conscience still begnaw thy soul!
> Thy friends suspect for traitors while thou liv'st,
> And take deep traitors for thy dearest friends!
> No sleep close up that deadly eye of thine,
> Unless it be while some tormenting dream
> Affrights thee with a hell of ugly devils!
>
> [I.iii.221–26]

Richard's sleeplessness, like Macbeth's, is the mark of a troubled condition of soul, the outward sign of an inward sin. Margaret in her self-chosen role as "prophetess" (I.iii.300) has called it down upon him, adding yet another to the series of omens which culminate in dream.

The terror which this dream evokes in Richard's mind is explicitly shown in his frightened soliloquy ("Is there a murderer here? No. Yes, I am" [V.iii.185]), and even more in his subsequent conversation with Ratcliff. "O Ratcliff," he exclaims, "I have dreamed a fearful dream!" This is a very dif-

ferent man from the bloodless Machiavellian who plants the
seeds of Clarence's execution in his brother's brain. His cry is
now the Shakespearean equivalent of Faustus's last speech:

> King Richard: O Ratcliff; I fear, I fear!
>   Ratcliff: Nay, good my lord, be not afraid of sha-
>   dows.
> King Richard: By the apostle Paul, shadows tonight
>   Have struck more terror to the soul of
>   Richard
>   Than can the substance of ten thousand
>   soldiers.
>
> [V.iii.215–19]

In his fear he hits the point precisely: the "shadows," because
they arise from the symbol-making unconscious, are more
threatening than the substance. The Richard who can say
"Richard loves Richard: that is, I am I" (V.iii.184) must create
his own omens if they are to strike him with terror. Consciousness is the one enemy he can neither trick nor silence. From
the controller of dreams he has become the controlled, the victim of his own horrible imaginings.

The Bosworth dream, like the predictive dream of Stanley,
serves a structural purpose as well as a psychological one. The
apparitions of murdered friends and kinsmen recall to the onlooker all the atrocities that have gone before, the perfidies
of *3 Henry VI* as well as the events of the present play. The
device is dramatically useful because of the complexity of the
historical events involved; many in the audience will probably
not remember whose corpse is being mourned at the play's
beginning, nor what relation the Lady Anne bears to the Lan-
castrian monarchy. Points of history are thus clarified at the
same time that a psychologically convincing "replay" takes
place in Richard's mind. The direct inverse of the prophetic
dream, this recapitulation simultaneously furthers the ends of
psychological observation, historical summation, and structural
unity, so that the sequence of dreams and omens which are

the formal controlling agents of *Richard III* are all embodied in the last revelation at Bosworth.

As useful a device as this final dream proves to be, it carries with it several inherent drawbacks. The apparatus of the serial ghosts is cumbersome and formal, analogous to (and probably derived from) the older pageantry of Deadly Sins and Heavenly Virtues. Holinshed, again a useful touchstone, describes the assemblage merely as "divers images like terrible devils" and rejects any supernatural interpretation: "But I think this was no dream but a punction and prick of his sinful conscience." [2] His eagerness to moralize causes him to miss a more significant point: the very equivalence of *dream* with "the punction and prick of conscience" goes deep into the structural and psychological roots of the play. But Holinshed's devils are simply punishment figures of a generalized and abstract sort; by replacing them with the pageant of Richard's victims seeking retributive justice, Shakespeare transforms the entire significance of the last dream. He will use such a formal array only once more, in the series of apparitions which address Macbeth on the heath. There, again, the ghostly figures will become part of the king's private and terrible mythology of symbols, at the same time that they recall the ominous, monitory procession of deadly sins common to Tudor drama.

But the interior world of dream in *Richard III* was to undergo yet another alteration and expansion, quitting the specific formalism of the Bosworth dream for a freer and richer exploration of the subconscious. Just as Richard's apparent control of "prophecies, libels, and dreams" was abruptly replaced by subjugation to internal terrors, so, in Clarence's dream, imagination and the creative unconscious begin to replace the mechanism of witchcraft and omen as the proper architects of dream. Clarence's prophetic dream falls into three structurally distinct parts, each of which is important to the pattern of dream use in the play. The first part (I.iv.9–20) recounts his supposed sea journey with Gloucester, their reminiscences of the wars, and Gloucester's accidental fall:

2. Ibid., p. 262.

>   As we paced along
> Upon the giddy footing of the hatches,
> Methought that Gloucester stumbled, and in falling
> Struck me (that thought to stay him) overboard
> Into the tumbling billows of the main.

>   [I.iv.16–20]

There is both psychological and symbolic truth in this passage. What Freud called the "dream-work," the process by which the latent dream thoughts are transformed into the manifest dream content, has rendered Clarence's latent suspicion of Richard, a suspicion he finds emotionally unbearable, into more reassuring terms. The subconscious thought "Gloucester wants to murder me," rejected by the conscious, here appears in the disguised form "Gloucester will kill me by accident, though he doesn't want to." Outwardly, of course, this prediction falls into the category of monitory dreams, the "tumbling billows of the main" anticipating the butt of malmsey in which Clarence is to be ingloriously drowned. We may, if we choose, regard it solely as another ignored or misunderstood omen, a class for which there is precedent in Shakespeare's works and in those of his contemporaries. But the passage, like the play, offers more than one possibility. While it fits into the pattern of unheeded warnings, it also begins to become an intrinsic part of the mind of the speaker, communicating to us something even he himself does not know.

Gloucester "stumbles" metaphorically in seeking the crown. This information is conveyed more directly in his own words; his soliloquies are psychological revelations, his disappointments and ambitions shown in psychological terms. He is a wholly new kind of character in Shakespeare, and we are able to follow the workings of his mind in a wholly new way. When he thinks aloud at the close of *3 Henry VI*, "Clarence, beware. Thou keep'st me from the light" (V.vi.84), he gives to us the same warning which is given in Clarence's dream. And though we enter Clarence's consciousness only once, in the dream itself, it is clear that some part of him suspects what we know to be a certainty: Richard's design on his life. To read the accident passage as merely another foreshadowing is to ignore the remarkably acute psychology with which the poet approaches the unique occasion of the dream. Through the dream device he permits us to enter Clarence's consciousness for a moment, in the same way we have entered Richard's. This is why the dream appears so different in style and imagery from anything else in the play. The latent suspicion Clarence harbors is authentically presented in masked form by his subconscious mind. And what is most interesting is that the process of masking here takes the form of *metaphor*.

The mention of the "tumbling billows" meantime precipitates the dream into its second phase, the lyrical description of a world undersea. The chief characteristic of this vision—for that is what it really appears to be—is a striking contrast of mortality and eternity, the obscenely decaying body and the insensate but highly valued jewels which endure unchanged.

> A thousand men that fishes gnawed upon;
> Wedges of gold, great anchors, heaps of pearl,
> Inestimable stones, unvalued jewels,
> All scatt'red in the bottom of the sea.
>
> [I.iv.25–28]

The ambiguity in "unvalued" is key to the whole. To Clarence in the extremity of his fear the jewels, though priceless, are without value as compared to human life. "Some lay in dead men's skulls," he continues,

> and in the holes
> Where eyes did once inhabit there were crept,
> As 'twere in scorn of eyes, reflecting gems
> That wooed the slimy bottom of the deep
> And mocked the dead bones that lay scatt'red by.
>
> [I.iv.29–33]

What is chiefly remarkable about this image is its sheer physicality, the fascinated horror of a man contemplating his own

imminent death. When the same image next appears in Shakespeare, it will have been curiously purified of passion:

> Those are pearls that were his eyes:
>   Nothing of him that doth fade,
> But doth suffer a sea change
>   Into something rich and strange.
>
> [*Tmp.* I.ii.401–04]

In Ariel's song mortality has become immortality, the eyes not
replaced by pearls but transformed into them. The difference
between this view and Clarence's suggests the direction in
which vision and dream will develop in the plays. In *Richard
III*, however, the undersea passage is nightmare to the
dreamer, though its language is touched with a strange and
haunting lyricism.

The passage which succeeds it, by contrast, is vividly dramatic, working through dialogue rather than through images.
Two spirits appear to Clarence and confront him with his
crimes, much as Richard's victims do on Bosworth Field. The
tradition here evoked is that of the underworld visit of classical
epic, the dead man greeted by the shades of those he knew on
earth.

> I passed, methought, the melancholy flood,
> With that sour ferryman which poets write of,
> Unto the kingdom of perpetual night.
>
> [I.iv.45–47]

Here is yet another sea journey, parallel to the channel cross-
ing of the dream's first section. This generally unnoticed parallel is significant, for it again utilizes authentic dream logic
to clarify the total meaning of the dream. In the first sea
journey, as we have seen, Clarence overtly ascribes the cause of
his fall to accident, though he betrays a latent distrust of his
brother Richard. Here, in the second journey, he pictures his
destination as hell, and supplies vivid reasons—in the forms of
Warwick and Edward Prince of Wales—why he deserves dam-
nation. The displaced figure of the stumbling Richard is
strongly related to Clarence's assessment of his own guilt: he

has perjured himself (i.e. dissembled about his allegiance) and slain the heir to the throne. But Richard, too, is a perjurer and will become a murderer; he has had Clarence falsely imprisoned and has then pretended ignorance and concern over the event; he will later have him killed because he stands in the line of succession. Clarence thus displaces his unacceptable distrust of Richard, by transferring his just suspicions to analogous episodes in his own life. Simultaneously he punishes himself for having these suspicions by turning them against himself. The ghosts of Warwick and Edward thus possess a multiple significance for the dream's meaning, establishing even further the psychological accuracy of its form.

The more direct significance of these figures is of course historical recapitulation, as it will be in the Bosworth dream. The magnificent tongue twister of a line,

> "What scourge for perjury
> Can this dark monarchy afford false Clarence?"
> [I.iv.50–51]

is meant to recall the elaborate chain of events by which, in *3 Henry VI*, Clarence first pledges his support to Warwick and then deserts him. On that occasion Warwick rebukes him as a "passing traitor, perjured and unjust" (V.i.106), and the charge is repeated by the Prince of Wales: "Thou perjur'd George," he taunts (V.v.34), and when Clarence joins with his brothers to stab the prince to death, he does so in a spirit of resentment as well as anger, retorting, "there's for twitting me with perjury" (40). The accusations made by the ghosts in his dream are thus authentic reminders of Clarence's history. The prince's ghost resembles the accusatory apparitions of Bosworth, but is much more closely assimilated into the consciousness of the dreamer:

> A shadow like an angel, with bright hair
> Dabbled in blood, and he shrieked out aloud,
> "Clarence is come, false, fleeting, perjured Clarence,
> Seize on him, Furies, take him unto torment!"
> [I.iv.53–57]

This is no ceremonial intoning, but rather a visionary visitation. The prince is not identified by name, but is only presented in fragmented detail, as if hastily glimpsed—"a shadow like an angel," "bright hair," "blood." We are inside the mind of Clarence, and we see the ghost through his eyes. In keeping with the play's general design, the ghosts of Clarence's mental landscape appear only secondhand, as related through his dream. It is Richard's consciousness with which we are continually in contact, and only Richard's ghosts make actual appearances on stage.

Yet there is something extremely important about the relationship of Clarence's vision of Warwick and Edward to the actual ghosts of act V. Clarence's dream internalizes the ghosts, portrays them directly as elements of imagination. Gone is the cumbersome apparatus of the Bosworth dream, and gone likewise is the aura of artificiality created by the mechanical pattern of omen and fulfillment. Dream here is an agency of liberation, a means of freeing prophecy from device and relating it to psychological intuition. Imagery bears a bigger part, and association is legitimately employed to make images into symbols. The materials of Clarence's dream are still embryonic, and its technique stands in marked contrast to that of the rest of *Richard III*. But it is the first real anticipation of a new use of dream, to be refined and expanded in the later plays.

Dream and Structure: *The Taming of the Shrew*

The "flatt'ring dream" (Ind.I.44) of noble birth, which is devised as a joke upon Christopher Sly, is a framing device in *The Taming of the Shrew*, permitting the story of the "taming" itself to be presented as a play-within-a-play. Such an induction is not uncommon in the plays of the period: the ghost of Don Andrea in Kyd's *Spanish Tragedy* (1584–88) is explicitly invited by Revenge to "serve for Chorus" (I.i.91) as the play unfolds, and the induction written by Webster for Marston's *Malcontent* (1604) places the actors of the King's

Men in their own persons on the stage. In these cases, however, the use of the introductory scene is different from that in *The Shrew;* Andrea has played a principal part in the circumstances surrounding the *Tragedy,* while the *Malcontent* induction is a way of explaining the company's pirating of Marston's play. *The Shrew*'s induction is both longer and more elaborate than either of these (it introduces ten characters who never again appear), and its personages are related neither to the main action nor to the circumstances of production. Sly's dream is in fact more of a play-within-a-play than the inductions of the *Tragedy* or the *Malcontent,* and the events it contains are connected to the Kate-Petruchio plot by analogy. The metaphor of dream, like the stage metaphor, presents the audience with the problem of comparative realities and juxtaposes a simple or "low" illusion with the more courtly illusions of the taming plot itself.

   The Shrew's induction owes its existence, at least in part, to identifiable sources and analogues. Its ultimate source is a story in the *Arabian Nights,* "The Sleeper Awakened," which made its way to England in three known forms: a letter from Juan Luis Vives to Francis, Duke of Béjar; a collection of stories assembled by Richard Edwards and published in 1570, now lost; and a story in the *De rebus burgundicis* of Heuterus (1584).[3] The Heuterus version alludes to a comedy to be presented to the gulled sleeper and is thus the most likely actual source. None of the versions, however, drop the framing device as Shakespeare does; in all of them the prologue is balanced by an epilogue in which the effect of the dream on the sleeper is made clear. This is also the case in the anonymous *The Taming of a Shrew, The Shrew*'s most celebrated analogue. The omission of the epilogue-frame is thus an important characteristic of Shakespeare's version of the dream; it marks the story's transformation from the narrative to the dramatic mode. The symmetry of prologue-epilogue is pleasing in a tale, but—as Shakespeare may have reasoned—less feasible in a comedy,

3. Richard Hosley, "Sources and Analogues of *The Taming of the Shrew,*" *Huntington Library Quarterly,* 27 (1963–64), 306.

where a return to the frame might constitute an awkward anti-
climax. Similarly, as has been frequently suggested,[4] the induction as it stands provides a thematic parallel for the later
action: Sly's acceptance of a new personality—after some initial resistance—foreshadows Kate's own. Contrary arguments
have been advanced by some scholars to suggest either (1) a
"lost" epilogue, or (2) a flaw in the play's construction because
of the lack of one; by and large these contentions are merely
the inverse of the others (an epilogue could be climactic rather
than anticlimactic; the thematic parallel was meant to operate
by contrast, when Sly loses his new identity at the close) and
seem more conjectural than persuasive. Robert B. Heilman's
contention that "surely most readers feel spontaneously that
. . . something is left uncomfortably hanging"[5] seems to take
insufficient note of the difference between reading a play and
watching one.

In any case, the formal device of the induction has a considerable effect upon the play as a whole, and its importance is
closely linked with the fact that it purports to tell a dream.
The frame performs the important tasks of distancing the later
action and of insuring a lightness of tone—significant contributions in view of the real abuse to which Kate is subjected
by Petruchio. Its most important single advantage, however, is
the immediacy with which it establishes the deliberate metaphorical ambiguity of reality and illusion. This is a role
which we are accustomed to ascribe to the play metaphor, and
the play metaphor is in some sense operative here. Because
of its inherently formal and concrete character, however—*The
Shrew* takes place upon a stage, and the recumbent Sly is pre-
sumably visible on the upper stage while the main plot unfolds
upon the lower—the play metaphor has limitations. Though
we may suspend our awareness of varying planes of reality in

4. E.g. Richard Hosley, "Was There a 'Dramatic Epilogue' to *The Taming of Shrew?*", *Studies in English Literature*, 1, no. 2 (1961), 17–34.
5. Robert B. Heilman, ed., *The Taming of the Shrew*, in *The Complete
Signet Classic Shakespeare*, p. 322.

drama, we can never wholly escape it: Sly is always present upon the upper stage, Theseus and Hippolyta comment throughout the "Pyramus and Thisby" play, Prospero summons and interrupts the pageant of the nymphs. Even "All the world's a stage" and "O what a rogue and peasant slave am I" are in a real sense set pieces, calling attention to the remarkable circumstance of a player on a stage comparing himself extensively to a player of a player.

By comparison, dream—and Sly's dream—escapes these limitations of structure. The content of the dream, like the content of the play-within-a-play, can be measured against the play of which it is a part: in just this way, commentators remark the similarity in theme between Sly's change from beggar to lord and Kate's from shrew to wife. But at the same time something more subtle is achieved by the suggestion made to Sly that he has been dreaming. The "dream" to which the lord and his servants refer is Sly's conviction that he is a tinker named Christopher Sly. Thus, what they call his dream is actually the literal truth, while the "truth" they persuade him of is fictive. When Sly wonders aloud, "Or do I dream? Or have I dreamed till now?" (Ind.ii.69), he states the general case of the problem of illusion. His own problem is concrete: he suspects that he has been awake and is now dreaming, while the servingmen attempt to persuade him that the opposite is the case. We know—or think we know—which judgment is correct, and thus Sly's pragmatic solution,

> I smell sweet savors and I feel soft things,
> Upon my life, I am a lord indeed
> And not a tinker nor Christopher Sly
>
> [Ind.ii.71–73]

strikes us as comic, while it permits a continued play upon the interchanged terms: "These fifteen years you have been in a dream / Or when you waked so waked as if you slept" (79–80). But in the later plays, and particularly in the romances, this rhetorical and formal interchange, which is in Sly's case simple confusion, becomes a serious interpenetration of planes. When Miranda says of her memory of Milan that it is "rather like a dream than an assurance" (*Tmp.* I.ii.45), or when Leontes tells Hermione that "your actions are my dreams" (*WT* III.ii.80), a much more highly refined version of the same handy-dandy is at work. The extremely formal, local, and concrete use of the dream figure in *The Shrew* thus provides a starting point of sorts. It is largely device in *The Shrew;* in later plays it will become part of the dream world of transformation.

At the moment when the drunken Sly is first discovered onstage by a lord and his huntsmen, the lord exclaims:

> O monstrous beast, how like a swine he lies!
> Grim death, how foul and loathsome is thine image!
>
> [Ind.i.34–35]

Although they are conventional epithets, terms like "beast" and "swine" immediately establish a line of significant imagery with which the induction—like the play as a whole—will be much concerned: the imagery of transformation or metamorphosis. The entire "supposes" plot based on Gascoigne turns on change of guise—Lucentio as a tutor, Tranio as Lucentio, the pedant as Vincentio, as well as the more symbolic changes undergone by Kate and Petruchio. With superb economy Shakespeare introduces the theme at once in a casual, almost accidental way. For part of the effectiveness of the "beast-swine" terminology lies precisely in the fact of its conventionalism: the imagery enters the play in the form of metaphors so common as to lack strong metaphorical force; yet as the play progresses this seeming convention becomes more and more relevant and particular. The lord's next lines point out the chain of development:

> Sirs, I will practice on this drunken man.
> What think you, if he were conveyed to bed,
> Wrapped in sweet clothes, rings put upon his fingers,
> A most delicious banquet by his bed,

And brave attendants near him when he wakes—
Would not the beggar then forget himself?

[Ind.i.36–41]

He appropriates to himself the role of a stage director, a play-wright, even a god; he will "practice" on Sly to make him "forget himself." This lord is no Prospero, and his transformation of Sly is of the most broad and external kind, but it is significant that even at this early point Shakespeare conceives of transformation in terms of dream. His seeming metamorphosis will appear to Sly "even as a flatt'ring dream or worthless fancy" (44). The lord, as one might expect, takes a contemptuous attitude toward dreams, which he equates not only with "worthless fancy" but with lunacy (63). He is the instrument of Sly's transformation but he stands outside of it, secure in his knowledge of the real state of affairs.

The sybaritic components of his intended charade—"wanton pictures," "warm distillèd waters," "sweet wood," "music," "a costly suit" (47–60)—anticipate the ministrations of Titania to the ass-eared Bottom (*MND* IV.i) whom Puck "translated" in similar fashion. The "wanton pictures" also continue the covert imagery of metamorphosis which began with "beast" and "swine."

2 *Servingman:*	Dost thou love pictures? We will fetch thee straight
	Adonis painted by a running brook
	And Cytherea all in sedges hid,
	Which seem to move and wanton with her breath
	Even as the waving sedges play with wind.
Lord:	We'll show thee Io as she was a maid
	And how she was beguilèd and surprised
	As lively painted as the deed was done.
3 *Servingman:*	Or Daphne roaming through a thorny wood,
	Scratching her legs that one shall swear she bleeds,
	And at that sight shall sad Apollo weep,

So workmanly the blood and tears are
drawn.

[Ind.ii.49–60]

These Ovidian reminiscences are of course a form of sexual
temptation, with emphasis on verisimilitude, leading to the
crowning jest of the substitution sequence, when the young
page impersonates Sly's supposedly love-sick lady. But Adonis,
Io, and Daphne are all associated with transformation myths,
which here stand in ironic contrast to the false metamorphosis
of Sly. The lord and his attendants are having a private joke,
which is all the more telling for its appositeness to the play's
major themes. They flatter Sly by comparing him indirectly
to such august personages as Jove and Apollo, whose beloveds
have undergone a number of startling transformations. When
the disguised page enters, as he does almost immediately, the
ribald joke is complete.

"Dream" in this context becomes a kind of code word, a
sign for the initial inversion which is the induction's central
trope. What the lord insists are "abject lowly dreams" (Ind.ii.
32) are the only truths Sly knows. But there is an element of
verbal ambiguity present as well. "Persuade him," the lord instructs his servants, "that he hath been lunatic";

And when he says he is, say that he dreams,
For he is nothing but a might lord.

[Ind.i.64–65]

"Nothing," here as always in Shakespeare, is a word of great
power. While the sentence means "He is nothing *except* a
mighty lord," articulating the deception, it is also capable of
meaning "He is nothing—*but at the same time* a mighty lord."
This is the essential ambiguity of the dream state, in which illusion and role playing reach their apex. So likewise the lord
will insist to Sly at the close of his Ovidian catalogue, "Thou
art a lord and nothing but a lord" (Ind.ii.61). His remarks have
one meaning to the gulled and another to the initiate. He himself is not confused as to Sly's identity, nor are we. Since we

observe the mechanics of alteration, we know that Sly's metamorphosis, unlike Bottom's, is not a metamorphosis at all. But
for Sly the situation is radically different. When he speculates

Or do I dream? Or have I dreamed till now?

he is weighing the same two possibilities occasioned by the
lord's unconscious pun on "nothing."

In a sense he is "dreaming on both," for the answer to both
of these questions is no. The whole matter of dream is a fiction
contrived by the lord. But Sly, accepting the dream hypothesis,
is at a loss to know which of the two contrary states—tinker
into lord or lord into tinker—corresponds to the facts. Since
he is (ostensibly) *inside* the dream, his evaluation of it can only
be subjective. As we have seen, this quandary is resolved in the
direction of humor when Sly wholeheartedly attempts to embrace the page-turned-lady. In the main plot of the play, however, the same ambiguity is turned to metaphor, and assumes
a more far-reaching significance.

Petruchio's device for controlling the quick-tongued Kate is
itself a species of metamorphosis; as one of the servants points
out, "he kills her in her own humor" (IV.i.169). The fiction
he constructs is that of the shrewish husband, irascible and
determined not to be pleased, totally unresponsive to fact and
reason—a personality wholly inconsistent with the Petruchio
who wooed her. He arrives for his wedding dressed in rags,
curses at the priest, announces he will not attend the wedding
feast, and abuses his servants without cause, reversing in the
process all her expectations about his behavior and calling into
question that which she has taken for reality. The final reversal comes as he leads her supperless into the bridal chamber,
where a servant reports that he is

Making a sermon of continency to her,
And rails and swears and rates, that she, poor soul,
Knows not which way to stand, to look, to speak,
And sits as one new-risen from a dream.
[IV.i.171-75]

Kate has now been placed in the same ambiguous position as
Sly found himself in the induction. The dream from which she
seems to have risen is a figure of speech, but her condition of
confusion is very like Sly's. Here again there is a manipulator
and a manipulated; Petruchio practices on Kate as the lord had
on Sly. Significantly, this stage of wonderment, this subjectivity
of experience and suspension of ordinary assumptions, is the
turning point in the transformation of the shrew.

We are very far, yet, from the healing and transforming sleep
of Lear, and further from the marvelous sleeps of *The Tempest*. Kate comes no closer to dream than a brief simile invoked
by a minor character. The image of the "one new-risen from a
dream" remains on the level of language and does not enter
the action. But the symbolic possibilities of the newly wakened
state are adumbrated here, and adumbrated the more clearly
for the parallelism of this image with Sly's condition. When
Juliet awakens from her deathlike sleep, when Hero returns
so surprisingly from the dead, there is about them, however
briefly, the same glow of maturation as we find in the transformed Kate. We are presented with a fundamentally psychological insight: the suspension of certainties and the inter-
changeability of reality and illusion result in a heightened self-
awareness.

The Taming of the Shrew is thus a significant early venture
for Shakespeare in the multiple meanings and uses of dream.
It contains the germ of the important idea of transformation
—an idea which was to become central to *A Midsummer
Night's Dream*. At the same time it experiments with the structural presentation of dream in a manner closely related to the
play-within-a-play. Perhaps its most interesting single element,
however, is a playful—though artistically polished—manipulation of the terms of reality and illusion seen through the image
of dream. The potential utility of such a manipulation, only
partially glimpsed here, is what changes dream from a device
to a subject matter; from *A Midsummer Night's Dream* to *The
Tempest* these beginnings made in *The Shrew* are implemented with increasing skill and power.

Dream and Language: *Romeo and Juliet*

Two doctrines of dream are expounded in *Romeo and Juliet* —one by Romeo, the other by Mercutio. That of Romeo looks backward to the old tradition of omen and portent; that of Mercutio looks forward to dream as fantasy, the significant product of the shaping imagination.

Mercutio is a pivotal figure in the play as a whole. Neither Montague nor Capulet, a kinsman to the prince and thus not party to the feud which circumscribes the actions of the other principals, he talks sense in the guise of nonsense, counseling most sagely when he speaks most wildly. Coleridge saw him, acutely, as "a man possessing all the elements of a poet." "The whole world," he wrote, "was, as it were, subject to his law of association. Whenever he wishes to impress anything, all things become his servants for the purpose: all things tell the same tale, and sound in unison. This faculty, moreover, is combined with the manners and feelings of a perfect gentleman, himself utterly unconscious of his powers." [6] The "law of association" is the organizing principle of his wit; puns and riddles, his weapons and signs. He is, in fact, a master of fencing with language. Deftly, he baits the blunt Tybalt to rage by deliberately misinterpreting him:

Tybalt:	A word with one of you.
Mercutio:	And but one word with one of us?
	Couple it with something; make it a word and a blow.
Tybalt:	You shall find me apt enough to that, sir, and you will give me occasion.
Mercutio:	Could you not take some occasion without giving?
Tybalt:	Mercutio, thou consortest with Romeo.
Mercutio:	Consort? What, dost thou make us minstrels?

6. Samuel Taylor Coleridge, *Lectures on Shakespeare and Milton* (1811-12), Lecture VII, in *Shakespearean Criticism*, ed. Thomas Middleton Raysor (London: Constable, 1930), II, 98.

> And thou make minstrels of us, look to hear
> nothing but discords.
>
> [III.i.39 ff.]

For the spectator, this is like watching an epéeist go after a pikeman. The confrontation, though it has tragic conse-quences, begins as a kind of play for Mercutio. Yet when his words draw blows in return, and the hapless intervention of Romeo renders one of those blows mortal, Mercutio's wit turns tragic and profound:

> 'tis not so deep as a well, nor so wide as a church
> door; but 'tis enough, 'twill serve. Ask for me
> tomorrow and you shall find me a grave man.
>
> [III.i.97 ff.]

His words have the authentic ring of the oracle, who speaks in riddle to hid his meanings and to reveal them. Mercutio's language, in short, is in the finest sense *poetical*. At the same time, in its shifting patterns of association and double mean-ing, its reliance on puns and serious wit, it is the language of dream. Freud has described "the extraordinarily important part played by puns and verbal quibbles" in dream interpre-tation,[7] and we have already observed the effect of associa-tionism upon the subconscious mind in Clarence's dream. Mercutio's agile manipulation of language—and most centrally his high-spirited, brilliantly modulated monologue on Queen Mab—is verbally related to the processes of dream logic. Like Clarence's dream it explores the subconscious mind while re-taining its manifest function as part of the ongoing plot.

The banter between Romeo and Mercutio concerning dreams begins in act I, scene iv, as Mercutio and the other masked revelers prepare to attend the Capulets' feast. The dialogue, which has heretofore remained bound in distinct speeches of two or four lines, now turns sharply stichomythic. Romeo and Mercutio are the two wits of the gathering, and

7. *Interpretation of Dreams*, chap. 2, p. 131.

there is an air of competition between them as they take up the topic of dream. Romeo is reluctant to participate in the masque, and he expresses his reluctance at first in serious terms. But the remarkable skill of Mercutio is to deal with the gravest issues in the lightest terms, and Romeo is unable to resist the temptation to cap him.

> *Romeo:* I dreamt a dream tonight.
> *Mercutio:* And so did I.
> *Romeo:* Well, what was yours?
> *Mercutio:* That dreamers often lie.
> *Romeo:* In bed asleep, while they do dream things true.
> *Mercutio:* O, then I see Queen Mab hath been with you.
>
> [I.iv.50–53]

The alternated rhyme is typical of the formalism of *Romeo and Juliet.* Used here it makes the deliberate "wittiness" of the exchange even more pronounced. Underneath the banter, however, lie some serious differences of approach. Romeo, in referring to his dream of the previous evening, presents it as a premonition of trouble; his disinclination to the feast is the result of a sense of foreboding which he elaborates in lines 106–11. According to his point of view, dreamers dream "things true," which is to say that dreams have an ability to forecast future events. This is an opinion we have frequently encountered before, and those who wish to argue for a deterministic reading of *Romeo and Juliet* properly seize upon Romeo's view of dream as evidence. Especially here in the early moments of the play, before the entrance of Juliet, the doctrines to which Romeo subscribes are received conventions, however wittily expressed.

By contrast, Mercutio, despite his verbal nonchalance, is making an important distinction between two kinds of dream. The dreamers who lie are those whose dreams are either wishes or fears; their dreams are self-deception in the one case, superstition in the other. The satiric catalogue of dreamers affected by Queen Mab is an anatomy of self-deception, to which— Mercutio implies—could be appended Romeo's elaborate passion for Rosaline. Likewise Romeo's premonition of disas-

ter at the feast is a superstitious fear, upon which Mercutio
looks with an equal suspicion. The world of the play admits
the possibility of such a premonition, and Romeo's fear is
finally justified by tragedy. But Mercutio is a character of a
different order, of the play and yet apart from it, and to him
such a use of dream rings false. His own doctrine of dream,
articulated at the close of the Queen Mab speech, is a creative
and visionary faith in the transforming power of fantasy.

The Queen Mab speech itself is the play's single most complex and important statement on dream. Often considered as
a kind of virtuoso performance, a showcase for the breezy
extravagance of Mercutio's volatile personality, it is less frequently examined for what it says than for how it says it. Yet
Mercutio's style, as we have seen, permits him to seem most
frivolous when his matter is most profound. In the disquisition
on Mab and her subjects he is at his most artful, progressing
through exaggerated lyrical and satirical passages to a characteristically veiled statement on the true meaning of dream.

The speech divides into three sections, the first of which (53–
69) is an extended description of Queen Mab and her chariot,
deliberately lengthy and "poetical" in tone. Mab, with

> Her wagon spokes made of long spinners' legs,
> The cover, of the wings of grasshoppers;
> Her traces, of the smallest spider web;
> Her collars, of the moonshine's wat'ry beams
>
> [I.iv.59–62]

would be at home in the Athenian wood of *A Midsummer
Night's Dream*. She is in fact the apotheosis of fairyhood, a
parody fairy queen, combining in her equipage all the legends,
old wives' tales, and ballad lore Mercutio can put together.
The length and particularity of his description has a cumula-
tively comic effect, as does the monotony of the syntax: "her
whip, of cricket's bone; the lash, of film" (63). Because she
delivers dreams, Mercutio calls her "the fairies' midwife";
this is his own kind of jest, and it shows us what he really
thinks of her. The rest of his description, however, is com-

pletely romantic, fantastical, without a hint of the earthy. It is Mercutio speaking in an assumed voice, the voice of the romantic daydreamer and fabulist, his words a compilation from the annals of folklore and superstition. Clearly this is meant to be a continuation of the mocking of Romeo with which the scene began.

Yet in a way Mercutio speaks more in earnest than in jest, because Mab exemplifies to him that power which he and the lovers alone will value—the creative power of imagination. More than a century later Addison, citing Dryden, was to call this *"the Fairy Way of Writing."* [8] Addison's remarks could have been designed especially to fit Mercutio's case:

> There is a very odd turn of Thought required for this sort of Writing, and it is impossible for a Poet to succeed in it, who has not a particular Cast of Fancy, and an Imagination naturally fruitful and superstitious. Besides this, he ought to be very well versed in Legends and Fables, antiquated Romances, and the Traditions of Nurses and old Women.

or again

> For the English are naturally Fanciful, and very often disposed by the Gloominess and Melancholy of Temper, which is so frequent in our nation, to many wild Notions and Visions, to which others are not so liable.

or yet again

> Among the English, Shakespear has incomparably excelled all others. That noble Extravagance of Fancy, which he had in so great Perfection, thoroughly qualified him to touch this weak superstitious part of his Reader's Imagination; and made him capable of succeeding, where he had nothing to support him besides the Strength of his own Genius.[9]

8. Joseph Addison, "Spectator 419," in *The Spectator*, ed. Gregory Smith (London: J.M. Dent, 1907), III, 299.

9. Ibid., pp. 300, 301.

This last, like the rest, might be a description of Mercutio
rather than of his creator: "Noble Extravagance of Fancy,"
with "nothing to support him besides the Strength of his own
Genius." Together with Coleridge's insight, these observations
of Addison do much to point out the degree to which Mercutio is a poet-persona. The first part of his speech on Queen
Mab thus deliberately relates him to the bardic tradition,
while at the same time its tone gently mocks that tradition and
Romeo as its votary.

In the second and by far the longest section of the speech,
the satirical tone reappears. This section (70–94) is really a
miniature "progress," the chariot of Mab hurtling across the
sleeping anatomies of dreamers. Its subject is wish fulfillment,
which is treated—characteristically—in a jocular manner with
a very serious meaning beneath the surface glitter. Wish-
fulfillment dreams are pictured as selfish, shallow, and not a
little ludicrous—another thrust at the love-sick and self-
centered Romeo. It is the *style* of the passage, however, which
is of special interest, because it demonstrates the inventive
mind of Mercutio at work, manipulating language for maxi-
mum richness and freedom. The language of this passage,
with its wealth of association and breathless pace, its fondness
for wordplay and puns, is a vivid record of the mind in process.

Mercutio's catalogue of dreamers begins, naturally enough,
with lovers, since it is the peculiar relation of love and dream
which has initiated the discussion. "And in this state," he says,
referring to Mab's finery,

> she gallops night by night
> Through lovers' brains, and then they dream of love;
> On courtiers' knees, that dream on curtsies straight;
> O'er lawyers' fingers, who straight dream on fees;
>
> [70–73]

These are relatively straightforward witticisms: lovers dream
of love; courtiers, confined to their most literal and mechanical function, dream of curtsies; lawyers' "fingers," apparently
their most responsive parts, dream immediately of alliterating

"fees." Dream for all three is mere wish fulfillment, and a fulfillment which reveals the shallowness of their ambitions. In the next series of dreams Mercutio begins to warm to his theme; the chiasmic simplicity of "lovers . . . and then they dream of love" gives way to small comic anecdotes in which Mab is made a kind of mock-heroine. The anatomical index of "brains," "knees," and "fingers" is extended to "lips," the lips of ladies who dream of kisses; but this romantic image is immediately undercut, for the lips are of that sort

> Which oft the angry Mab with blisters plagues,
> Because their breath with sweetmeats tainted are.
>
> [75–76]

The contiguity of "blisters," "plagues," and "sweetmeats" suggests self-indulgence rather than romance. Mercutio's favorite verbal device, the pun, is here the pivot of his wit. The courtier's proverbially delicate nose is use for "smelling out a suit"; and the dreaming soldier, feeling the press of Mab's chariot on his neck, dreams of slitting throats, but also of drinking. It is human nature which is his subject here, and he treats it with loving mockery. The soldier, awakened suddenly, "swears a prayer or two / And sleeps again." Mab in her role as midwife "presses" maids and "learns them first to bear, / Making them women of good carriage." In pointing out to Romeo the superstition inherent in wish-fulfillment dreams, Mercutio commends the imagination of the dreamer-as-myth-maker, and himself becomes the dreamers' dreamer, master of these smaller fantasies, controlling illusion and reality through the multiple meanings of words.

Little of any of this is comprehended by Romeo, however, and he has grown impatient with Mercutio's purposeful hyperbole. "Peace, peace, Mercutio, peace!" he cries, "Thou talk'st of nothing" (95–96). Here is the significant word "nothing" again, and again it is the center of a conflict of understandings. Romeo is concerned with his own premonitory dream and not with Mercutio's wider speculations. And Mercutio for his part replies

> True, I talk of dreams;
> Which are the children of an idle brain,
> Begot of nothing but vain fantasy;
> Which is as thin of substance as the air,
> And more inconstant than the wind, who wooes
> Even now the frozen bosom of the North
> And, being angered, puffs away from thence,
> Turning his side to the dew-dropping South.
>
> [96–103]

This is the third and last part of his speech, the fledgling doctrine of creative dream. With characteristic dramatic tact he phrases his praise of dream in such a way that Romeo and the others can take it for disparagement. And when Benvolio reacts with irritation to his long poetical discursus on the wind, remarking, "This wind you talk of blows us from ourselves" (104), we may wonder whether that is not precisely Mercutio's purpose. Just as Berowne in *Love's Labor's Lost,* proposing that the lords masque themselves as Muscovites, suggests "Let us once lose our oaths to find ourselves" (*LLL* IV.iii.358), so Mercutio is here suggesting something other than the internal pretense of everyday life; the dreams which are but "vain fantasy" are more revealing than the "selves" Benvolio is zealous to recall. Benvolio himself is the perfect counterfoil; like the later figures of Horatio and Enobarbus, he is the stolid and reasonable confederate, unpersuaded by poetry or passion. With his intervention the visionary world of Mercutio's fantasy, which has for moments dominated the scene, is allowed to recede as quickly as it has grown. As he began the dialogue, Romeo ends it, returning to his dream:

> my mind misgives
> Some consequence yet hanging in the stars
> Shall bitterly begin his fearful date
> With this night's revels and expire the term
> Of a despised life, close in my breast,
> By some vile forfeit of untimely death.
>
> [I.iv.106–11]

Mercutio has spoken for us, and not for Romeo. The night will indeed bring "some consequence," though he cannot guess it, and its terminus will be the "vile forfeit of untimely death" for many as well as him. Yet now, having acknowledged the premonition and given it some credence, he chooses deliberately to ignore it:

> he that hath the steerage of my course
> Direct my sail!
>
> [112–13]

This is a heroic action within the play's context. Voluntarily Romeo enters the world of the tragedy. There is no question but that he believes in the efficacy of dreams of warning, but he chooses nonetheless to disregard them. His dream is of a type we have seen before, the valid premonition which is ignored by the dreamer. It is true that his decision is influenced by a regard for the good opinion of his fellows; it is also true that the Romeo of this first act tends to take himself too seriously, to play at roles. But the mode here is tragedy; Romeo's denial of the dream is more than behavior, more than device. It seals him as an actor in a world he only partially comprehends. It is an act and a sign at once. From this point the tragedy extends.

As the play unfolds, the subject of dream continues to be evident, for it is a thematic as well as a structural consideration. In the orchard or balcony scene Romeo muses to himself, as Juliet departs,

> I am afeard,
> Being in night, all this is but a dream,
> Too flattering-sweet to be substantial.
>
> [II.ii.139–41]

Here "dream" is used in its conventional sense of imaginary vision. Romeo's words have a hidden significance in them, for his fears are accurate, though it is not Juliet's literal existence but the hope of their happiness which is illusory. His fear is another version of the premonitory "beauty too rich for use"

theme, which once more subjects to scrutiny those poles of
reality and illusion which are fundamental to the dream state.
And when "dream" becomes "fear," rather than "wish," at the
play's close, Romeo too is willing to wonder which is which.

> What said my man when my betossèd soul
> Did not attend him as we rode? I think
> He told me Paris should have married Juliet.
> Said he not so, or did I dream it so?
> Or am I mad, hearing him talk of Juliet,
> To think it was so?
>
> [V.iii.76–81]

These are very like the choices of reality open to Christopher
Sly: fact, dream, or madness. It is a mark of Shakespeare's
artistry that they here carry the full and somber weight of
tragedy.

But if all this attests to the traditionalism of Romeo's view
of dream, the unheeded omen and the illusion which might
be reality, how are we to consider his interpretation of the one
dream he narrates in full? This final dream is recounted at the
the opening of act V, as Romeo waits confidently in Mantua
for news of Juliet. "If I may trust the flattering truth of sleep,"
he exults,

> My dreams presage some joyful news at hand.
> My bosom's lord sits lightly in his throne,
> And all this day an unaccustomed spirit
> Lifts me above the ground with cheerful thoughts.
> I dreamt my lady came and found me dead
> (Strange dream that gives a dead man leave to think!)
> And breathed such life with kisses in my lips
> That I revived and was an emperor.
> Ah me! How sweet is love itself possessed,
> When but love's shadows are so rich in joy!
>
> [V.i.1–11]

At this point, his servant Balthasar arrives in haste from
Verona with the misleading news that Juliet is dead, and
Romeo cries out "I defy you, stars!" anticipating the Hamlet

of act V who would defy augury. His wistful dreams collapse in a moment and turn to action.

Several aspects of this "strange dream" deserve attention. Romeo presents the dream as another "presage," a prediction that Juliet will find him dead and revive him with her kisses, transforming him into "an emperor." The first half of this—that she will find him dead—comes literally true; the second half—that he "revived and was an emperor"—does not. Yet this is not really a false dream, though its optimistic mood is designedly at variance with the tragic occurrences that follow. What happens in the course of the dream as Romeo tells it is that the prediction ceases to be literal and becomes metaphorical. Indeed, this is the only way we can satisfactorily account for the supernatural note, the revival or resurrection. Because of Juliet's love for him, Romeo will be ironically revived and enshrined by the Capulets, as she by the Montagues. "For I will raise her statue in pure gold," declares Montague, viewing the bodies of the lovers,

> That whiles Verona by that name is known,
> There shall no figure at such rate be set
> As that of true and faithful Juliet
>
> [V.iii.300–03]

and Capulet, chastened but competitive to the last, replies

> As rich shall Romeo's by his lady's lie—
> Poor sacrifices of our enmity!
>
> [304–05]

In effect the lovers are to be transformed into a monitory artifact, a pair of golden statues, just as their story is transformed into a greater, living artifact, the play of *Romeo and Juliet*. Neither Montagues nor Capulets grasp the real significance of their expiatory impulse to make a monument out of tragedy, and from the point of view of the lovers their action is as futile as it is belated. Yet as is true of so many characters in Shakespeare, their impulse toward transformation carries a truth beyond what they intend.

The transposition of Romeo's dream thoughts from the literal to the metaphorical plane, from the predictive almost to the mythic, is marked by a curious reflexive interpolation.

> (Strange dream that gives a dead man leave to think!)

This is a new note for Romeo, contemplative rather than active. It is an analytical and not a narrative observation. In fact at this point we are witnessing Romeo in the act of analyzing, or at least of scrutinizing, his own dream. There seems no question but that he considers it as some kind of figurative expression: the dreams presage "some joyful news," but he is not sure of what kind. Similarly, with

> Ah me! How sweet is love itself possessed,
> When but love's shadows are so rich in joy!

the pleasant dream of awakening from the dead at Juliet's kiss is but a "shadow," a dream or figment, which he feels to be indicative of some unspecified good tidings. Characteristically the "shadow" is more real than the substance: Romeo never from this moment has a chance to possess "love itself." But from this point of view the significance of the dream is general rather than specific—"some joyful news"—just as his earlier dream suggested "some consequence" of misfortune. The dream's "message," its prediction, is for us rather than for him.

The importance of this is manifest. Dream, which we have generally been regarding here as in the other early plays as a device of plot, has once more—as with Clarence and with Mercutio—begun to enter the subconscious mind of the dreamer. Romeo's vision here is substantially different from his earlier concept of the dream state. It would be greatly misleading to suggest that Romeo, even at this point, begins to grasp what Mercutio has intimated about the possibilities of dream; he is still its instrument, rather than its master. But the dream here goes beyond monition, beyond plot manipulation. It becomes part of the mythos of the play. Though it has its functional role in plot—Romeo is elated by it, so that his mood is abruptly and dramatically reversed by Balthasar's message—it also imparts a further significance. Again we are faced with the reality-illusion problem and the subjectivity of the dreamer. As he tells his dream, even the words in which he speaks show a new self-awareness. Though his expectations are to be cruelly reversed in the actions which follow, for a moment the world of the dream holds sway.

In *Romeo and Juliet*, then, dream is beginning to extend itself in the direction of myth. The truth function of the dream perception, and the inability and unwillingness of the rational mind to accept it, has been expanded to encompass truths of a much more complex order than the fundamental monitory truth of Richard III's Bosworth dream. By contrast the last dream of *Romeo* is a myth or romance in little, to be measured against the play as a whole. The remarkable strength and intricacy of the play's last act, with its many misunderstandings and partial enlightenments, its suggestion of an *ekphrasis* which fails and a spirit which conquers, is due in large part to the power of dream and to the tension which develops between dream and action. Romeo's final dream brings him close to a poetic understanding of his own situation and makes him into an interpreter of the play as well as its protagonist. The language of dream as myth, in fact, as Mercutio knows it and as Romeo will come to glimpse it, works in the play's final moments to enlarge—and transform—the tragedy of *Romeo and Juliet;* its ultimate form is not that of private chronicle, but of exemplum and metamorphosis, a tragedy which takes place so that other tragedies may be averted. The youthful Romeo and Juliet, in their rash passions and idealistic expectations, are not so very different from their older and more magniloquent successors, Antony and Cleopatra; and the overt myth-making of the later play is already making itself felt in *Romeo*'s language of dream, love, and transformation.

Dream and Interpretation: *Julius Caesar*

In the final act of *Julius Caesar,* Cassius, fearful of defeat at Philippi, dispatches Titinius to discover whether the surround-

ing troops are friends or enemies. He posts another soldier to
observe, and when the soldier sees Titinius encircled by horse-
men and reports that he is taken, Cassius runs on his sword
and dies. Shortly afterward, Titinius reenters the scene bearing a "wreath of victory" from Brutus. When he sees the dead
body, he at once understands Cassius's tragic mistake. "Alas,
thou has misconstrued everything!" (V.iii.84), he cries out, and
he too runs on Cassius's sword.

That one cry, "thou hast misconstrued everything!", might
well serve as an epigraph for the whole of *Julius Caesar*. The
play is full of omens and portents, augury and dream, and almost without exception these omens are misinterpreted. Calpurnia's dream, the dream of Cinna the poet, the advice of the
augurers, all suggest one course of action and produce its
opposite. The compelling dream imagery of the play, which
should, had it been rightly interpreted, have persuaded Caesar
to avoid the Capitol and Cinna not to go forth, is deflected by
the characters of men, making tragedy inevitable. For *Julius
Caesar* is not only a political play, but also a play of character.
Its imagery of dream and sign, an imagery so powerful that it
enters the plot on the level of action, is a means of examining
character and consciousness.

Much of the plot of *Julius Caesar*, like that of *Richard III*,
is shaped by the device of the predictive dream or sign. The
two plays also have another point of similarity, not unrelated
to the device of dream: each divides men into two camps, those
who attempt to control dream and destiny and those who are
controlled by it. In *Richard III* only Gloucester thinks himself able to master dream and turn it to his own purposes; Edward, Clarence, and Hastings are its helpless victims. *Julius
Caesar*, on the other hand, presents a number of characters
who declare themselves indifferent to dream or contemptuous
of its power: Cassius, who so firmly places the fault not in our
stars but in ourselves; Decius Brutus, who deliberately misinterprets Calpurnia's prophetic dream to serve his own ends;
Octavius, in whom the whole dimension of emotion seems
lacking; and Caesar himself. Caesar's conviction, however, is

notably wavering as the play begins. As Cassius points out to
the conspirators,

> he is superstitious grown of late,
> Quite from the main opinion he held once
> Of fantasy, of dreams, and ceremonies.
>
> [II.i.195–97]

Caesar struggles against this tendency, repeatedly invoking his
public persona to quell his private fears: "Danger knows full
well," he boasts, "That Caesar is more dangerous than he"
(II.ii.44–45). Yet he protests too much.

In his susceptibility to dream and introspection he stands
midway between the coldness of Decius Brutus and the blind
self-preoccupation of Brutus. For Brutus is in a way the least
self-aware of all these characters, because he thinks of himself
as a supremely rational man. Again and again he confronts his
situation and misinterprets it, secure in his own erroneous
sense of self. His frequent solitary ruminations have a certain
poignancy about them; they approach a truth and reject it
through lack of self-knowledge. Thus he meditates,

> Between the acting of a dreadful thing
> And the first motion, all the interim is
> Like a phantasma, or a hideous dream:
> The genius and the mortal instruments
> Are then in council; and the state of man,
> Like to a little kingdom, suffers then
> The nature of an insurrection.
>
> [II.i.63–69]

Yet in the next moment he turns his back on this foreboding
and welcomes the conspirators to his house. It is Brutus who
sees the ghost of Caesar and is indifferent to him; Brutus who
is afflicted with a revealing insomnia: "Since Cassius first did
whet me against Caesar," he says, "I have not slept" (II.i.61–
62). Like Gloucester, Macbeth, and Henry IV, all similarly
blind to self, he bears his crime on his conscience and cannot
sleep, though he is visited by an apparition which seems to

come from the dream state. There is a poignant moment after
the ghost's first appearance, when he tries in vain to convince
his servants and soldiers that they have cried out in the night:

Brutus:	Didst thou dream, Lucius, that thou so criedst out?
Lucius:	My lord, I do not know that I did cry.
Brutus:	Yes, that thou didst. Didst thou see anything?
Lucius:	Nothing, my lord.
Brutus:	Sleep again, Lucius. Sirrah Claudius! (*To Varro*). Fellow thou, awake!
Varro:	My lord?
Claudius:	My lord?
Brutus:	Why did you so cry out, sirs, in your sleep?
Both:	Did we, my lord?
Brutus:	Ay. Saw you anything?
Varro:	No, my lord, I saw nothing.
Claudius:	Nor I , my lord.

[IV.iii.291–301]

Nowhere is the quintessential loneliness of the conscience-
stricken man more forcefully portrayed. "Nothing, my lord."
Brutus, too, has misconstrued everything, and his tragedy is
that he suspects it. Trapped by his high-minded vanity and his
inability to function in the world of action—trapped, that is,
by his own character—he sees the Rome he tried to rescue in
ruins as a result of his act.

Caesar's ghost appears to Brutus in the source for *Julius
Caesar*, Plutarch's *Lives of the Noble Grecians and Romans*.
Its presence is also related to the Senecan theatrical tradition
we have discussed above. Psychologically, it can be seen as an
extension of Brutus's guilt feelings; like Richard III's Bosworth dream or the appearance of Banquo's ghost, the apparition here presents itself to one man only and is not sensed
by the others present. Such visionary dream figures are found
in Shakespeare only in plays which are directly concerned
with the psychological condition of the characters; the disap-

pearance of the ghost as a type in the plays following *Macbeth* is a sign, not merely of dramaturgical sophistication, but also of a shift in emphasis. For *Julius Caesar* is, in a way, the last play of its kind. The uses of dream, vision, and omen will change sharply in the plays that follow.

The motif of the misinterpreted dream in this play becomes a main factor in the dramatic action, demonstrating, always, some crucial fact about the interpreter. In the second scene of the play the soothsayer's warning goes unheeded, though in the same scene Caesar betrays his superstitious cast of mind. The contrast is adeptly managed: Antony is reminded to touch Calpurnia in the course of his race on the Lupercal, to remove her "sterile curse" (I.ii.9). But when the soothsayer cautions Caesar to "beware the ides of March" (18), he rejects the intended warning out of hand;

> He is a dreamer, let us leave him. Pass.
>
> [I.ii.24]

The inference is that dreams, like omens, are of no value; "dreamer" is a pejorative dismissal, akin to "madman." Calpurnia may have need of supernatural aid, but not the public Caesar. Already in this early scene we see him assuming a position closer to that of gods than men, a thoughtless hubris which is in itself dangerous. The omen, intrinsically a kind of dramatic device, is chiefly significant because it indicates his lack of self-knowledge.

The next scene, like much of the play, is in part at least a landscape of the mind. Casca, who is to be one of the conspirators, apprehensively reports to Cicero the strange events of the day. The heavens are "dropping fire" (I.iii.10), a slave's hand flames but does not burn, a lion walks in the Capitol, an owl sits in the marketplace at noon. These omens are all reported by Plutarch,[10] but Shakespeare turns them to drama-

---

10. "The Life of Julius Caesar," trans. Thomas North (1579), in *Shakespeare's Plutarch*, ed. C.F. Tucker Brooke (New York: Haskell House, 1966) II, 95–96.

tic purpose, making them mirror the conspirators' mood. "When these prodigies / Do so conjointly meet," says Casca,

> let not men say,
> "These are their reasons, they are natural,"
> For I believe they are portentous things
> Unto the climate that they point upon.

[I.iii.28–32]

To this superstitious view Cicero has a wise and moderate reply.

> Indeed, it is a strange-disposèd time:
> But men may construe things after their fashion,
> Clean from the purpose of the things themselves.

[33–35]

This is Titinius's lament: "Thou hast misconstrued everything." Like all the quasi-oracular pronouncements in this play, it is two-edged. Men may construe things as they like for their own purposes; just so Cassius plays on Brutus's fears of monarchy to enlist his help. And men may also misconstrue through error; so Caesar misreads the signs which might have kept him from death. But if Cicero's answer is apposite, it is also bloodless and dispassionate. What he does not consider is the element of humanity, the energy of men's passions inflamed by supposed signs. He is outside the tragedy, a choric figure who does not reenter the drama.

More and more it becomes evident that signs and dreams are morally neutral elements, incapable of effect without interpretation. By structuring his play around them, Shakespeare invites us to scrutinize the men who read the signs—to witness the tragedy of misconstruction. The two senses of Cicero's maxim, the willful deceiver and the willingly deceived, are the controllers of dream and the controlled. Decius Brutus, perhaps the coldest in a play replete with cold men, states the position of the former unequivocally. No matter how superstitious Caesar has lately become, he, Decius Brutus, is confident of his ability to manipulate him.

> I can o'ersway him; for he loves to hear
> That unicorns may be betrayed with trees,
> And bears with glasses, elephants with holes,
> Lions with toils, and men with flatterers;
> But when I tell him he hates flatterers,
> He says he does, being then most flattered.
> Let me work;
> For I can give his humor the true bent,
> And I will bring him to the Capitol.
>
> [II.i.203–11]

Willful misconstruction is his purpose and his art. And, fulfilling his promise, it is Decius Brutus who artfully misinterprets Calpurnia's dream and coaxes Caesar to the scene of his death.

Calpurnia's dream is one of the play's cruxes. By this time in the course of the drama an internal convention has been established regarding dreams and omens: whatever their source, they are true, and it is dangerous to disregard them. Shakespeare's audience would certainly have been familiar with the story of Julius Caesar, and such a collection of portents and premonitions would have seemed to them, as it does to us, to be infallibly leading to the moment of murder. Calpurnia herself adds to the catalogue of unnatural events:

> A lioness hath whelped in the streets,
> And graves have yawned, and yielded up their dead;
> Fierce fiery warriors fought upon the clouds
> In ranks and squadrons and right form of war,
> Which drizzled blood upon the Capitol;
> The noise of battle hurtled in the air,
> Horses did neigh and dying men did groan,
> And ghosts did shriek and squeal about the streets.
>
> [II.ii.17–24]

This is in fact an apocalypse of sorts, the last judgment of Rome. Unlike the events narrated by Casca, those reported by Calpurnia are not specified in Plutarch; it is noteworthy how

much more *Shakespearean* they are, and how economically
chosen to foreshadow, metaphorically, the later events of the
play. The lioness is Wrath, and from her loins will spring
forth "ranks and squadrons and right form of war," while the
ghost of Caesar appears solemnly in the streets. Shakespeare
was to remember this moment soon again, upon the appearance of the most majestic of all his ghosts.

> In the most high and palmy state of Rome,
> A little ere the mightiest Julius fell,
> The graves stood tenantless, and the sheeted dead
> Did squeak and gibber in the Roman streets.
>
> [*Ham.* I.i.113–16]

Calpurnia's *bona fides* as a prophetess is thus firmly established
by the time we hear her dream, and so too is the blind ob-
stinacy of Caesar. He willfully misinterprets a message from
his augurers, who advise him to stay away from the Capitol,
alarmed by the sacrifice of a beast in which they found no
heart. "Caesar should be a beast without a heart," he declares,
"If he should stay at home today for fear" (II.ii.42–43), thus
completely reversing the message of the haruspices. In this
mood he is interrupted by Decius Brutus, whose wiliness out-
lasts his own more heedless cunning. Caesar is one of those
elder statesmen who visibly enjoys causing discomfort to his
underlings; it is partially for this reason that he now abruptly
changes his mind upon the entrance of Decius and declares "I
will not come" (71). We have not yet heard the dream; Shakespeare leaves it for Caesar himself to recount, as he does now to
Decius.

> She dreamt tonight she saw my statue,
> Which, like a fountain with an hundred spouts,
> Did run pure blood, and many lusty Romans
> Came smiling and did bathe their hands in it.
> And these does she apply for warnings and portents
> And evils imminent, and on her knee
> Hath begged that I will stay at home today.
>
> [II.ii.76–82]

We may notice that here, as in our interpretation of Romeo's last dream, the dead man becomes a statue; this is a recurrent conceit in Shakespearean dreams, and in *The Winter's Tale,* as we will see, the dream action becomes plot as Hermione "dies," becomes a "statue," and is reborn. In Calpurnia's dream the latent dream thoughts are not far removed from the manifest content. She interprets the statue as the body of Caesar and also his funerary monument, and the gushing forth of blood she reads as death. As a prophetic dream this is both an accurate and a curiously lyrical one, graceful in its imagery. It forecasts directly the assassination before the Capitol.

Decius, however, is prepared for the event, and he begins immediately to discredit Calpurnia's prediction. He commences with what is by now a familiar note: "This dream is all amiss interpreted," and offers instead his own "interpretation":

> It was a vision fair and fortunate:
> Your statue spouting blood in many pipes,
> In which so many smiling Romans bathed,
> Signifies that from you great Rome shall suck
> Reviving blood, and that great men shall press
> For tinctures, stains, relics and cognizance.
> This by Calpurnia's dream is signified.
>
> [83–90]

It is the dissimulator now who cries, "thou hast misconstrued everything." He takes the manifest content of Calpurnia's dream and attributes to it a clever if wholly fabricated set of latent thoughts, which are the more impressive for their psychological insight. Caesar is flattered, as Decius had predicted, and resolves to go to the Capitol. His last doubts are abruptly erased when Decius suggests that he will be offered a crown and warns that refusal to go will seem like uxoriousness:

> it were a mock
> Apt to be rendered, for someone to say
> "Break up the Senate till another time,

When Caesar's wife shall meet with better dreams."

[II.ii.96–99]

This is a thrust well calculated to strike home. But there is a curious ambiguity about Calpurnia's dream, and the real irony of the situation is that Decius's spurious interpretation of it is as true in its way as Calpurnia's.

The content of her dream, it may be pointed out, does not itself appear in Plutarch. "She dreamed," he writes, "that Caesar was slain, and that she had him in her arms," and he also tells us that "Titus Livius writeth, that it was in this sort. The Senate having set upon the top of Caesar's house, for an ornament and setting forth of the same, a certain pinnacle, Calpurnia dreamed that she saw it broken down." [11] But the dream as we have it, the spouting statue and the smiling Romans, is a Shakespearean interpolation. Like Romeo's last dream, which we have already examined, it is chiefly remarkable for the fact that it permits two opposite interpretations, the one literal and the other metaphorical. For Decius's flattery,

> that from you great Rome shall suck
> Reviving blood, and that great men shall press
> For tinctures, stains, relics, and cognizance

is also a truth. Antony's funeral oration turns on precisely this point, elevating the slain Caesar to the status of a saint or a demigod, exhibiting the bloody wounds to win the hearts of the crowd. And at the play's end Antony shares hegemony—however uneasily—with the *novus homo* Octavius, literal descendant of Caesar's "blood."

The presence of Calpurnia's dream at this crucial point in the plot is thus trebly determined: (1) it has Plutarchan authority and is thus an original element in the story; (2) it acts as a functional device to further the action, showing the deliberate blindness of Caesar to a warning which would have saved his life and demonstrating the cold-blooded manipulation of the conspirators; (3) it symbolically foreshadows events

11. Ibid., p. 97.

to come, supporting the theme of "all amiss interpreted" which is central to the play's meaning. Interestingly, the accustomed tension between the men who aspire to control dream and those who are controlled by it is diminished in this episode; Decius, who means to assert control, is in a larger sense controlled, since he does not see that his interpretation is true.

For all its richness, however, the scene of Calpurnia's dream is rivaled in significance by a much more tangential scene, which seems at first glance oddly out of place in the plot. The scene of Cinna the poet is in many ways the most symbolically instructive of the whole play: it demonstrates in action the same theme of misinterpretation with which we have been so much concerned. Cinna the poet, a character unrelated to his namesake Cinna the conspirator, appears only in this scene, which may be seen as a kind of emblem for the entire meaning of *Julius Caesar*. We encounter him as he makes his way along a Roman street, and his opening lines describe his dream.

> I dreamt tonight that I did feast with Caesar,
> And things unluckily charge my fantasy.
> I have no will to wander forth of doors,
> Yet something leads me forth.
>
> [III.iii.1–4]

To "feast with Caesar" here means to share his fate—we may remember Brutus's "Let's carve him as a dish fit for the gods" (II.i.173). Cinna admits that he has had a premonition of danger, but that he has chosen to disregard it; "something"—misconstruction again—leads him forth. He is set on by a group of plebians, their emotions raised to fever pitch by Antony's oration, and they rapidly catechize him on his identity and purpose.

Third Plebian:	Your name sir, truly.
Cinna:	Truly, my name is Cinna.
First Plebian:	Tear him to pieces! He's a conspirator.
Cinna:	I am Cinna the poet! I am Cinna the poet!
Fourth Plebian:	Tear him for his bad verses! Tear him for his bad verses!

| *Cinna:* | I am not Cinna the conspirator. |
| *Fourth Plebian:* | It is no matter, his name's Cinna; pluck but his name out of his heart, and turn him going. |

[III.iii.27 ff.]

The scene is a perfect illustration of Cicero's verdict: "Men may construe things after their fashion, / Clean from the purpose of the things themselves." The taking of the name for the man—a thematically important element throughout this play, where Caesar is at once a private man and a public title—is symbolic of the overt confusion manifest in much of the action. Cinna's dream is a legitimate cause for anxiety, which he chooses to ignore at peril to himself. Plutarch supplied him with a practical motive: "When he heard that they carried Caesar's body to burial, being ashamed not to accompany his funerals: he went out of his house"; [12] in Shakespeare's version the cause is deliberately less exact, more psychological than circumstantial. The warning is given and ignored; the plebians do not care that they attack the wrong man. In one short scene of less than forty lines the whole myth of the play is concisely expressed.

Julius Caesar is a complex and ambiguous play, which does not concern itself principally with political theory, but rather with the strange blindness of the rational mind—in politics and elsewhere—to the great irrational powers which flow through life and control it. The significance attached to the theme of "thou hast miscontrued everything" clearly depends to a large extent upon the reading—or misreading—of the play's many dreams. Here, in the last of his plays to use dreams and omens primarily as devices of plot, Shakespeare again demonstrates the great symbolic power which resides in the dream, together with its remarkable capacity for elucidating aspects of the play which otherwise remain in shadow.

12. "The Life of Marcus Brutus," in Brooke, *Shakespeare's Plutarch*, II, 139.

2

Spirits of Another Sort:
A Midsummer Night's Dream

If we shadows have offended
Think but this, and all is mended:
That you have but slumb'red here,
While these visions did appear.
And this weak and idle theme,
No more yielding but a dream.

V.i.422–27

Puck's closing address to the audience is characteristic of the tone of *A Midsummer Night's Dream;* it seems to trivialize what it obliquely praises. All the key words of dream are here, as they have been from the play's title and opening lines: "shadows," "slumb'red," "visions," and "dream" itself. Puck is making an important analogy between the play and the dream state—an analogy we have encountered before in Shakespeare, but which is here for the first time fully explored. For *A Midsummer Night's Dream* is a play consciously concerned with dreaming; it reverses the categories of reality and illusion, sleeping and waking, art and nature, to touch upon the central theme of the dream which is truer than reality.

Puck offers the traditional apologia at the play's end; if the audience is dissatisfied, it may choose to regard the play as only a "dream" or trifle and not a real experience at all. The players, as Theseus has already suggested, are only "shadows" (V.i.212); the play, in short, is potentially reducible to a "weak and idle theme" of no significance. Yet everything which has gone before points in precisely the opposite direction: sleep in

A Midsummer Night's Dream is the gateway, not to folly, but
to revelation and reordering; the "visions" gained are, as Bottom says, "most rare" (IV.i.208), and the "shadows" substantial.
Puck's purposeful ambiguity dwells yet again on a lesson
learned by character after character within the play: that reason is impoverished without imagination, and that we must accept the dimension of dream in our lives. Without this acknowledgment, there can be no real self-knowledge.

The fundamental reversal or inversion of conventional categories which is a structuring principle of this play is familiar
to us in part from the framing device of *The Taming of the
Shrew*. The Athenian lovers flee to the wood and fall asleep,
entering as they do so the charmed circle of dream. When
Puck comes upon them and anoints their eyes, the world of the
supernatural at once takes over the stage, controlling their
lives in a way they cannot guess at, but must accept, "appre-
hending" "more than cool reason ever comprehends." In the
great dream of the forest experience and the smaller dreams
within it, we might say paradoxically that their eyes are
opened; this is the fundamental significance of the key word
"vision," which appears several times in the play, offsetting the
deliberately disparaging use of "dream" to mean something
insignificant, momentary. "Swift as a shadow, short as any
dream" (I.i.144), says Lysander in the first scene, describing
what he takes to be the inevitable tragedy of romantic love,
and Hermia replies that they must have patience, "As due to
love as thoughts and dreams and sighs" (154), where dreams are
once again the customary furniture of passion, illusory and
conventional.

By contrast "vision," as it is introduced into the play, is a
code word for the dream understood, the dream correctly
valued. Often the user does not know that he knows; this is another of the play's thematic patterns, supporting the elevation
of the irrational above the merely rational. As a device it is related to a character type always present in Shakespeare, but
more highly refined in the later plays, that of the wise fool.
Thus Bottom, awakening, is immediately and intuitively im-

pressed with the significance of his "dream," which we of course recognize as not a dream at all, but rather a literal reality within the play.

> I have had a most rare vision. I have had a dream, past the wit of man to say what dream it was.
>
> > [IV.i.205 ff.]

Similarly Oberon, to conceal the truth of events, instructs Puck to straighten out the mismatched lovers by crushing a magic herb into Lysander's eye, "and make his eyeballs roll with wonted sight" (III.ii.369). When the lovers wake, then,

> all this derision
> Shall seem a dream and fruitless vision.
>
> > [370–71]

The "vision" has been true, but he will make it appear to have been "fruitless," illusory, with the submerged Eden pun in "fruit" underscoring one of the play's principal mythic themes. Again, Titania, roused from her sleep, cries out

> My Oberon, what visions have I seen!
> Methought I was enamored of an ass.
>
> > [IV.i.77–78]

Her "visions," like the others, were "play" reality, and not dream or illusion. Moreover, the mental concept of "vision" in her phrase is picked up again in the more literal and physical reference in the next line (80) to his face or the way he looks. The association with images of sight, literal and metaphorical, is thematically significant. Early on, Helena suggests that "Love looks not with the eyes, but with the mind" (I.i.234):

> Things base and vile, holding no quantity,
> Love can transpose to form and dignity.
>
> > [232–33]

She does not, of course, comprehend the larger implications of this doctrine; yet this is what the mind of Titania in the dream

state does to the loathsome visage of Bottom, and the mind of
the bewitched Demetrius to the formerly despised Helena. It is
this transposition or transformation which is the special pre-
rogative of the dream state and the center of interest of the
whole of *A Midsummer Night's Dream*. Dream is truer than
reality because it has this transforming power; it is part of the
fertile, unbounded world of the imagination.

Standing in opposition to this world, which exists only
within the wood, is the practical everyday world of Athens, in
which reason and law hold sway. Interestingly, reason is a
limiting rather than a liberating force for Shakespeare, close
to Blake's "bound or outward circumference of energy," and
this is particularly true in *A Midsummer Night's Dream*.
Theseus attempts to impose a "reasonable" solution upon the
lovers without regard for passion or imagination, with the result that no one's happiness is taken into account. Lysander, his
eyes anointed in error by Puck so that he swears his devotion
to Helena, given "reason" as the excuse for his change of
heart:

> The will of man is by his reason swayed
> And reason says you are the worthier maid.
> Things growing are not ripe until their season:
> So I, being young, till now ripe not to reason.
> And touching now the point of human skill,
> Reason becomes the marshal to my will,
> And leads me to your eyes, where I o'erlook
> Love's stories, written in love's richest book.
>
> [II.ii.115–22]

It is characteristic of *A Midsummer Night's Dream* that Lysander should produce this speech at a point when his actions
are completely supernaturally or subconsciously controlled,
without the slightest hint of either reason or will. Delusion is
the prelude to illusion. Likewise it is fitting that the oracular
Bottom, unknowingly transformed into a monster, should observe placidly to Titania that "reason and love keep little company together nowadays" (III.i.142–43). Reason has no place in

the dream state, which possesses an innate logic of its own; and when characters attempt to employ it, they frustrate their own ends. Thus the lovers, awakened in act IV by the arrival of Theseus's hunting party, are bemused by what has taken place:

Demetrius:	These things seem small and undistinguishable,
	Like far-off mountains turnèd into clouds.
Hermia:	Methinks I see these things with parted eye,
	When everything seems double.
Helena:	So methinks:
	And I have found Demetrius like a jewel,
	Mine own, and not mine own.
Demetrius:	Are you sure
	That we are awake? It seems to me
	That yet we sleep, we dream.

[IV.i.188–95]

Although they reap the benefit of the night's dreams, they do not fully apprehend them. Significantly the images they choose to describe their experiences are those of ambiguous and incomplete vision: "parted eye," "far-off mountains turnèd into clouds." The memory of the dream is itself obscuring, because as the mind tries to rationalize what has occurred, it inevitably distorts. The instinct of the mind is to set boundaries, while the process of dream blurs and obliterates those boundaries. Demetrius's hypothesis—"that yet we sleep, we dream"—is literally incorrect, but there is another sense in which these dreamers are not, and will not be, awakened. We as audience are made aware of the primacy of the dream state, but the lovers, the means of our enlightenment, remain themselves unenlightened.

The pattern of the play is thus in part controlled and ordered by a series of vital contrasts: the opposition of the sleeping and waking states; the interchange of reality and illusion, reason and imagination; the disparate spheres of influence of Theseus and Oberon. All of these are structurally re-

lated to portrayal of the dream state; while the lovers sleep, the
world of dream and illusion inhabited by the fairies dominates
the stage. For the world over which Oberon presides, peopled
by Puck and Titania, by Peaseblossom and Mustardseed, is itself a dramatic metaphor for the dream world of the subconscious and the irrational. "Spirits" are moods and energies as
well as sprites, and the fruitful ambiguity of the word may
stand as a sign of the multiplicity of the world they inhabit.
As was the case with Queen Mab, and will be again with Ariel,
the diminutive fairies of Shakespearean fantasy are elemental
indwellers of the imagination, quicksilver manipulators of
dream. The simultaneity of dream world and spirit world is
central to an understanding of the special magic of *A Midsummer Night's Dream.*

There is, of course, a traditional literary basis for the dream
world, which extends back to the French and Middle English
dream visions of the fourteenth century. Throughout *A Midsummer Night's Dream* formal reminders of this tradition appear, often characteristically transformed into sophisticated
commentaries on the received forms. Particularly prominent
among these motifs are those of the god of love, the enchanted
garden, the journeying lovers and the May morning, all present in whole or in part in the play. Of these the most important for our purpose is the traditional figure of the god of love,
who acts as intermediary between the lover and the beloved.
This role is taken in *A Midsummer Night's Dream* by Oberon,
the fairy king, whose intent it is to bring together the right
pairs of lovers in the forest. Essentially he appropriates to himself the role of stage manager, a role we have seen utilized by
the lord in *The Shrew* for the purpose of controlling Christopher Sly's "dream," and one which will attain its greatest
prominence in the later and richer dream management of
Prospero and Autolycus.

Oberon's stage-managing falls somewhere between the relatively mechanistic deception of the *Shrew* lord and the
apocalyptic hegemony of Prospero. His intentions are in the
main benevolent; when he tells Puck to bring "death-counter-

feiting sleep" (III.ii.364) to the lovers, so that what has occurred may appear to them "a dream and fruitless vision," he
is attempting to redress an inadvertent error by his mischievous and unreliable messenger. The relation of sleep to death,
which will be strongly emphasized in *The Tempest,* is here
deliberately underplayed; Oberon, though he is a god of sorts,
is not trafficking in resurrection. Shakespeare has made him a
kind of tongue-in-cheek fairy king, a little pettish, something
of a buffoon. But like so many characters in this play, Oberon
speaks fairer than he knows; what to him are independent and
pragmatic actions, the putting to sleep of the lovers and of
Titania, have a much more far-reaching thematic significance
for the play as a whole. It is no accident that he regards the
events of the night as "accidents" (IV.i.69), which can be made
to seem to all "but as the fierce vexation of a dream" (70). He
undervalues dream and mechanizes "translation," and he,
like the lovers, is an accidental rather than a controlling instrument of the doctrine of creative dream.

As the play's god of love, Oberon is structurally comple-
mented by Peter Quince, who casts and manages the "most
lamentable comedy" of Pyramus and Thisby; and both are
deliberately made parallel to Theseus, Duke and arbiter of
Athens, so that the cognate worlds of reason, art, and imagination are juxtaposed through plot. It is notable that all three
authorities manage with more zeal than skill; Theseus appears
to appropriate the role of the reasonable adjudicator, but in
fact he fails to analyze the situation of the lovers properly and
later is persuaded to reverse his earlier ruling. The events of
the "dream" have altered his sense of reality, just as they have
ours. The dream vision situation, in which the lover is
thwarted by jealousy, idleness, and false appearances and is
both helped and hindered by the god of love, is here simultaneously echoed and commented upon.

If Oberon may be usefully compared to the much more complex figure of Prospero, there is also a sense in which Puck
looks forward to Ariel. Puck is a more deliberately earthbound
figure, a local British spirit not unlike Mercutio's Queen Mab.

He emerges from a world of regional superstition and old
wives' tales. "I jest to Oberon and make him smile," he tells
us,

> When I a fat and bean-fed horse beguile,
> Neighing in likeness of filly foal:
> And sometimes lurk I in a gossip's bowl,
> In very likeness of a roasted crab;
> And when she drinks, against her lips I bob
> And on her withered dewlap pour the ale.
> The wisest aunt, telling the saddest tale,
> Sometime for three-foot stool mistaketh me;
> Then slip I from her bum, down topples she,
> And "tailor" cries, and falls into a cough;
> And then the whole quire hold their hips and laugh,
> And waxen in their mirth, and neeze and swear
> A merrier hour was never wasted there.

[II.i.44–57]

This is the same theme of transformation we have observed
before, and to which we shall want to return at greater length.
Puck is a quicksilver figure, capable of lightning transformations and astonishing impersonations; he is a true denizen of
dream. Yet he lacks the sublimity of Ariel, the moral and spiritual grace. He is mischievous, and he makes mistakes. When
he leads the mechanicals astray, frightening them with the apparition of the transformed Bottom, he so reverses their ideas
about perception and comprehension that he places them in
the midst of nightmare:

> Their sense thus weak, lost with their fears thus strong,
> Made senseless things begin to do them wrong;
> For briers and thorns at their apparel snatch;
> Some sleeves, some hats, from yielders all things catch.
> I led them on in this distracted fear,
> And left sweet Pyramus translated there:
> When in that moment, so it came to pass,
> Titania waked, and straightway loved an ass.

[III.ii.27–34]

Likewise, when commanded by Oberon to keep Lysander and Demetrius safe from harm, he impersonates first one, then the other, in a frantic round robin that leads them both to abandon the chase for sleep. But there is a significant difference between Puck's coltishness, even on a supernatural level, and the more apocalyptic and controlled transformations of Ariel. The unholy triumvirate of Stephano, Trinculo, and Caliban poses a much more profound threat to art and humanity as represented by Prospero than does anything in *A Midsummer Night's Dream*. Prospero is severely distressed when, in the middle of the pageant of fertility, he remembers the existence of the plot against his rule; and Ariel's treatment of the rebels, though in many ways formally related to Puck's horseplay with the lovers and mechanicals, sounds a far deeper note which takes cognizance of tragedy:

>   I beat my tabor;
> At which like unbacked colts they pricked their ears,
> Advanced their eyelids, lifted up their noses
> As they smelt music. So I charmed their ears
> That calf-like they my lowing followed through
> Toothed briers, sharp furzes, pricking goss, and thorns
> Which ent'red their frail shins. At last I left them
> I' th' filthy mantled pool beyond your cell,
> There dancing up to th' chins, that the foul lake
> O'erstunk their feet.
>   [*Tmp.* IV.i.175–84]

This is a profoundly moral landscape, the projected vision of the internal state of a soul. It is a dimension which, with the less ambitious and more playful Puck, Shakespeare is careful to leave unexplored.

But the problem of the nature of the spirit world extends beyond Puck, even beyond Oberon. These are not apparitions, such as we found in *Richard III* and in *Julius Caesar*, nor are they creatures clearly contained within the fancy, as was the case with Mercutio's Queen Mab. They partake in part of the spirit of genius loci, especially in the account of Puck as a hobgoblin and in the names given to Peaseblossom, Cobweb, and Mustardseed—all, in Theseus's phrase, precisely "airy nothing" given "a local habitation and a name." But the fairies are predominantly inhabitants of an in-between world, neither wholly fictive nor wholly explainable in natural or even psychological terms. An important dialogue between Puck and Oberon touches usefully on this in-between state, a state which, like dream vision, takes place in half-light, between sleeping and waking.

> Puck: My fairy lord, this must be done with haste,
>   For night's swift dragons cut the clouds full fast,
>   And yonder shines Aurora's harbinger;
>   At whose approach, ghosts, wand'ring here and
>   there,
>   Troop home to churchyards: damnèd spirits all,
>   That in crossways and floods have burial,
>   Already to their wormy beds are gone.
>   For fear lest day should look their shames upon,
>   They willfully themselves exile from light,
>   And must for aye consort with black-browed
>   night.
> Oberon: But we are spirits of another sort.
>   I with the Morning's love have oft made sport;
>   And, like a forester, the groves may tread,
>   Even till the eastern gate, all fiery-red,
>   Opening on Neptune with fair blessèd beams,
>   Turns into yellow gold his salt green streams.
>   But, notwithstanding, haste; make no delay.
>   We may effect this business yet ere day.
>   [III.ii.378–95]

"But we are spirits of another sort"—Oberon's reminder charts a distinction without which we can hardly comprehend the importance of dream in the play. All the spirits of which Puck makes mention, ghosts and damned spirits immured in dusty churchyards, are the creatures of a superstitious supernaturalism, allied to witchcraft and fear. Not only the ghost of Caesar, but also old Hamlet and the *Macbeth* witches are inhabitants of this realm. We may usefully call them night or evening spirits, because they were thought to roam only in darkness; hence Horatio recounts the Christmastime phenomenon when "the bird of dawning singeth all night long" and no spirit dares to stir abroad. But they are evening spirits in another way as well, spirits which recall and recollect what has gone before, shadows whose substance is past. As such they stand in marked contrast to Oberon's "spirits of another sort" —morning spirits, or spirits of dawning. It is perhaps not too fanciful to compare such spirits with the impulse to creation, working in the half-light of the subconscious, shadows in place of and in some ways greater than the substance they portend.

This redemptive view of dream and its creatures arises in part from a new emphasis upon transformation as a creative act. We have seen that somatic dreams function through the use of transformations, described by Freud as displacements and condensations, by means of which the underlying meaning is bound into an apparently fictive plot. This process is clearly analogous in many ways to that of conscious fiction-making in literature; words like "symbol," "image," and "meaning" are common analytic terms for both the psychoanalyst and the literary critic, and the patterns of interpretation they employ each involve, at some stage, a search for subconscious and associative meanings which have been transformed or translated into the finished artifact, poem or dream. Our word "translate" overlaps both categories; when Peter Quince exclaims, "Bless thee, Bottom! Bless thee! Thou art translated" (III.i.117–18), he is describing the appearance of Bottom in an ass's head as a kind of awful change. The spectator knows, however, that Bottom is metaphorically an ass, a fool or buffoon. His "translation" is therefore in other terms a kind of identity, bringing the hidden to the surface through a literal symbol, the ass's head. The stage event has become a metaphor.[1] This is, as we have said, the special provenance of the dream world, that it presents the imagined as actual and that it does so by means of transformation.

1. It is interesting to note that Quintilian (*Institutio Oratione* VIII.2.6) equates *translatio*, "transfer," with the Greek figure Μεταφορά. See Ernst Robert Curtius, *European Literature and the Latin Middle Ages*, trans. Willard R. Trask (New York: Pantheon Books, 1952), p. 128.

In *A Midsummer Night's Dream* this transforming creative process becomes the subject as well as the technique of the play. The structural paradigm of transformation is the overall movement from court to wood and back, the transition from childhood and innocence to experience and adulthood. This is the fundamental Shakespearean pattern of growth and renewal, and it is anticipated in this play by the transformation which has already taken place in the lives of Theseus and Hippolyta. Theseus, the warrior and abductor, who "wooed [Hippolyta] with his sword" (I.i.16), is now the governor of a city, the guardian of the Athenian law, who will wed her "in another key" (18); Hippolyta, the warlike Amazon, erstwhile forest companion of Hercules and Cadmus (IV.i.113–19), is to be his wife in Athens. As the play opens these changes have already taken place, and they provide a frame or prologue for the works of transformation yet to come. Theseus now appears as the ostensible embodiment of civilized reason. Yet the choice he offers to Hermia between an unwelcome marriage and life in a nunnery is more like tyranny than reason or justice, and either alternative would run counter to the concept so often stressed in this play—that fertility is an important component of a creative and harmonious order. Throughout the play, and even at its close, Theseus stands as the apostle of reason against imagination, and therefore as a kind of limit to the transforming world of dream.

Not only the court-wood-court structure, but also the very nature of the landscape itself, form part of this spatial pattern of natural and supernatural transformation. We have touched upon the question of the landscape of the mind, the correlation between psychological and geographical description. This phenomenon might well be called "visionary landscape," because it is a projection of the subconscious state of mind upon the external state of terrain and climate—what Wallace Stevens was in his poetry to call "weathers." Early in the play we learn from Titania that her quarrel with Oberon has in fact brought about such a change; what was formerly a fairy place, *locus amoenus,* is now all disordered, its rivers overflowing

their banks, its corn rotten before it is ripe, its cattle dead or
dying.

> And thorough this distemperature we see
> The seasons alter: hoary-headed frosts
> Fall in the fresh lap of the crimson rose,
> And on old Hiems' thin and icy crown
> An odorous chaplet of sweet summer buds
> Is, as in mockery, set. The spring, the summer,
> The childing autumn, angry winter, change
> Their wonted liveries; and the mazèd world,
> By their increase, now knows not which is which.
> And this same progeny of evils comes
> From our debate, from our dissension;
> We are their parents and original.
>
> [II.i.106–17]

This is a strangely solemn note for a comedy. Suggestions of
the fall from paradise are unmistakable, yet the ostensible
cause (possession of the Indian page boy) seems insufficient.
Here we are directly confronted with the terrifying and inexplicable world of the irrational unconscious. What was once
perfect, regular, and orderly is now out of all proportion. Even
the place of ritual joy-making and fertility rites, the "nine
men's morris," is now "filled up with mud" (98). The overwhelming impression is that of sterility, and this is important
because it is the opposite of fruitful creation and change.
Everywhere in the plays of Shakespeare the progression of the
seasons is taken as a significant figure for the just and orderly
progression of life; in the most season-oriented of all the plays,
The Winter's Tale, Leontes greets the disguised Perdita as
"Welcome hither, / As is the spring to th' earth" (*WT* V.i.151–
52). Titania is describing the world of *A Midsummer Night's
Dream*, and it is a world which greatly needs this seasonal
change. In a sense the Athenian wood is at this point a parodic
version of Eden, a timeless but paradoxically disordered realm
which seeks a fortunate fall into knowledge.

    This pattern of fall and redemption is clearly a valuable

mythic analogue within the play. Both the Bible and the dream vision tradition classically present the image of a time-less garden, invaded and despoiled by a snake or its human counterpart. In Shakespeare's plays the same motif appears many times indirectly, as for example in the death of King Hamlet in the orchard, but it is nowhere so clearly and directly set forth as in *A Midsummer Night's Dream*. The innocent or unfallen version of the image is that of Titania as pictured by Oberon:

> I know a bank where the wild thyme blows,
> Where oxlips and the nodding violet grows,
> Quite overcanopied with luscious woodbine,
> With sweet musk roses, and with eglantine.
> There sleeps Titania sometime of the night,
> Lulled in these flowers with dances and delight;
> And there the snake throws her enameled skin,
> Weed wide enough to wrap a fairy in.

> [II.i.249–56]

Here we have a harmonious composition, suggestively Eden-like: the garden, the flowers, the unsuspecting lady, signifi-cantly asleep, and the amiable snake, herself engaged in be-nevolent natural transformation. Yet Oberon is describing this retreat in order that Puck may go there with the transforming love juice, to "make her full of hateful fantasies" (258). Thus Titania's apparently secure world is actually in the process of a fall—a fortunate fall, as it turns out, since the fantasy ex-perience in the wood helps to reunite her with Oberon and to restore order to the fairy world.

An equivalent structure can be perceived in Hermia's dream, the only literal dream in the play. Highly evocative, full of fruitful associations, the dream—in which Hermia is at-tacked by a serpent, while Lysander sits by "smiling at his cruel prey" (II.ii.150)—is especially susceptible to the kind of dream analysis we have been attempting. The snake, long a representative of violation and betrayal in scripture and in emblem books, is also a familiar Freudian image for male sexuality, and sexual fears are clearly in Hermia's mind:

"gentle friend, for love and courtesy," she says before they sleep, "Lie further off, in human modesty" (II.ii.56–57). At the same time her dream is monitory and predictive, describing in metaphorical terms the estrangement which is actually taking place. Puck has anointed Lysander's eyes, and his love has been transferred from Hermia to Helena. The snake image is vivid and literal within the dream, just as the ass's head was literal in the dream world of the enchanted Bottom. Interestingly, however, when Hermia awakes, into a world which is now for her fallen, she begins to use the same image in a figurative, allusive way. Demetrius, whom she suspects of doing away with Lysander, is a "worm," an "adder," a "serpent":

> with doubler tongue
> Than thine, thou serpent, never adder stung.
> [III.ii.72–73]

Where she was controlled by the snake image while dreaming, she here controls it with her conscious mind. We may note the difference in technique between the conscious and unconscious formulations. A protective distortion operates in the dream; by means of what Freud calls "displacement," Hermia separates Lysander, the beloved, from the serpent with whom she instinctively identifies him. The serpent eats at her heart, as does her love for the perfidious Lysander; and Lysander himself is made merely a passsive onlooker. She reproaches him for smiling, but she does not take the further step of blaming him directly for her unhappy condition. The splitting of the menacing figure into two, Lysander and the snake, may thus be considered as a compensatory action on the part of the subconscious. By contrast Hermia feels no such compunctions about accusing the despised Demetrius. She is able to use the snake image as a direct metaphor. The imputation of the "double tongue" is clearly the culmination of her outburst, and this is appropriate, because the question of duplicity and its near relative, ambiguity, is central to the concerns of the play.

Duplicity in Demetrius's case is really a matter of lack of self-knowledge; Berowne's maxim that we "lose our oaths to

find ourselves" is again apposite here. Hermia, however, like
so many others in this play, is afraid of ambiguity and double
meanings and equates them with guile. Fiction to her is a
species of deceit. Hers is a regressive attitude, antithetical to
the potentialities of dream, which is itself ambiguous and contains many things in one. The activities of condensation and
displacement, essential elements in the dream work, are based
upon the concept of multiplicity of meaning. In fact, this
positive pluralism is at the heart of the whole question of
dream, as we began to perceive in our examination of "truth"
and "fiction" in *The Taming of the Shrew*. The exchange of
shadow and substance, illusion and reality, is implicit in the
dream state, and it is the very impatience of the Athenians
with such an exchange which renders them insensible for a
while to the play's subtlest discoveries. Hermia's experience
in the woods, however, is a first step toward a heightened
awareness, a necessary incident in the pursuit of self-knowledge. Both specifically Edenic moments in the play thus utilize
a fundamentally comic form: the fortunate fall leads ultimately to reintegration, and the apparently innocent unfallen
state is seen to be fraught with danger and concomitant with
an interior disorder. Experience and change are clearly necessary if the persons of the play are to progress toward a fuller
understanding of themselves.

Change itself is essentially an aspect of creativity in the
realm of time; from the opening lines of the play it is evident
that time, too, is in a state of fallenness or disorder which requires reparation.

> *Theseus:*   Four happy days bring in
>   Another moon; but O, methinks, how slow
>   This old moon wanes! . . .
> *Hippolyta:*   Four days will quickly steep themselves in
>   night,
>   Four nights will quickly dream away the
>   time.
>
> [I.i.2–4,7–8]

Hippolyta uses "dream" here to mean "make to seem unreal." She is suggesting an illusion, the compression of an objective span, "four days and nights," into a subjective experience, "short as any dream." This imaginative compression is achieved in part through the "reality" of theatrical time, the fictive "four days" presented in two hours on the stage. "This palpable-gross play hath well-beguiled / The heavy gait of night," (V.i.366–67) says Theseus at the close of the "Pyramus and Thisby" play, underscoring the point, as the lovers depart for their nuptial beds. With the wedding night comes the promise of fertility, the reunion of Oberon and Titania and the consequent restoration of fertility and change to the landscape. Puck's last speech is appropriately concerned with progeny, since here at the play's close the fertility theme intersects with the theme of creativity and imagination.

Seasonal and temporal change are thus for *A Midsummer Night's Dream* active agents of transformation. With the initial premise "our quarrel has caused a disruption in the seasons" we are abruptly ushered into a world in which dream logic takes precedence over reality. Moreover, this impression is heightened when the proper personae of the wood appear. For one of the essential properties which is shared by Puck and Oberon is the ability to change shape at will—to present the illusion of something they are not. In a long jubilant passage we have already examined Puck reports his successive metamorphoses from "filly foal" to "roasted crab" and then to "three-foot stool" (II.i.44–57). Setting out to bait the Athenian lovers, he boasts

> Sometime a horse I'll be, sometime a hound,
> A hog, a headless bear, sometime a fire;
> And neigh, and bark, and grunt, and roar, and burn,
> Like horse, hound, hog, bear, fire, at every turn.
>
> [III.i.107–10]

Similarly Oberon is taxed by Titania for his impersonation of a love-struck shepherd:

> I know
> When thou hast stolen away from fairy land
> And in the shape of Corin sat all day,
> Playing on pipes of corn, and versing love
> To amorous Phillida.

[II.i.64–68]

Puck's antics seem largely drawn from the native folkloric tradition, though they may owe something as well to the figure of
Proteus; Oberon's more explicitly pastoral posturing recalls
Jove, another king of gods, and hints at a classical parallel.
These associations help to place the play in a larger imaginative context, to give it dimension and depth by suggesting a
body of tradition. But in all cases these allusions are subsidiary
to the central purpose, which is to develop and refine the growing sense of a dream world whose essence is change.

Physical transformations of this type are of necessity metaphorical in the language of the Athenian lovers: Helena at one
time calls herself a "spaniel" (II.i.203), and at another laments
"I am as ugly as a bear" (II.ii.94). Oberon, because of his fairy
powers, is able to transmute the metaphor into literal reality
at will, sending Puck for the flower whose juice will bewitch
Titania's eyes:

> What thou seest when thou dost wake,
> Do it for thy true love take;
> Love and languish for his sake.
> Be it ounce, or cat, or bear,
> Pard, or boar with bristled hair,
> In thy eye that shall appear
> When thou wak'st, it is thy dear.
> Wake when some vile thing is near.

[II.ii.27–34]

This is the literal enactment of Helena's homily on blind
Cupid, which was only meant as a figure: "Love looks not with
the eye but with the mind." The effect is a devastating parody
of romantic love, not unlike Mercutio's relentless baiting of
Romeo. Women "dote" beyond all control—"How I dote on

thee!" exclaims Titania to Bottom (IV.i.46)—and "dote" is throughout Shakespeare's plays a sign word for shallow, meaningless affection; men are literally turned into asses by romantic folly. Further, these literal transformations are echoed and answered by the behavior of the Athenian lovers, since it is a fundamental structural principle of the play that the creatures of the dream world enact literally what is undergone figuratively or metaphorically by the citizens of the court. The result is a kind of visual punning, with the metaphors physically present on the stage, as we have seen in the case of Bottom. At the same time, moreover, this process is a dramatic counterpart of the workings of the dream state, in which ideas and concepts are conveyed as visual symbols.

Metaphor, then, is a condition structurally analogous to the dream state. Moreover, in *A Midsummer Night's Dream,* the spectator's eye is continually directed to the act of metaphor-making, the visible exchange of literal for figurative and fictive. The whole play is almost a tour de force in this regard, and its sustaining creativity is developed, at least in terms of felt energy, as a crucial counterpart to the literal comedic values of fertility and marriage. Almost inevitably, then, the play begins to take on meanings which are at once direct and reflexive. The act of artistic creation, so clearly a conscious parallel to the subconscious activities of memory and imagination, is now brought before our eyes directly in a series of fictional artifacts: a sampler, a ballad, and a play. The availability of art as an ultimate form of transformation, a palpable marriage of dream and reason, emerges as a logical extension of the recognized dream state. Thus Helena, distraught and offended, reminds her childhood playmate of their earlier contentment together:

> We, Hermia, like two artificial gods,
> Have with our needles created both one flower,
> Both on one sampler, sitting on one cushion,
> Both warbling of one song, both in one key.
>
> [III.ii.203–06]

She pictures them as twin creators, "artificial gods," that is, gods of artifice, although the other meaning of "artificial" is also present in a muted and fallen way. As an image this anticipates the later and more resounding recollection of Polixenes, "We were, fair queen, / Two lads that thought there was no more behind / But such a day tomorrow as today, / And to be boy eternal" (*WT* I.ii.62–65). "Artificial" is thus darkly predictive, but the memory itself remains joyous. The girls are singing, an act with creative associations, as they perform the godlike act of creating flowers, transforming nature into art. The incident itself is lightly stressed within the play, a momentary glimpse rather than a vivid occurrence. As a memory, however, it retains a certain understated power, anticipating the more direct creative moments to come.

A more central incident for the play as a whole, and one crucial to the question of art as transformation, is the recapitulation of "Bottom's Dream." Significantly, as we have noted, the "dream" is of course not a dream at all; as was the case with Christopher Sly and others, the dreamer thinks he is awakening when he is actually moving from one kind of real experience to another. Bottom is the quintessential naïve percipient, and his approach to his "dream" is unfettered by reason:

I have had a most rare vision. I have had a dream, past the wit of man to say what dream it was. Man is but an ass, if he go about to expound this dream. Methought I was— there is no man can tell what. Methought I was—and methought I had—but man is but a patched fool if he will offer to say what methought I had. The eye of man hath not heard, the ear of man hath not seen, man's hand is not able to taste, his tongue to conceive, nor his heart to report, what my dream was. I will get Peter Quince to write a ballet of this dream. It shall be called "Bottom's Dream," because it hath no bottom; and I will sing it in the latter

end of a play, before the duke. Peradventure to make it the
more gracious, I shall sing it at her death.

[IV.i.205 ff.]

His text is well chosen; the passage from Saint Paul he quotes
in scrambled form [2] is not only a sign of his ignorance but
also, and more importantly, of his radical wisdom. Paul is
expounding the doctrine of the spirit in its primacy over the
letter—an important crux for metaphorical expression itself
and one which has a bearing upon the symbolic medium of
dream. "God," he says, "hath chosen the foolish things of the
world to confound the wise; and God hath chosen the weak
things of the world to confound the things which are mighty"
(I Cor. 1:27). The allusion is more meaningful to author and
audience than it is to Bottom; though he would doubtless
acknowledge himself one of the "foolish things of the world,"
he is not taking the context of his quotation into account—he
is intent merely upon utilizing an orthodox expression of
wonder. In part, the biblical quotation is thus a learned joke
at Bottom's expense. But we have learned by now that this
kind of joke is almost always superseded in *A Midsummer
Night's Dream* by a greater joke upon the learned perceiver.
Bottom's multiple confusion—"the eye of man hath not heard,
the ear of man hath not seen, man's hand is not able to taste,
his tongue to conceive, nor his hand to report"—is a synes-
thetic mixture highly characteristic of dream sensation. The inversion of "eye" and "ear" is a structural parody of the Pauline
original; that "tongue" should "conceive," however, is both
more profound and more relevant to the interests of the play.
In each of these phrases Bottom unconsciously warns us that
the senses are untrustworthy; at the same time, his malapropisms are related to the important theme of transformation. He
remains himself unaware of these further implications; like
the others in the play, he sees and says more than he con-

2. "Eye hath not seen, nor ear heard, neither have entered into the
heart of man, the things which God hath prepared for them that love
him" (I Cor. 2:9).

sciously knows, and like them he is fundamentally a determined realist. But his words speak to us with a special significance; like the porter in *Macbeth,* and the clown in *Antony
and Cleopatra,* he unknowingly hits upon the central themes
of the play. Despite his intellectual and cultural limitations,
his inadvertent role as the wise fool and his willingness to
suspend disbelief in the world of dream place him closer to the
top than to the bottom of an evaluative scale. This is the same
handy-dandy with which we are becoming familiar; what
Sidney called with disapprobation "mingling Kinges and
Clownes" [3] has a supreme logic of its own in the world of
dream.

Language as well as scriptural allusion seems to have a
transforming energy of its own within "Bottom's Dream." The
pun on "duke" and "gracious," for example, is doubtless hidden from Bottom himself, following the pattern of a more or
less oracular diction, truer than it is conscious of being. The
obvious irony of "man is but an ass," and the fleeting invocation of the "patched fool," a figure which throughout
Shakespeare's plays is representative of the imaginative capability of mankind, hint at deeper meanings than Bottom can
rationally perceive. But perhaps the clearest evidence of the
creative impulse to transformation is present on the level of
art, in Bottom's avowed desire to have Peter Quince "write a
ballet of this dream." The writing—and perhaps the perform-
ing—of the ballad is conceived as a kind of verification, the
manufacturing of a palpable artifact from the material of a
transient experience. In Bottom's eyes to "expound" the
dream is a fruitless and foolhardy task; what can be done instead is to transform it into an independent, unchanging work
of art. The choice of "ballad" again emphasizes the enormous
difference between the intellectual and cultural assumptions
of Bottom and the author and audience, while the unerring
movement from spiritual transformation through dream to

3. *Defence of Poesie,* in *The Prose Works of Sir Philip Sidney,* ed. Al-
bert Feuillerat (Cambridge: Cambridge University Press, 1962), II, 39.

ekphrasis, transformation into art, mirrors the informing structural design of the play as a whole.

The ballad of "Bottom's Dream" is of course never performed for the Duke. Instead the play's two audiences—the court of Theseus and ourselves—are privileged to witness an even more gloriously flawed artifact, "the most lamentable comedy, and most cruel death of Pyramus and Thisby," which in its parodic form summarizes and unites the themes of transformation in art, in nature, and in language. In part a failed transformation, a transformation out of control which keeps on transforming, the "Pyramus and Thisby" play is ultimately nothing less than a countermyth for the whole of *A Midsummer Night's Dream,* setting out the larger play's terms in a new and revealing light. In the body of the playlet, the audience sees before it a transformed vision of the events of the play. For "Pyramus and Thisby," while comic in performance, is unrelievedly tragic in conception. In it we see the spectacle of a father who harshly opposes the marriage of his daughter, just as was the case with Egeus and Hermia. But here the result is not reconciliation, but tragic death for the lovers. Similarly the menacing forest of the playlet, which contains the fatal lion, stands as a tragic alternative to the amiable world of the Athenian wood, where animal shapes are mischievous but benevolent, and natural spirits are agents of amelioration rather than of harm. Misconceptions and misinterpretations dominate both situations—the delusion of crossed loves among the Athenians is balanced by Pyramus's mistaken belief in the death of Thisby—but in the cathartic world of art the outcome is death, not marriage. The play-within-a-play thus absorbs and disarms the tragic alternative, the events which did not happen. Art becomes a way of containing and triumphing over unbearable reality.

Here, too, language has its part in demarcating patterns of transformation. The prologue, spoken by Peter Quince, is an accurate forecast of what will take place throughout the play-within-a-play.

Consider, then, we come but in despite.
    We do not come, as minding to content you,
Our true intent is. All for your delight,
    We are not here.

[V.i.112–15]

"Like a tangled chain; nothing impaired, but all disordered"
(V.i.125–26) is Theseus's opinion of this performance. The
clear intention of the text is amusingly and totally reversed by
the delivery of the speaker. "Nothing impaired, but all disordered," is in fact the prevailing condition of the world of
A Midsummer Night's Dream—a fruitful disordering in a
comic realm which leads to a renewed understanding. Its ar-
ticulation here in a most literal way, through the collision of
a rationally intended text and a passionate Peter Quince caught
up in his role as actor, makes plain the kinship of unreason
and imagination while hinting at their real dangers.

Characteristically, Bottom is vividly aware of the dangers of
imagination and illusion, while at the same time he is at-
tracted by them. He is eager, for example, to protect the court
audience against untoward effects of illusion. Thus his first
thought at the rehearsal of the mechanicals is that "Pyramus
must draw a sword to kill himself; which the ladies cannot
abide" (III.i.9–11). His answer, again characteristic, is to extend his own part:

I have a device to make all well. Write me a prologue, and
let the prologue seem to say, we will do no harm with our
swords, and that Pyramus is not killed indeed; and, for the
more better assurance, tell them that I Pyramus am not
Pyramus, but Bottom the weaver. This will put them out
of fear.

[III.i.15 ff.]

This is comic in part because the play as we perceive it is
hardly realistic enough to contain the dangers he fears for it.
But what is most telling about Bottom's plan here is his em-

phasis upon the literal truth: "Pyramus is not killed indeed"; "I Pyramus am not Pyramus, but Bottom the weaver." He sees the principal fiction of the "Pyramus and Thisby" play as somehow dangerous and misleading. By seeking to destroy or control the illusion, he demonstrates his faith in its power, together with his own limited understanding of that power. The same is true in the case of the lion's part: "To bring in— God shield us!—a lion among ladies, is a most dreadful thing" (III.i.29–30). Snug the joiner is therefore instructed to reassure the audience:

> If you think I come hither as a lion, it were pity of my life.
> No, I am no such thing. I am a man as other men are.
>
> [41 ff.]

"And there indeed," says Bottom, "let him name his name, and tell them plainly, he is Snug the joiner" (44–45). Part of the humor, as is usual with a play-within-a-play, comes from the doubling of the illusion: in trying to strip off artifice ("not Pyramus, but Bottom the weaver"; "tell them plainly, he is Snug the joiner") the speaker substitutes something equally artificial, since "Bottom" and "Snug" are fictions as surely as are Pyramus and the lion. But the limits of illusion for Bottom are not the same as those for the spectator. Distanced by our vision of the whole play, we can see that nothing is but what is not; Bottom is and is not Pyramus the mythical lover, just as he possesses and does not possess an ass's head, and has seemed to Titania both an "angel" (III.i.128) and a monster. The equality of all roles in a fictive world is vividly clear, just as in dreams a "composite person" [4] may simultaneously represent father, teacher, and lover. But to Bottom the artifice of imagination is more literal and more threatening. Insulated by laughter, the spectator can view the doomed lovers and the lurking lion without a sense of tragic identity. To Bottom, for whom they are not comic at all, the imitation and the tragedy are dangerously persuasive. The prologue serves as a deliber-

4. See Freud, *Interpretation of Dreams*, pp. 297ff.

ate breaking of the frame, paralleled by illusion-shattering
asides from Wall, Moon, and Pyramus in the body of the play.
In the analogy of dream, these are manifest content and latent
thoughts at once, and their clear purpose is to warn against
the dangers of the irrational: for the world of art, the lion in
the fictional forest; for the subconscious imagination, the
equally frightening serpent of Hermia's dream.

But if illusion and the imagination are not without their
dangers, they are nonetheless, in the terms of this play, pref-
erable to their radical opposite, "cool reason," in Theseus's
phrase. We have already observed the follies of Lysander when
he claims to be acting on the promptings of "reason," and considered the wisdom of Bottom's conclusions about reason and
love. *A Midsummer Night's Dream* is throughout a celebration
of the irrationality of love, not a criticism of the failure of
reason. The indistinguishable Athenian lovers and their
changeable passions are emblems, not of love's disorderliness,
but of its creative power, more akin to the logic of dream
than to that of waking reason. Yet it is part of the play's design
that none of the Athenians, including even Theseus and
Hippolyta, should fully comprehend the lessons of the dream
state. It might be said of them that they have had the experience and missed the meaning—missed it in part because of
the preoccupation with reason and the rational which dominates the civilized world of Athens. Puck's highly suggestive
closing words, with which we began this examination of *A
Midsummer Night's Dream*, are thus fittingly juxtaposed to
Theseus's great speech on imagination, a speech so frequently
considered out of context that it is rivaled only by Polonius's
"This above all, to thine own self be true," for distorted interpretation within the Shakespearean canon.

Theseus's position as a rational lawgiver has been somewhat impugned by the tyrannous sentence he imposes upon
Hermia, an exercise of "cool reason" without imagination or
generosity which calls into question his own understanding of
love. By the end of the play he has amended these rigorous
views; he approves the love matches of the Athenians and is

generously inclined toward the performers of "Pyramus and Thisby." His fundamental ideas about the relative values of reason and imagination, however, remain largely unchanged, and stand in sharp contrast to the doctrine of dream and the dream state as articulated by events in the interior world.

> *Hippolyta:* 'Tis strange, my Theseus, that these lovers speak of.
> *Theseus:* More strange than true. I never may believe
> These antique fables, nor these fairy toys.
> Lovers and madmen have such seething brains,
> Such shaping fantasies, that apprehend
> More than cool reason ever comprehends.
> The lunatic, the lover, and the poet
> Are of imagination all compact.
> One sees more devils than vast hell can hold,
> That is the madman. The lover, all as frantic,
> Sees Helen's beauty in a brow of Egypt.
> The poet's eye, in a fine frenzy rolling,
> Doth glance from heaven to earth, from earth to heaven;
> And as imagination bodies forth
> The forms of things unknown, the poet's pen
> Turns them to shapes, and gives to airy nothing
> A local habitation and a name.
>
> [V.i.1–17]

In these lines words like "fantasies" and "fables" are clearly deprecatory, as indeed is "fairy"; fictions and the world of the supernatural, because not "true," become suspect and of little value. Imagination itself is equated with madness and with the irrational—qualities which, in this play of "midsummer madness," have demonstrated enormous energies and the ability to bring about self-knowledge through transformed vision. The triad of lunatic, lover, and poet is meant to demean the

roles of poet and lover and comes oddly from a Theseus who
has won Hippolyta by the sword. Yet in this association
Theseus, like Bottom before him, speaks truer than he knows
and defines the very creative and imaginative unities toward
which all of *A Midsummer Night's Dream* has been striving.
The image of the poet's transforming power to make "shapes"
of the "forms of things unknown" follows closely the processes
of dream as we have seen them; the "airy nothing" which is
the raw material of poetic vision is clearly related to the
volatile "nothing" of other early plays. Though "nothing"
may be pejorative to Theseus, from his stance of practical
rationality, it is akin to Puck's "shadows" and imparts the
same sense of transcendent wonder. "Airy nothing" is clearly
an appropriate figure for the fairy folk who inhabit the
Athenian wood. It is equally telling as a description of the
subconscious dreams and conscious fictions which preoccupy
the play's human characters. And, even more, it is an emblem
of the spirit of creative gaiety which is so important to the
festive world of *A Midsummer Night's Dream*. Theseus himself intends his words in a critical and instructive sense as a
defense of reason. Yet with the ambiguity so characteristic of
utterances throughout the play, he sets forth, as well, an un-
exampled praise of imagination.

Theseus would partition experience into the true and the
false, the dream and the reality, much as did Christopher Sly
in *The Taming of the Shrew:* "Or do I dream? Or have I
dreamed till now?" But the transforming effect of the dream
world upon the Athenian lovers has been to teach them to
suspend disbelief in order to inhabit two worlds at once. "It
seems to me / That yet we sleep, we dream" says Demetrius
(IV.i.194–95) as the lovers follow Theseus out of the wood,
and significantly, a moment later, "Why then we are awake.
Let's follow him, / And by the way let us recount our dreams"
(199–200). This final impulse to recount is a counterpart of
the ballad projected by Bottom, a creative transformation
turning experience and insight into a self-contained verbal
form. Like the "winter's tale" and *The Winter's Tale*, a sym-

bolic artifact within the play and the play itself as a symbolic artifact, the dreams in *A Midsummer Night's Dream* have attained an important reflexive function as emblems of the visionary experience. In Hippolyta's perceptive phrase, the lovers see now with "minds transfigured" (V.i.24)—the ultimate turning inward of the world of dream. Moreover, the impulse to recount and remember is merged with the impulse to return, so that the redemptive energies of the play come to rest at last in a harmonious moment of self-realization. At the last, as Puck alone remains upon the stage, the "shadows" of *A Midsummer Night's Dream* have become inexhaustibly evocative, "no more yielding but a dream," in a dramatic world where dreams are a reliable source of vision and heightened insight, consistently truer than the reality they seek to interpret and transform.

3

A Dagger of the Mind:
Dream and "Conscience" in the Tragedies

Conscience is but a word that cowards use.
                    Richard III V.iii.310

Thus conscience does make cowards of us all.
                    Hamlet III.i.83

Richard III, as we have observed, is Shakespeare's first truly psychological play. The long, self-revelatory soliloquies, the apparitions, and the narrated dreams all create a reality both inside and outside Richard, wedding the subjective condition of consciousness to the objective conditions of London and Bosworth Field. The word "conscience" echoes repeatedly throughout the play: Margaret rails at Richard "the worm of conscience still begnaw thy soul" (I.iii.221); one of Clarence's murderers, though he acknowledges "certain dregs of conscience" (I.iv.122–23) in himself, concludes that conscience is a thing he'll "not meddle with," since it "makes a man a coward" (136–37). Richard himself, badly shaken by the parade of apparitions at Bosworth Field, for a moment concedes that

> My conscience hath a thousand several tongues,
> And every tongue brings in a several tale,
> And every tale condemns me for a villain.

> [V.iii.194–96]

But the play is really a systematic rejection of conscience, the tragic record of a failed self-knowledge. Richard's last defiant assertion, that "conscience is but a word that cowards use," is a denial of that interior reality, a desperate attempt to obliterate from mind all the reflective events of the play. We have been preparing for this rejection since the play's first moments: the refusal by Clarence to heed the warning of his own dream, Hastings's disregard of omen, the apparent emptiness of Margaret's curse—all of these are failed recognitions, moments when the realm of self-conscious awareness tries and fails to assert its primacy. It is appropriate that all of these moments are part of that complex of supernatural occurrences, omens, ghosts, and warnings, which we have come to associate with the world of dream. The dream world is able to exercise a controlling power beyond that of any of the play's characters, although none of them acknowledge its sovereignty. The undervaluing of conscience becomes, for the play as a whole, a sign of a larger misunderstanding. For, like those of *A Midsummer Night's Dream,* the characters of *Richard III* are affected by the subconscious and the dream state without ever fully realizing it. We see the play largely through Richard's persona, as a simultaneous portrait of his history and his soul; but he himself refuses to accept the correlation of the two spheres, and his final flaw is lack of self-knowledge.

"Conscience" in *Richard III* is predominantly a moral term, having its modern meaning of "sense of duty" or "remorse." When Richard associates conscience with cowardice, he is talking about feelings of guilt and responsibility, essentially societal values internalized into a moral system. But "conscience" in Shakespeare's time also carried the primary meaning of "consciousness." Hamlet's "conscience does make cowards of us all" is a tacit recognition of the primacy of "consciousness" in the human spirit; "conscience" in his phrase contains both of its root meanings and yet goes beyond them, to express the essential condition of man. To Richard, only cowards capitulate to conscience; by the time of *Hamlet,* though Richard's meaning is retained, "conscience" in the sense of "consciousness" has reversed the terms; and cowardice, if one equates it with a sensitivity to the subjectiveness of human experience, is finally the condition which draws us all

together. That man should be in this state, confronting rather
than avoiding the problem of his own consciousness, is a prelude to the tragic experience. And in the great tragedies from
Hamlet to *Antony and Cleopatra* Shakespeare develops the
theme of consciousness to a point where the world of one
man's imagination, the psychological dream state, takes over
the landscape and the characters of the drama.

The relationship between subjective and objective experience, the thing thought and the thing done, is a constant
concern in Shakespeare's plays from the earliest histories to
the last romances. Of all the plays, *Hamlet* perhaps best illus-
trates the problem of subjectifying experience, the reduction
of "what happens" to "what is thought," the temporary, often
playful, yet always significant exchange of the fictive for the
"real." This is a reversal we have considered at some length
in relation to *A Midsummer Night's Dream;* in *Hamlet* the
means of exchange is subtly different, because it has its root
in Hamlet's own conscience. Dream here, as in the other great
tragedies of the middle period, is most nearly equivalent to
consciousness, the world subjectively glimpsed through the
lens of imagination. At one pole this encompasses all that is
terrifying, irrational, inexplicable: the ghost of old Hamlet,
the *Macbeth* witches, the storm on the heath in *King Lear.*
At the other, equally true, are the redemptive moments,
grounded in common experience uncommonly viewed: Cleopatra's dream vision of Antony, the awakening of Lear. Literal, encapsulated dreams of the sort of Clarence's dream have
almost entirely disappeared: the only traditionally "told"
dream in all these plays is the supposed dream of Cassio, and
significantly it is not really a dream at all, but rather a fiction
crafted and controlled by Iago. This replacement of the episodic dream by the dream state is a dramaturgical advance,
permitting a steady flow of plot and language without the in-
terruption of artificially impacted flashbacks or recapitulations.
At the same time, however, refinement in dramatic construction is paralleled by refinement in thematic development, as

the dream state more and more encompasses the entire world of the play. The theme of consciousness, which unites the inner world of private vision with the outer world of visible reality, deliberately blurs distinctions between the factually "real" and the purportedly "imagined," so that the audience, as much as the protagonist, is forced to make wholly subjective choices among equally possible truths.

The familiar supernatural background of shaded omen and sign is established for *Hamlet* by the remarkable opening scene. The time is midnight, midway between dusk and dawn, and the night so dark that the sentries cannot see. That they tensely mistake one another for intruders is our first symbolic indication of a danger which lurks within Denmark, rather than without. Almost immediately the subject of the ghost is introduced, together with the crucial question "Is it real?"

> *Marcellus:* What, has this thing appeared again tonight?
> *Barnardo:* I have seen nothing.
> *Marcellus:* Horatio says 'tis but our fantasy,
> And will not let belief take hold of him
> Touching this dreaded sight twice seen of us;
> Therefore I have entreated him along
> With us to watch the minutes of this night,
> That, if again this apparition come,
> He may approve our eyes and speak to it.
> *Horatio:* Tush, tush, 'twill not appear.
>
> [I.i.21–30]

The terrifying vagueness of "this thing" immediately intensifies the mood of mystery: the ghost is unclassifiable, uncontrollable, and therefore frightening. Barnardo replies with the factual "I have seen nothing," which is meant to convey the fact that the ghost has not yet appeared. Yet our experience of the word "nothing" and its potential for ambiguity should alert us here; behind Barnardo's assertion is the covert meaning "I have seen a ghost; I have seen something made of 'nothing.'" Barnardo, of course, does not intend this meaning; the poet's adroit manipulation of language preserves verisimilitude on the literal level while permitting the audience a glimpse of deeper symbolic significance. It is a pattern we have seen before, and it here once more reinforces the important fact that dream goes beyond reason into the subjective realm of poetry. Having lightly but unmistakably established this theme, the scene moves away from it with superb economy. Horatio, rational man in his most attractive guise, is also present on the ramparts, and Marcellus makes it clear that he finds the idea of the ghost incredible. According to him it is "fantasy," meaning not creation but delusion, a phantom vision induced by an atmosphere of terror. For a moment we are drawn to agree with him, as we are meant to; the reassuring finality of "tush, tush" is a prosaic and welcome assertion of the boundary between the actual and the fantastic. But the well-bred control which is later to caution against considering "too curiously" is almost immediately demonstrated as the limited gift it is, as the appearance of the ghost on the platform abruptly negates all Horatio's scholarly assumptions.

Each of these independent figures represents an aspect of the mind of Hamlet; it is part of Shakespeare's astonishing craftsmanship that he should be able to present characters and settings simultaneously as subjective interior perceptions and objective exterior realities. In its treatment of the dream state *Hamlet* may therefore be viewed as an internal landscape projected by the protagonist, a shadowy world inhabited by figures inseparable from the "conscience" of Hamlet himself. Thus the ghost can be interpreted both as superego and as old Hamlet, guardian of ancient values; Horatio, both as Freudian censor and as the wise and temperate scholar from Wittenberg. Laertes and Fortinbras also appear in the play as alter egos for Hamlet—Laertes a skilled fencer and fiery champion of Ophelia, Fortinbras a "most royal" prince—and Hamlet's progress toward self-knowledge in the play depends in large part upon his readiness to recognize these identities within himself.

The metaphorical equivalency of interior and exterior
worlds is set forth with great clarity in an early exchange between Hamlet the father and Hamlet the son. Fading from
the battlements, the ghost enjoins at the last, "Remember me"
(I.v.91), and Hamlet cries

> Remember thee?
> Ay, thou poor ghost, whiles memory holds a seat
> In this distracted globe.
>
> [I.v.95–97]

Clearly, the phrase "distracted globe" here carries a primary
meaning of "confused mind"; metaphorically, Hamlet pledges
to remember as long as he has a memory, which is to say, as
long as he lives. But the literal meaning of "globe" is also
appropriate here, since the world of the play is likewise "distracted" by the murder of the king, all the personae of the
kingdom blighted in language and action; the madness Hamlet assumes when he puts on his "antic disposition" (I.v.172)
is a madness already present in the state of Denmark. Moreover, the "distracted globe" may well carry a third relevant
meaning, since the theater in which the play's Elizabethan
audience "held a seat" was also called the Globe. Hamlet's
pledge thus takes on the added meaning "as long as the play
is remembered or performed," a sense enriched further by the
traditional belief that Shakespeare himself appeared in the
original production in the role of the ghost: not only will old
Hamlet be remembered, but so too, through him, will the
playwright and the play. The mysterious world of theatrical
illusion of course becomes itself a principal subject for the
play as a whole, and it is a "distracted" world in part because
of the difficulty of distinguishing actor from audience. Claudius
thinks of himself as merely a spectator watching a play in the
"Mousetrap" scene (III.ii); he is not aware that he is at the
same time a character in a larger play of Hamlet's devising, or
that he and Gertrude are soon to be revealed as an actual
"player king" and "player queen." Polonius, considering that

"more audience than a mother" (III.iii.31) should hear Hamlet's conversation with the queen, conceals himself behind the
arras in her chamber; he is tragically transformed into an
actor when his shouts for help provoke Hamlet to stab him
blindly through the curtain. Everywhere reality has become
elusive, as we have already seen in Horatio's confident rejection of the supernatural and the immediately subsequent
entrance of the ghost. Just as boundaries between Norway and
Denmark, youth and age, life and death seem to be constantly
shifting in this play, so too do boundaries between reality and
illusion. "My father, methinks I see my father," exclaims
Hamlet to a startled Horatio. "Where, my lord?" "In my
mind's eye, Horatio." "My lord, I think I saw him yesternight"
(I.ii.184–85, 189). This sudden transition from conventional
recollection to supernatural vision, especially when voiced by
the supremely rational Horatio, is a leap into the world of
illusion.

Hamlet himself is of course perfectly capable of distinguishing in basic terms between the actual and the dreamlike or
fictive. The challenge of the ambiguity comes in his conscious
refusal to sort these aspects of experience according to conventional classification. There is something electric in the emotion which seizes him when confronted, suddenly, with the
denizens of the imagination. It is important to keep in mind
that in *Hamlet* the ghost and the players are parallel entities,
compounded of fact and fiction, reason and something beyond
reason. In *Richard III* the characters of dream were ghosts,
apparitions, omens which impinged upon the passive consciousness of Richard and of Clarence; in *A Midsummer
Night's Dream* the dream world was inhabited by creative and
fertile sprites whose presence was inseparable from concepts
of play and imagination. In *Hamlet,* fittingly, the two senses
come together, fused by the imagination of Hamlet himself,
now in the condition of Everyman, the man of "conscience" or
consciousness. Thus there is a strange but unmistakable triumph in his reply to Horatio, as the ghost cries in the cellar-
age:

Horatio:	O day and night, but this is wondrous strange!
Hamlet:	And therefore as a stranger give it welcome.
	There are more things in heaven and earth, Horatio,
	Than are dreamt of in your philosophy.

[I.v.164–67]

Horatio's exclamation is an admission that the appearance of the ghost violates his canons of experience. We would expect this to be more or less the same for Hamlet, as it has been for the other members of the watch. But the effect of the apparition on Hamlet is in fact one of liberation rather than of amazement. In part this is because the reality of the ghost is validated by his own imagination. "Touching this vision here, / It is an honest ghost" (137–38), he assures the frightened watchmen. Its message, in fact, has apparently been subconsciously suggested to him before the actual apparition—"O my prophetic soul!" (40), he cries out at news of the usurpation, in a phrase at once wonderfully expressive and remarkably condensed. The foreboding of prophecy, which in the earlier plays required the extensive narration of monitory dream, is here magically contained in a moment.

Hamlet's exchange with Horatio is made even more significant, however, by the addition of the element of wordplay. "And therefore as a stranger give it welcome," he urges. He alludes in part to the courtesy proverbially accorded to visitors from foreign parts, a category in which he affects, somewhat whimsically, to include the ghost. Horatio is thus urged to accept the presence of the apparition without question, extending his cautiously delimited concept of the logical and the real. But at the same time the resonant word "stranger" in folklore denotes "something foreboding the arrival of an unexpected visitor," in effect an omen or sign. The ghost is an apocalyptic forecast of a later revelation. As such it represents the rich and proper sphere of dream, implicitly contrasted by Hamlet with the conventional things "dreamt of," or envisioned, in Horatio's study. The puns and double meanings here are of great importance, as they will be throughout the play. Hamlet, an inveterate punster and wit whose caustic, ribald humor resembles that of Mercutio, repeatedly attempts to control his environment and indeed the entire external world through the manipulation of language. In doing so he asserts the primacy of the imagination, the dream state of creation in which "words, words, words" are greater than and different from the mere "matter" they contain.

His starting point, of course, has been the message of the ghost, a message itself delivered in a tone strikingly different from that of the surrounding drama. The ghost of old Hamlet has within the play a dual reality: as an apparition he is really more closely related to the omens and oracles of earlier plays than to spirits of imagination, and he appears only to give his fateful report, reappearing once to Hamlet to "whet [his] almost blunted purpose." (III.iv.112) He is a "real" illusion in the sense in that he can be seen, not only by Hamlet, but by Horatio and the sentries. Yet the queen will see "nothing at all" (III.iv.133) when he appears in her closet; though the audience, once more included in Hamlet's interior consciousness, can both see and hear him. The ghost is in fact an intuition or perception in the mind of Hamlet at the same time that he is corporeally distinct from him, and a willingness to accept this seeming paradox is essential to an understanding of the dynamics of dreaming throughout the play.

A revenge figure descended not only from Elizabethan and Senecan models but also from Patroclus of the *Iliad*, old Hamlet cones, like his Homeric predecessor, to press his dilatory champion to action in an epic world. His associations with the epic are manifold: he is dressed in "complete steel" (I.iv.52), and his mode of warfare is the single combat in which he defeated old Fortinbras; both costume and martial demeanor contrast as sharply as possible with the luxurious furnishings of the Claudian court and its twin weapons, the rapier and the "painted word." His language, too, is epic in style: "List, list, o list," he intones, (I.v.22); "Of life, of crown, of queen at once dispatched" (75); "unhouseled, disappointed,

unaneled" (77); "O, horrible! O, horrible! Most horrible!"
(80); and finally, "Adieu, adieu, adieu" (91). We have heard
these portentous triplets before, in "The most lamentable
comedy, and most cruel death of Pyramus and Thisby," where
Shakespeare was clearly burlesquing the language of early
tragedy in a play obviously intended by its actors to rival the
best of the genre: "Thou wall, O wall, O sweet and lovely
wall" (*MND* V.i.176); "O grim-looked night! O night with hue
so black! / O night, which ever art when day is not!" (170–71);
"And farewell, friends. / Thus Thisby ends. / Adieu, adieu,
adieu" (344–46). The voice of the ghost in *Hamlet*, of course,
sounds quite a different note; his incitement to revenge is a
plea for Hamlet to return to an Old Testament world as well
as to a world of epic values and heroic wrath. But with the
murder of the king and the ascension of the political Claudius
such a return is rendered impossible, as it will be after the
death of Hector in *Troilus and Cressida* or the defeat of
Antony in *Antony and Cleopatra*—both, like old Hamlet, epic
heroes anachronistic in a modern world.

Yet the voice of epic is close to the voice of myth, and the
tale of horror the ghost comes to tell has the spare authority
of myth and the symbolic form of dream. Significantly, it is a
tale of a sleep and a visitor to sleep; equally significantly, it is
a tale which has been misconstrued and which requires a new
interpretation.

> 'Tis given out that, sleeping in my orchard,
> A serpent stung me. So the whole ear of Denmark
> Is by a forged process of my death
> Rankly abused. But know, thou noble youth,
> The serpent that did sting thy father's life
> Now wears his crown. . . .
>
> . . . Sleeping within my orchard,
> My custom always of the afternoon,
> Upon my secure hour thy uncle stole
> With juice of cursed hebona in a vial,

And in the porches of my ears did pour
The leperous distillment. . . .

[I.v.35–40; 59–64]

This is an Edenic myth of corrupted innocence, the invasion
of a medieval *hortus conclusus*. In the ghost's interpretation,
the metaphorical "serpent" is replaced by the specific "thy
uncle," Claudius, the literal invader of the peaceful orchard.
The version of his death widely accepted in Denmark is un-
masked as a fiction which hides the truth through metaphor:
"The serpent that did sting thy father's life / Now wears his
crown." The tale is important because it interprets the dream
which deludes Denmark; its images will recur repeatedly
throughout the play and dominate its plot and imagery, constantly reminding us—as well as Hamlet—that old Hamlet was
killed in a *garden*, by a human *serpent*, who poured *poison*
in his *ears*. " 'A poisons him i' th' garden for his estate"
(III.ii.265), as Hamlet will gloss the play-within-the-play.

The garden or orchard assumes the character of a despoiled
Eden of the purer past, a garden of attempted innocence which
is literally associated with its biblical antecedents by the
gravedigger's punning joke about "Adam's profession" (V.i.
31), now shared by "gard'ners, ditchers, and grave-makers"
(30). It is a garden in which Gertrude's marriage to Claudius
"takes off the rose / From the fair forehead of an innocent
love, / And sets a blister there" (III.iv.43–45), bringing together the themes of garden and poison. Ophelia calls Hamlet
"th'expectancy and rose of the fair state" (III.i.153); she herself, addressed as a "rose of May" (IV.v.158) by Laertes, sings
mad songs which are all too apt in their scattering of telltale
flowers, and her watery death, "When down her weedy
trophies and herself / Fell in the weeping brook" (IV.vii.174–
75), seems to translate into action the language of Hamlet's
first bitter soliloquy on self-slaughter: "Fie on't, ah, fie, 'tis an
unweeded garden / That grows to seed" (I.ii.135–36).

The "serpents" who infiltrate this garden are many: not
only Claudius, but also his willing instruments, the insinuating

Rosencrantz and Guildenstern, whom Hamlet vows he will trust "as I will adders fanged" (III.iv.204). The poison administered by such "serpents" is that which is rotten in the state of Denmark: the ulcers beneath the skin, cosmeticked over with lies, the contagion that spreads unwholesomely through the night, and above all the poisonous language of deceit and pretense which is everywhere in the play poured into unsuspecting ears. There is, too, the "certain convocation of politic worms" (IV.iii.20) to whom Hamlet consigns the body of Polonius, and the all-conquering Lady Worm, a special and victorious serpent who abides as the genius loci of that ultimate garden, the graveyard.

The ears of the ghost's tale are also omnipresent in *Hamlet:* in the advices of fathers to sons which occupy so much of the first act; in the "ear of Denmark" which is abused by the false account of the king's death; in the constant practice of eavesdropping: Claudius and Polonius behind the arras listening to Hamlet and Ophelia; Polonius again concealed, this time in the queen's chamber; Claudius sending for Rosencrantz and Guildenstern to eavesdrop on Hamlet's plans; Polonius dispatching Reynaldo to ascertain "by indirections" Laertes' reputation in France. Words enter like daggers into Gertrude's ears; Hamlet seeks to know if the king will "hear this piece of work" (III.ii.46–47) as he prepares the play; and the ghost himself, who has initiated the theme, enjoins his son to "List, list, O list."

Indeed there is a sense in which, by the very act of telling his tale, old Hamlet pours poison into the ear of young Hamlet, inflaming him to agony, soul-searching, and revenge, so that the "antic disposition" and the protective cloak of "words, words, words" become for him a temporary but necessary means of escape from the sudden burden of fact and responsibility for action. Thus we find in *Hamlet* the same triple pattern we have elsewhere observed, from exterior "real" world to interior psychological landscape and back—in *A Midsummer Night's Dream,* the journey from court to country to court. Here it emerges as a journey into the world of art, play,

and fiction, whose own proper personae are the players—
players who almost seem to materialize out of his own sudden
awareness that the world about him is replete with posture
and pretense. Hamlet's journey is a journey into the mental
territory of the irrational, and the later "real" voyage to England, where the gravedigger will jest that all men are "as mad
as he" (V.i.154), becomes its metaphorical counterpart.

The interior landscape is deftly described by Hamlet himself in a deceptively playful dialogue with Rosencrantz and
Guildenstern on the subject of his "bad dreams," (II.ii.243–
70), a dialogue which ends with the defiant assertion, "I cannot
reason." The entire scene is highly reminiscent of Mercutio's
dry disquisition on Queen Mab, contained within a verbal
pattern closely analogous to dream logic. But unlike the amiable linguistic duel of Romeo and Mercutio, this contest of
wits is a mask for pointed accusation and revelation. There is
a heady recklessness in Hamlet's tone, for he is playing with
his schoolmates as skillfully as he later intercepts their attempt
to "play upon" him. He is wise enough to recognize the limitations of rationality in a world in which fear and death play
major roles. His delight in badinage sharpened by double
meaning is especially keen when the recipients of his verbal
thrusts—Rosencrantz, Guildenstern, Polonius, Osric—perceive
only the deceptive surface. In his remarks to Rosencrantz and
Guildenstern, the form with which he is playing is *argumentum,* or syllogistic reasoning, a favorite university game and
one well suited to the occasion. His final abjuration, "I cannot reason," rejects not only the triviality of the *argumentum*
but also the self-interest, policy, and cold-blooded "reasoning"
of these "indifferent children of the earth" (230). For Hamlet
himself is far from indifferent. In an attempt to discover meaning and moral values in a world without them, he places the
boundaries of that world metaphorically within himself. Thus
he argues that the world is a "prison" (255) not because of the
"ambition" suggested by the ambitious Rosencrantz, but
rather because he has "bad dreams." He is confined not by
physical boundaries, but instead by boundaries which are

psychological, part of the realm of imagination. His "bad dreams" are a clear reversal of outer and inner worlds, for the "dreams" are not dreams at all, but rather intimations of the truth behind real events in Denmark. Unprotected by a "nut-shell" to insulate him against the pain of sensibility, he moves forward into an area of willed subjectivism, in which "dream" becomes a term synonymous with his own vision. "I cannot reason" thus announces his readiness to abandon logic for emotion. Verbally, at least, he embraces the irrational, pre-ferring Guildenstern's disparaging "dream," and Polonius's "madness," to a world in which logic has replaced human values.

We have noticed that the world of Denmark contains at least three distinct, if related, kinds of illusion: the apparently real illusion of the ghost, verified by the evidence of Hamlet's eyes and ears; the patently false illusion which is the common language of pretense in Claudius's court; and the deliberately fictive illusion of the players, whose world is the world of crea-tive imagination, and whose materials are the same materials as those of the larger play, *Hamlet,* which contains them. In choosing the world of the creative irrational, the players' world, Hamlet attempts to penetrate the atmosphere of "seeming" which so vexes the court. The instinctive desire to play a part, to escape from the prison of unyielding reality into the interior world of dream and illusion, is a fundamental aspect of his character, and nowhere is it more clearly shown than in his sincere affection for "the tragedians of the city" (II.ii.336). The players' stock-in-trade is this very business of illusion, and it is clear that he feels far more comfortable in their world than in his own. When they are announced, Hamlet once more assumes that strange gaiety which informs his other moments of "playing." Yet he remains mindful of his own limitations; while urging the first player to recite a half-remembered speech, he is suddenly struck by the contrast with his own reaction to actual events. As in *Richard III,* the solil-oquy here becomes the instrument of his own psychological revelation; it is yet another indication of the unity of physical

and psychological worlds in Hamlet's persona that we hear
his thoughts as if they were spoken aloud:

> Is it not monstrous that this player here,
> But in a fiction, in a dream of passion,
> Could force his soul so to his own conceit
> That from her working all his visage wanned,
> Tears in his eyes, distraction in his aspect,
> A broken voice, and his whole function suiting
> With forms to his conceit?

> [II.ii.556–62]

"Dream" is here explicitly equated with "fiction," and also
with the poetical terms "forms" and "conceit." Hamlet is ap-
palled that the player can evince more emotion in a fictive
circumstance than he himself in a real one. But once more the
implication is of the strangely extended power of dream and
creative imagination over reality. The players' element is
dream; Hamlet for a moment covets both the element and the
response. Later in the same speech he will deprecate himself
further, drawing the parallel directly:

> Yet I,
> A dull and muddy-mettled rascal, peak
> Like John-a-dreams, unpregnant of my cause,
> And can say nothing.

> [572–75]

The short line is a pivot turning the subject from the player
to Hamlet himself. Where dream in the player's world was
a powerful creative tool, dream in Hamlet's bitter estimate
of himself is the nonproductive daydream of the village idler,
concomitant of inaction. Yet we might observe that the self
of whom Hamlet speaks has ceased in part to exist some thirty
lines before, at the point when he determined to become not
only an actor but also a playwright and director. In conceiv-
ing the plan to play "The Mousetrap" before the king, he has
begun to exchange the unprofitable musings of John-a-dreams
for "dreams of passion" which will provoke passion itself. His

self-castigation is once again couched in terms of utterance: he "can say nothing." Yet when he asks for "The Mousetrap," he calls for speech in its most carefully crafted form; and with the insertion of "some dozen or sixteen lines" of his own he speaks through the play, transforming it into a new and private artifact of his own. "Nothing," as always, is a clue to ambiguity here. But what is most significant is that Hamlet has chosen poetry, the realm of the imagination, as the most congenial instrument here; he, too, will "by indirections find directions out" (II.i.66), controlling the world of dream for a moment to make it reveal a hidden truth in the realm of reality.

In all of these instances, concepts of truth and reality have become subjective quantities, controlled and defined by Hamlet's consciousness. It is often remarked that the entire play is full of questions, verbal and thematic, which are never satisfactorily resolved, and which seem to exist for the sake of the question rather than in the hope of any answer. Maynard Mack, in his classic essay "The World of *Hamlet*," [1] points out that "Hamlet's world is pre-eminently in the interrogative mood," and that this is an aspect of a prevailing mood of "mysteriousness" throughout the play. Indeed it is this very atmosphere of mystery which is most hospitable to the world of dream. Dreaming for Hamlet becomes a kind of private and individual myth-making, in which we are included through the vehicle of the play, but which remains a closed system of coordinated symbols and images all related to one fulcrum: "conscience," the moral and spiritual dilemma of man.

This central question of conscience and its relation to the dream state is explicitly introduced in the great soliloquy which marks the play's midpoint, the "To be or not to be" speech of act III, scene i. As in so many cases we have examined, the position of the speech is of extreme importance; for a moment Hamlet stands suspended between the real and the illusory, the returning and the going o'er. His is a position very like that described by Keats in a letter to J. H. Reynolds

1. *Yale Review*, 41 (1952), 502–23.

(3 May 1818)—a letter which itself takes the form of a modern
dream vision. In it Keats recalls

> that tremendous (effect) of sharpening one's vision into
> the heart and nature of Man—of convincing one's nerves
> that the world is full of Misery and Heartbreak, Pain,
> Sickness and oppression—whereby this Chamber of
> Maiden Thought becomes gradually darken'd and at the
> same time on all sides of it many doors are set open— but
> all dark—all leading to dark passages—We see not the
> ballance of good and evil. We are in a Mist. *We* are now
> in that state—We feel the "burden of the Mystery." [2]

The "burden of the Mystery" is exactly what grips Hamlet at
this moment; he will accuse Rosencrantz and Guildenstern of
wanting to pluck out its heart. He, too, "see[s] not the ballance
of good and evil," for his view of life, like his view of reality,
is rendered wholly subjective by the workings of his mind.
Yet even in the extremity of moral crisis he plays with verbal
images, drawing out a long conceit to make it yield a crypto-
logical solution. The image he chooses, significantly, is once
more the central metaphor of sleep and dream.

> To die, to sleep—
> To sleep—perchance to dream; ay, there's the rub,
> For in that sleep of death what dreams may come
> When we have shuffled off this mortal coil
> Must give us pause. There's the respect
> That makes calamity of so long life:
> For who would bear the whips and scorns of time,
> Th' oppressor's wrong, the proud man's contumely,
> The pangs of despised love, the law's delay,
> The insolence of office, and the spurns,
> That patient merit of th' unworthy takes,
> When he himself might his quietus make
> With a bare bodkin? Who would fardels bear,
> To grunt and sweat under a weary life,

2. *The Selected Letters of John Keats*, ed. Lionel Trilling (Garden
City, N.Y.: Doubleday, 1951), p. 99.

> But that the dread of something after death,
> The undiscovered country, from whose bourn
> No traveler returns, puzzles the will,
> And makes us rather bear those ills we have,
> Than fly to others that we know not of?
> Thus conscience does make cowards of us all,
> And thus the native hue of resolution
> Is sicklied o'er with the pale cast of thought,
> And enterprises of great pitch and moment,
> With this regard their currents turn awry,
> And lose the name of action.
>
> [III.i.64–88]

Even here both language and meaning suggest that the "undis-covered country" of dream is more real to him than his imme-diate surroundings. The magic of sleep is here made meta-phorically equivalent to death, so that "to dream" means to take part in some life after death. It is striking that to him "what dreams may come" are more real and more terrifying than the physical fact of dying, just as the world of playing is more real than the world of fact. Yet there is a curious academicism here, a verbal detachment in the midst of this Mercutian catalogue of wrongs. In this speech Hamlet speaks as the philosopher of Everyman, articulating the crucial ques-tions of the human spirit. For all its solitude, it is a formal and public utterance in which the fears and discouragements of all mankind are brought forward and examined. Denmark is a prison; so is all the world. Even the "dreams" of the afterlife are frightening and limiting images, the ultimate case of the embodied irrational. What Hamlet speaks in these lines is a manifesto of the human condition, a subjectivism so far advanced that he identifies with all men rather than with his individual conscience. He is well on his way to the graveyard scene, where the dust of Alexander may be discovered stop-ping a bunghole.

What happens to Hamlet—and it is a paradigm, in part, for what will happen in each of the tragedies—is that out of his subjectivity grows acceptance and consequent strength. His victory lies in the fact that at last he is able to perceive both the world of dream and the world of reality, the inner world of conscience and the outer world of event. It is this comprehension upon which the drama depends. Hamlet's triumph is an equivocal one, compact of sorrow and resignation, but grounded in an increased self-knowledge. For there comes to him at the last a species of revelation—as Brutus says of himself, his state, "like to a little kingdom, suffers then / The nature of an insurrection" (*Julius Caesar* II.i.68–69). Most appositely, the revelation comes in the graveyard scene, when Hamlet's confrontations with the world of dream and the supernatural have expanded from the individual (the ghost) to the collective (the human condition) and so to the spiritual or eternal. The eternity of the graveyard is the ultimate leveler, in which Lady Worm claims indifferently the homage of lord and jester. Once more the tone of Hamlet's serious wit may remind us of Mercutio, as he catalogues the residents of the place: politician, courtier, lawyer, jester—again, all aspects of his own complex role. The gravedigger is his final and most telling counterpart, succeeding the ghost and the first player as a repository of values against which he consciously measures himself.

Yet the gravedigger's language differs sharply and significantly from the sonorous epic triplets of the ghost and the mimetic rhetoric of the player; his is no voice of fiction or illusion, but rather one of uncompromising fact, and he speaks a determinedly literal language of spades, shrouds, and skulls. The Hamlet whom he addresses, much altered by his confrontation with the world of dream, is an apt pupil whose psychological landscape may now be identified with the churchyard in which he finds himself; he is at last prepared to accept the literal realities of human frailty and the mortal condition. That he comprehends the lesson of the gravedigger's determined literalism is made plain by his approving aside to Horatio:

> How absolute the knave is! We must speak
> by the card, or equivocation will undo us.
>
> [V.i.137–38]

The state of equivocation, or ambiguity, has been his own dominant characteristic for much of the play and is of course central to the processes of dream. But in act V the "absoluteness" of the churchyard enforces a rejection of metaphor, euphemism, and verbal disguise; Yorick's skull is literally "chapfall'n" (192) as well as figuratively so. The apparently reductive and often disconcertingly comic literalism of the gravedigger's language, like that of the equally literal and equally comic clown in *Antony and Cleopatra*, carries with it an insistence on viewing things as they are. Civilizing fictions are stripped away and seen from the perspective of eternity: "let her paint an inch thick, to this favor she must come" (193–94), just as Claudius's "painted word" will be belied by his deeds.

Hamlet's return to the "real" world, the world literally of things, is made possible by his experience of "equivocation" in language and action—of doubt, fear, misunderstanding, subjectivism, and deliberate ambiguity and pretense. At the play's close he is able to reenter the political world of action because he has made this private journey through the transforming world of dream. And just as a chapfallen skull is remembered because it "had a tongue in it and could sing once" (75–76), so the world of the mortal and "real" is immortalized in the world of art. Thus Hamlet's dying request to Horatio,

> Absent thee from felicity awhile,
> And in this harsh world draw thy breath in pain
> To tell my story
>
> [V.ii.349–51]

is in a political sense an instruction to inform Fortinbras and the English ambassador of the true state of affairs in Denmark. In another, equally valid sense, however, it is an injunction to perform the play, to tell *The Tragedy of Hamlet, Prince of*

Denmark. We have seen parallel resolutions to recount in
Romeo and Juliet and *A Midsummer Night's Dream,* and we
will see them again in *Othello, King Lear,* and *Antony and
Cleopatra.* The play as an artifact—"my story"—becomes in
each case a surrogate and an example, precluding the necessity for a literal repetition of human tragedy. As life becomes
history and history becomes "story," both the audience in the
theater and that on the stage—in Hamlet's phrase, "mutes or
audience of this act" (337)—are offered a new opportunity for
self-knowledge; just as Claudius and Gertrude were the play
Hamlet watched, while they themselves watched a play, so we
as audience watch ourselves in *Hamlet.* By viewing the world
of Hamlet's interior imagination as dramatically and symbolically equivalent to the exterior political world of Denmark,
and the personae of the play as aspects of his consciousness,
Shakespeare explores a new dimension of the nature of dream;
by further resolving those worlds into a self-conscious fiction,
he hints once more at the inseparability of dream from what
we loosely call "reality" and suggests that redemption can be
approached, and perhaps achieved, by transmutation into art.

The essential relation between "conscience," awareness of
self, the self as a lens of the drama, and "equivocation," ambiguity of word and action, thus has a central importance for
the question of dream in *Hamlet.* Significantly, equivocation is
also a pivotal concept in *Macbeth,* where again the crucial
problem of conscience alters the boundaries of dream and
reality through "th' equivocation of the fiend / That lies like
truth" (V.vi.43–44). This "fiend" is another of those paradoxical spirits located simultaneously within and without the
protagonist; Macbeth refers literally to the witches' prophecy,
the apparent impossibility of the moving grove, but in fact he
himself is the play's greatest equivocator.

> I am in blood
> Stepp'd in so far that, should I wade no more,
> Returning were as tedious as go o'er.
>
> [III.iv.136–38]

Uttered at the midpoint of the play, this statement of moral abdication, so close in wording to that of Richard III, lays bare the destructive subjectivity at which Macbeth has arrived. Because he is in some sense a villain, committing murder for gain rather than for revenge, it is easier to appreciate the psychological landscape of his own "horrible imaginings" than it was in the case of Hamlet. For in Macbeth the crucial boundary between the dream—here close to Freudian "wish"—and the facts as objectively recounted dissolves completely, and the recriminations of conscience displace and obscure reality.

We may notice that the dissolution of this boundary is in Macbeth's situation an almost completely negative achievement. In *A Midsummer Night's Dream* the temporary confusion of the real and dream states, the transformation of the court into the enchanted wood, was a positive alteration, which enabled characters to discover hidden truths about themselves and prepared them for the necessary return to the court world of mortality. In *Hamlet,* although the exchange of states is more episodic, important truths are likewise revealed to Hamlet himself by the worlds of vision and play. Macbeth, however, is held captive by his imagination; it does not release him into a world of sudden self-knowledge, but rather imprisons him in a present reality in which the acting out of his fantasies leads to his exposure and ruin. Dream to him, as to Lady Macbeth, becomes a literal reenactment of a reality from which neither can escape except through death.

As in *Hamlet,* dream in *Macbeth* is closely related to the entire realm of witchcraft, omen, and the supernatural, as well as to the imagination. On the point of committing the murder of Duncan, and terrified by the waking dream of the dagger, Macbeth reflects anxiously on the nature of reality:

> Art thou not, fatal vision, sensible
> To feeling as to sight, or art thou but
> A dagger of the mind, a false creation,
> Proceeding from the heat-oppressèd brain?
>
> [II.i.36–39]

The apparition is a "fatal vision" because it portends the death of Duncan, but also because it seems to point to a murder fateful and foreordained. Macbeth's horror is mixed with self-discovery; the suggestion that this is a "dagger of the mind" represents a momentary inward glance which is all too revealing, while the alternative, that it is a "false creation," hints at the already present confusion between reality and illusion, the entrapment of the dreamer within the confines of his own subjective imagination. The witches are apparitions shared by Banquo and by the audience; like the ghost of old Hamlet, they have a dramaturgical existence which purposely straddles the line between the real and the imagined. But the dagger is a pure dream, wholly illusory, and Macbeth makes no attempt at a disinterested interpretation of it; instead he uses it to reinforce ideas he already holds. "Thou marshal'st me the way that I was going" he says (42); the dagger has become a self-made omen, a sign unambiguously produced by the mind of the man who interprets it. When he rejects its corporeal reality ("There's no such thing. / It is the bloody business which informs / Thus to mine eyes" [47–49]), he nonetheless accepts its message; and, further, he interprets the message in a certain way. For the dream, as we have before remarked, is almost always subject to the moral interpretation of the dreamer; it is the construction he puts upon it, often at variance with what we should consider its meaning, which exerts the primary influence upon thought and action.

Immediately after the dagger vision, Macbeth passes to a tableau of the sleeping world. It is a curiously malign and disturbing picture, compact of history, mythology, and superstition:

> Now o'er the one half-world
> Nature seems dead, and wicked dreams abuse
> The curtained sleep; witchcraft celebrates
> Pale Hecate's offerings; and withered murder,
> Alarumed by his sentinel, the wolf,
> Whose howl's his watch, thus with his stealthy pace

> With Tarquin's ravishing strides, towards his design
> Moves like a ghost.
>
> [II.i.49–56]

This is simultaneously a vision of Macbeth's world and of the state of his soul. "Wicked dreams," here as in Hamlet's "bad dreams," refer in actuality to a state of his own mind and perceptions; night is both an internal and an external time. It is typical of Macbeth's thinking that "Nature seems dead"; it is precisely this finding of the natural unnatural, the need to force the hand of nature, which gives rise to his dilemma. Here, as in the suggestion that fate presents it, the impulse to evil-doing is abstracted and personified into "witchcraft," while the more elaborately drawn figure of "withered murder" replaces the covert pronouns "I" or "we." The syntax in this passage supports the denial of conscience; a remarkable number of interpolations, appositives, comparisons, and parenthetical descriptions divide even the abstractly allegorical "murder" from the verb ("moves") of his act.

But the condition of Macbeth's conscience and his appraisal of inside and outside worlds undergoes a much more considerable reversal once the deed is done. If hesitation was his mode then, fragmenting and disordering his language, now speech seems his refuge, a "fictive covering," in Wallace Stevens's phrase, for the act he cannot name. Again there is a fragment of a vision, this time reported rather than portrayed, and again the vision attempts to deal directly with the problems of the dream state:

> Methought I heard a voice cry "Sleep no more!
> Macbeth does murder sleep"—the innocent sleep,
> Sleep that knits up the raveled sleave of care,
> The death of each day's life, sore labor's bath,
> Balm of hurt minds, great nature's second course,
> Chief nourisher in life's feast—
>
> [II.ii.34–39]

The succession of metaphors—"death," "bath," "balm," "course," "nourisher"—is an attempt to distance the terror of the vision. With understandable impatience Lady Macbeth cuts him off—"What do you mean?" she asks, and "Who was it thus cried?" (39, 43), pulling him forcibly out of the spell of the dream. Yet the dream itself is a truth he cannot so easily avoid. Like Richard III and Henry IV, he is indeed now unable to sleep, with the result that the subconscious dream world of conscience becomes for him at one with the literal world of reality. The two worlds merge into one, and the interior visions of voices, ghosts, and daggers become palpable realities he tries in vain to share. He is trapped in the dream world, a world which is for him more like nightmare. From the moment of the murder he stands in the balance of his own equivocation, isolated by conscience.

The moral relativism induced by this consolidation of worlds is clearly demonstrated in Macbeth's discussion with Lady Macbeth on the subject of Banquo. Banquo had shared the vision of the witches—although in the first scene they indicate that they have come specifically to speak with Macbeth. If the witches were to be viewed in wholly psychological terms, it could be argued that Banquo, too, has had a temptation, a revelation of what might be. Through the battle the thought of personal advancement has "come to mind" for both. But Banquo, though he is curious, has not been moved to action. And now Macbeth feels vulnerable, trapped. There seems no reason to stop at one murder, when two would make him secure. It is Richard's reasoning, but without Richard's delight in manipulation. Macbeth is a man whose imagination has already condemned him; he is controlled, he does not control. Of Banquo he now says to his wife,

But let the frame of things disjoint, both the worlds suffer,
Ere we will eat our meal in fear, and sleep
In the affliction of these terrible dreams
That shake us nightly.

[III.ii.16–19]

Again he is talking about a present state of affairs as if it were a conditional possibility. He *does* eat his meals in fear; the ter-

rible dreams of night are doubtless both literal nocturnal imaginings and pure memory, pure daily experience. His assertion here is very like his portrait of the world on the eve of Duncan's death; here, too, cosmic results are foreseen from a private
act. Macbeth is drawing an overt parallel between the cosmos,
the "frame of things," and the state of his own mind and soul.
"Both the worlds" is provocative; probably, it means "life and
the hereafter," both realms in which he knows he is condemned
to suffer. Later in the same passage he will observe with curious
envy, "Duncan is in his grave; / After life's fitful fever he
sleeps well" (22–23), and again we are aware of the chasm of
consciousness which yawns between Macbeth and this healing
sleep.

The consequences of Macbeth's imprisonment in the dream
state, an imprisonment which intensifies as the play moves
toward Dunsinane, are numerous and far-reaching. We have
examined several instances in which the wall between illusion
and reality has been breached and not repaired, and we have
observed the externalization of psychological landscape to the
point where the play's scene is also the scenario of Macbeth's
sense of self. Two principal excursions into the irrational dominate and crystallize the problem of dream in *Macbeth,* and
they are fittingly placed, one at the very beginning, the other
very near the end. The first is the apparition of the "weird
sisters"; the second is the sleepwalking and sleeptalking of
Lady Macbeth.

Speaking of the encounter on the heath moments before the
murder of Duncan, Banquo remarks to Macbeth:

> I dreamt last night of the three weird sisters:
> To you they have showed some truth.
>
> [II.i.20–21]

Banquo's "I dreamt" is the record of a literal dream, the only
one so described in the play with the exception of Lady Macbeth's sleeping monologue. The "some truth" which has been
shown Macbeth accords with the principle we have developed
earlier that "the dream is always true"; yet we do not know

what Banquo has dreamt about the witches; and Macbeth is
determined to feign indifference:

> I think not of them:
> Yet, when we can entreat an hour to serve,
> We would spend it in some words upon that business,
> If you would grant the time.
>
> [21–24]

Here we can see the playwright shifting patterns he has previously established; the indifference of the dreamer to the
prophetic dream, which so often in earlier plays led to his
downfall, is here assumed rather than real. Banquo has
"dreamt" of the witches in a literal sense; Macbeth, on the
other hand, is preoccupied with them in the waking state,
which for him has merged with dream. Banquo's dream is
largely a provocative device which reminds Macbeth of the
danger posed by his erstwhile friend and, at the same time, underscores the degree to which dream, for Macbeth and Macbeth alone, has left its proper nocturnal sphere and become
obsessive.

The witches themselves have been subject to almost endless
speculations, the consensus of which, following A. C. Bradley,
is that they are both real and unreal, at once external manifestations and psychological entities. Bradley points out that while
the taking of the throne and the distrust of Macduff are ideas
which could logically be expected to have lain dormant in
Macbeth's mind, he clearly can have had no foreknowledge of
the peculiar circumstances of Macduff's birth, nor of the phenomenon of the moving grove.[3] The witches are thus deliberately made to seem both real and illusory, defying logical explanation at the same time that they seem tantalizingly close
to being "explained." We should remember, also, that Banquo
has seen them, a fact which renders their appearance qualita-

---

3. A. C. Bradley, *Shakespearean Tragedy*, 2d ed. (London: Macmillan,
1905), pp. 346–47.

tively different from that of the dagger or the oracular voice. In effect the witches perform the functions of many of the more static prophetic devices of earlier drama, combining omen, riddle, and warning. But the form in which they are cast signals a dramaturgical advance of considerable moment. They are integrated into the plot as characters who appear physically onstage and impart their supernatural messages. In this way they replace a cumbrous structural survival, the retold dream, with action and characterization—in effect substituting drama for narrative. The effect is both structural and thematic, achieving with Shakespeare's customary superb economy a synthesis of telling insight and striking dramatic effect. For the dual nature of the witches' reality, the fact that they both exist and do not exist as external figures, is a suggestive demonstration of the extent to which the dream state has taken over the play. No literal dreams are recited, and the element of supernaturalism is inseparable from the plot as it develops. The witches are a manifestation of conscience in Macbeth, and they are something more—inhabitants of the world of the irrational into which he has entered and into which we must all enter before the tragic events of *Macbeth* move toward a close. They are spirits of a dream world in which mischief is malicious and irreversible. Macbeth's journey to the heath to see them—and it is noteworthy that in their second confrontation it is he who deliberately seeks them out—is the tragic concomitant of the journey to the wood in the comedies. The truth they reveal is the dark side of the subconscious, and Macbeth's misinterpretation of the omens is as inevitable as his belief that they encourage him. Once more, an unheeded warning brings ruin upon a man who underestimates the full significance of dream.

Yet in a way the disintegration of Lady Macbeth is even more disturbing than that of Macbeth himself, because it is so sudden and so complete. Dream in her case reverts to its conventional sphere, the nocturnal thoughts of the sleeper; where with Macbeth vision and illusion invaded the real world of daylight, in Lady Macbeth's case the deeds of reality, the murders of Duncan, Banquo, and Lady Macduff, usurp the nighttime realm of dream. It is a variation on the crucial theme of "murdering sleep." The sleepwalking monologue thus provides a situation cognate with that of Clarence's dream, in which we are suddenly offered a glimpse into the subconscious mind of a character other than the protagonist.

The scene begins with a conversation between a doctor and a waiting gentlewoman, both of whom will observe and comment upon Lady Macbeth's actions throughout. The gentlewoman has heard these revelations before—we may be reminded of Barnardo's and Marcellus's previous visions of old Hamlet—but she refuses to divulge them. Again like Barnardo and Marcellus, the doctor says he has watched for two nights, but in his case he has seen nothing; he can "perceive no truth" (V.i.2) in her report. When Lady Macbeth appears with a taper, the pair observe that she is going through the motions of washing her hands. What is unique about this situation from the point of view of dream narration is that the dreamer is still asleep: the dream is not recounted, but actually experienced in front of us, with its dramatic character still further emphasized by the interjections of doctor and gentlewoman. Again this is both a dramaturgical and a thematic advance— the moment is supremely dramatic, rather than narrative; and the dichotomy in the character of Lady Macbeth, the conscious as against the unconscious woman, is forcefully described.

The monologue itself is an accurately presented stream of consciousness, the image of the bloody hands leading the dreamer from the memory of one murder to that of another. Images within the dream narrative are variations on images which have appeared throughout the play: her inability to cleanse her hands recalls her assurance to Macbeth, "A little water clears us of this deed" (II.ii.66). She has ordered that there be "light by her continually" (V.i.25–26); and the candle she carries is an unnatural reversal of Banquo's placid observation, "There's husbandry in heaven. / Their candles are all out" (II.i.4–5). Because she remains asleep throughout, the dream symbols and dream memories come through to the listeners relatively undistorted; we may note that her remarks are almost entirely literal, devoid of the wordplay and ambiguity we have come to associate with retold dreams. The sleepwalking scene is in fact as much a play-within-a-play as it is a dream. Its basic form is dialogue ("Fie, my lord fie! A soldier, and afeard?" "Come, come, come, come, give me your hand!" [39, 69–70]), crystallizing the symbolic events which have gone before. The doctor and gentlewoman are the inner audience, and we ourselves, of course, the outer. Gesture (the washing of the hands) is the scene's crucial medium, and here becomes a sign which tells us what is in her mind as plainly as do her words. This coming together of dream and play is something we have seen several times before, but each time the union produces new and appropriate effects. Here it becomes a final reversal, the substitution of the unconscious truth for the conscious fiction which has heretofore been Lady Macbeth's life. It is entirely fitting that her husband, on hearing of her death, should employ a metaphor which is a literal description of her last tragic scene:

> Life's but a walking shadow, a poor player
> That struts and frets his hour upon the stage
> And then is heard no more.
>
> [V.v.24–26]

Conscience, in Hamlet's phrase, has indeed made cowards, finally, of them all.

"Conscience" in *Hamlet* meant both consciousness and awareness of mortality; in *Macbeth*, consciousness and knowledge of guilt. In *Othello* "conscience" represents consciousness yet again, but it also connotes morality. Iago, speaking with characteristic disingenuousness to Othello, disclaims any inclination for killing:

> Though in the trade of war I have slain men,
> Yet do I hold it very stuff o' th' conscience
> To do no contrived murder.
>
> [I.ii.1–3]

Likewise, alluding to the adulterous habits of Venetian wives, he says

> their best conscience
> Is not to leave 't undone, but kept unknown.
>
> [III.iii.203–04]

Neither of these allegations is true, and the deliberate choice of the word "conscience" by the unscrupulous Iago suggests that "conscience," in this play, is a word and an attitude to be wary of, a virtue assumed although one has it not. It is part of the emphasis on rules, and by extension signs and taboos, which marks this play from the first scene to the last. Conscience and its concomitants, honesty, self-knowledge, and knowledge of human nature, are rare qualities in *Othello;* it is no surprise, therefore, that dream in this play, more than in any other, is used to mislead, control, and deceive. The conscious use of dream as a device, not by the playwright, but by a character within the play, is nowhere more clearly demonstrated.

Iago's valuation of dream is slight at best, and he tends to use the term in its most impoverished sense. "If ever I did dream / Of such a matter, abhor me" (I.i.4–5), he says to Roderigo on the subject of Othello's match with Desdemona. "Dream" here means simply "imagine," and as with so many of Iago's utterances this one has the ring of falsehood. Iago, in fact, is incapable of dream in any wider sense; he is a man in whom imagination has given place to rigid order, Theseus's "reason" without Theseus's benevolence. His only other use of the word comes in his soliloquy at Cyprus, as he expounds to himself and to the audience his plans to undo Cassio and Roderigo. "If consequence do but approve my dream," he exults, "My boat sails freely, both with wind and stream" (II.iii.62–63). The couplet form is functional here, since it heralds the arrival of Cassio and the Cypriots, but it is also pat, complacent. His "dream" is more properly a plot, in which little is left either to the imagination or to chance.

In contrast to Iago's imperviousness, the other characters of the play are immensely susceptible to dream and the suggestion of dream. The play opens in a scene of darkness and confusion, disembodied voices in the night, nightmare accusations. Iago and his puppet Roderigo control the moment, and their object is to startle as well as to anger, to break into the placid sleep of Brabantio with a reality worse than any dream. In these moments we can see once more how Shakespeare has expanded the dream state to a state of mind, a pervasive mood which puts all realities and identities into question, distorting facts and values. Beneath the window of Brabantio's house the shrill voice of Roderigo shouts its lewd insinuations, and Iago again and again exhorts him to awaken. Brabantio's response is consonant with the mood so carefully set: at first he resists the message of Desdemona's elopement, so graphically and coarsely set forth in animal metaphors which are keenly appropriate dream symbols; then, capitulating, he calls anxiously for light, to banish the night and the night thoughts it has brought. It is at this moment, when all the shouting has ended, that he makes his admission: "This accident is not unlike my dream" (I.i.139).

There are a number of things about this dream of Brabantio's which make it interesting in light of what we have already discovered about dream in the tragedies. We may notice that he mentions the dream only after its "fulfillment" (the union of Othello and Desdemona) has been described. He never tells his dream or refers to it again, so that the dream is not a prediction or prophecy comparable to the monitory dreams we have discussed. As was the case with the sleepwalking scene in *Macbeth,* this way of introducing a literal dream into the plot has distinct dramatic advantages over the older narrative method. The static recitation of fact is again avoided and is here replaced by violent accusation and uncompromising imagery. Shakespeare's remarkable insight into the process of the dream work is again discernible: specific visual images like those of the ram, the ewe, and the Barbary horse are overtly libidinal symbols.[4] These images, of course, are voiced

4. Freud, *Interpretation of Dreams,* p. 445.

by Iago and Roderigo and not by Brabantio himself; yet there
is a way in which the whole dark scene deserves to be called
Brabantio's dream. Iago and Roderigo then become characters
of that dream, speaking aloud those metaphors which Brabantio finds repugnant to say or think himself. We should also
take note of the extremely literary quality of Iago's and
Roderigo's descriptions, most particularly Roderigo's long and
adroit speech on the "gross clasps of a lascivious Moor" (117–
37). His phrasing is imaginative and acute, much more intelli-
gent and well crafted than we should ordinarily expect of him.
Both his and Iago's remarks are in a major sense fictional, fabricated, though instantly convincing. They provide yet another example of the intricate relationship between the worlds
of art and dream.

But the supreme example of the fabricated dream, here
wholly misleading, is of course that supposed dream of Cassio
which Iago expounds to an outraged Othello. If we postulate
that dream in the tragedies is at least partially a state of mind,
a series of psychological insights into the conscience or consciousness of the protagonist as he interprets the outside world,
we must here assume that this "dream" does not come to
Othello entirely as a surprise. Iago has contrived it in order
that it produce a certain predictable effect; like Richard III's
opportunistic use of the prophecy about "G," which set in
motion the train of events culminating in Clarence's death,
this purported dream of Cassio is a device employed by a man
of "hard heart" to undo and control more passionate and
human characters. It preys upon Othello's considerable susceptibility to the supernatural and the irrational. But at the same
time it is a "true" dream as far as he is concerned, because it
so exactly fits what he expects and suspects. Iago's management
of the entire affair is adept in the extreme:

> *Iago:*   I lay with Cassio lately,
> And being troubled with a raging tooth,
> I could not sleep.
> There are a kind of men so loose of soul

> That in their sleeps will mutter their affairs.
> One of this kind is Cassio.
> In sleep I heard him say, "Sweet Desdemona,
> Let us be wary, let us hide our loves!"
> And then, sir, would he gripe and wring my
>   hand,
> Cry "O sweet creature!" Then kiss me hard,
> As if he plucked up kisses by the roots
> That grew upon my lips; laid his leg o'er my
>   thigh,
> And sigh, and kiss, and then cry, "Cursèd fate
> That gave thee to the Moor!"

Othello: O monstrous! monstrous!

Iago: Nay, this was but his
                                     dream.

Othello: But this denoted a foregone conclusion,
'Tis a shrewd doubt, though it be but a dream.

Iago: And this may help to thicken other proofs
That do demonstrate thinly.

[III.iii.410–28]

In form this "dream" is quite different from the actual Shakespearean dreams we have examined; its internal development is exceedingly clear and logical, without any of the disguising elements which characteristically transform dream thoughts into dream content. But Othello is blind to this revealing rationality of design, and the narration of the "dream" itself is highly skilled. The presence of internal dialogue heightens the dramatic immediacy of the alleged situation at the same time that it avoids the static narrative quality we have frequently noticed in earlier dreams. The intrusion of aphorism into what purports to be direct description is highly effective, because it seems to impart credibility to the verdict of Cassio's "looseness of soul." In describing the supposed lovemaking scene, Iago deliberately inserts words like "leg," "thigh," "plucked," which emphasize the physicality of the scene he has invented. The fact that he is describing an en-

counter between two men gives to the entire picture an added
unsavoriness, a physical disgust which by contrast seems to
augment Iago's own moral rectitude. Finally, the excoriation
of fate, in which Othello believes much more strongly than
Cassio or Iago, seems to underscore the contempt of the dream-
Cassio for all that Othello symbolizes.

The effect of the "dream" is immediate and dramatic.
Othello is prepared to interpret the entire scene as truth, but
Iago shrewdly heads him off. "Nay, this was but his dream,"
he says. The reversal is dizzying. We know that this was *not*
Cassio's dream, but rather something Iago has "dreamed up"
as a ruse. Yet Iago solidifies Othello's credulousness by seeming
to denigrate what he secretly urges. His surface attitude toward
dream is consistent; he sets little store by it. Yet he affects to
be persuaded by Othello's insistence. Othello, for his part, is
pretending less conviction about the absolute truth of dreams
than he actually possesses. " 'Tis a shrewd doubt, though it be
but a dream." Everything we know about him, and about his
sense of self, must lead us to believe that there is no "but" about
it. Dreams are part of that illogical and superstitious world
from which the Othello of the Anthropophagi, the Othello of
the handkerchief, can never wholly be separated. It is this side
of Othello that makes the drama possible. We may say without
exaggeration that when he vows, earlier in this same scene,

> Perdition catch my soul
> But I do love thee! And when I love thee not,
> Chaos is come again
>
> [III.iii.90–92]

the chaos of which he speaks is the collapse of reality into
dream, or dream into reality. Desdemona has, so to speak,
only offended in a dream—in "Cassio's dream" and in Othello's
own deluded mind.

The final sorting out of apparent truths from real ones
comes in the deathbed scene, of which Dr. Johnson wrote
without hyperbole that it is "not to be endured." [5] There are

5. *The Plays of William Shakespeare*, with notes by Samuel Johnson and
George Steevens (London: C. Bathurst, 1778), X, 605.

no dreams in this scene, and yet there is one occurrence of central importance for our line of argument: the unexpected outcry of Desdemona, whom we, as well as Othello and Emilia, have supposed dead. This is not really a resurrection scene; when she speaks she is still alive, and when she finishes speaking she dies. But the pattern is very similar to supernatural restoration; indeed, Othello must for a moment think it is her fleeing spirit which speaks. The boundaries of death and life seem to flow into one another here, as have the worlds of fiction and fact. It is the final illusion, the final reversal; where *Hamlet* began with the ghost of a dead man crying for revenge, *Othello* ends with that impossibility, a living ghost, who speaks from a twilight realm between life and death to plead for forgiveness.

The pattern of apparent resurrection is one which will become increasingly important in the later plays, in a development parallel to the increased scope and importance of the dream state. Lear's conviction that Cordelia still lives and Cleopatra's false message of her own death are comparable examples in the tragedies; in the romances there occur the still more striking fictive "deaths" and restorations of Hermione, Thaisa, and Imogen. We will want to examine these "deaths" much more closely when we come to consider the romances in detail (chapter 4); for now, it will suffice to note that there is no straining of belief in these situations. The dream state has by this point taken over the entire play. Logic and psychology are for the romances no longer viable methods of analysis; the tidy categories of illusion and reality are in these plays intermingled to form an indissoluble whole, which is the world of dream. But in *Othello* the resurrection theme is still intensely psychological in tone. The unexpected outcry of Desdemona is a natural or explicable occurrence; yet at the same time it is a unit of Othello's conscience, a ghostly voice which gives the lie to everything he has passionately believed. Psychology, and the psychological dream state, are central to an understanding of the tragedies, and the uses of dream and illusion are ultimately all framed so as to let us share the subjective inner world of the protagonist.

Just such a crux of awareness is provided by the "resurrection" scene in *King Lear,* which suggests a kind of descent of the supernatural into the here and now. Of all the plays, perhaps *Lear* is the easiest in which to demonstrate Shakespeare's tendency to unify inner and outer worlds, objective fact and subjective feeling; clearly the court, the heath, and the cliffs of Dover are symbolic loci at the same time that they are local habitations. The underplot of the journey, from court to heath and back again, marks a discovery of self parallel to that of *Othello* or of *A Midsummer Night's Dream.* But Shakespeare never repeats himself, never employs a device without extending its possibilities; and the awakening of Lear at the close of the fourth act reaches out to unify more than inner man and outer world—for a moment it unifies time itself, obliterating the differences between death and life, this world and the next.

Only metaphorically can this scene be called a dream. The agitated Lear, driven past the point of sanity, has been rescued from the heath and laid to sleep by Cordelia in the French camp. As was the case with Lady Macbeth, an intermediary is present in the form of a doctor, ministrant at once to soul and body, and we learn of the circumstances through his words. "In the heaviness of sleep," he tells Cordelia, "we put fresh garments on him" (IV.vii.21–22). Sleep is for Lear what it can never be for Macbeth: "balm of hurt minds, great nature's second course." There is an acute significance in the fact that Lear's solace, however temporary, comes from nature itself, as his rage and madness too found their concomitants in the elements. But there is something more than natural in Lear's sleep, an inescapable symbolism which is underscored by the mention of "fresh garments." Clothing here is an outward sign of an inward alteration, a changing of interior scene. Confusedly awakening from sleep, Lear peers up at the face of Cordelia and says with poignant grace,

> You do me wrong to take me out o' th' grave:
> Thou art a soul in bliss; but I am bound

> Upon a wheel of fire, that mine own tears
> Do scald like molten lead.
>
> [45–48]

As we have noted, this is not really a dream. It is, however, a waking vision, and as such it is closely related to the ideas of internal symbolism and consciousness of self with which we have been concerned. Lear has actually been asleep, and when he awakens imagines himself dead—translated into hell and bound like Ixion upon a wheel of fire. The comparison with Ixion is curiously apposite: Ixion had promised a large bride-price for his wife, but reneged, and instead murdered his father-in-law. Lear's assumption—that he is dead, and that Cordelia is a spirit—is the direct inversion of Hamlet's metaphor, "to die, to sleep." Hamlet compares death to sleep; Lear, sleep to death. At the same time there is a further reversal, one with which we are by now familiar: the hell to which Lear feels he has been condemned is his present condition. As he regains consciousness and conscience, he, like Hamlet, Macbeth, and Othello before him, might justly borrow the phrase of Marlowe's Mephistopheles: "Why this is hell, nor am I out of it" (*Faustus* I.iii.80). Conscience is his captor here, and reality his hell; so too the vision of his ostensible rebirth is simultaneously a metaphor and a literal fact. "Lear" in this play stands not only for the individual man himself, but also for kingship, order, England—collective and idealized quantities beyond individual mortality. And though Lear the man is not reborn in this moment of translated awareness, there is a resurgence of the collective metaphorical concept for which he stands. Dream here comes closer to allegory than at any point we have previously noted. Later, when the masked Edgar defeats Edmund at the call of the third trumpet, there is a kind of apocalypse which completes this cycle of renewal.

In the later tragedies, then, Shakespeare moves from the representation of naturalistic behavior and psychological versimilitude toward a new treatment of dream: a transitional stage in

which symbols greater than the facts themselves overtake and
dominate the world of the play. It is a movement from the particular toward the universal, from the story of one man to the
story of all. W. B. Yeats, in an essay called "Emotion of Multi-
tude," perceptively suggests that "there cannot be great art
without the little limited life of the fable, which is always the
better the simpler it is, and the rich, far-wandering, many-
imaged life of the half-seen world beyond it." [6] This second
"life," that of the "half-seen world" beyond the fable, is dream
as we have described it. Yet Yeats's two kinds of artistic life
can hardly be separated; as he says elsewhere in the same essay,
they copy one another "much as a shadow upon the wall copies
one's body in the firelight." [7] It is the merging of these two
lives, the growing unity of dream and fable, that takes place
in the last plays. And in the last of the "great tragedies," *Antony and Cleopatra*, this unity is in part achieved by the continued growth of subjectivity, the eradication of the boundaries between seeming and being in the consciousness of the
protagonists.

It has frequently been pointed out that *Antony and Cleopatra* is not a tragedy of the same type as the preceding four.
The most popular alternative designation has been "Roman
play," a category which includes *Julius Caesar* and *Coriolanus*
as well as *Antony and Cleopatra* and which seems to stress a
classical as opposed to a Christian framework. With equal
validity, perhaps, we may regard it as the last and greatest of
the chronicle plays. For our purposes we may accept a mixture
of categories without strain, since we are predominantly concerned with a chronological development, and observe that
Antony partakes at once of tragedy, chronicle, "Roman play,"
"problem play," and even, to a certain extent, comedy. This
mixture of modes is in fact exactly what we should expect of
Shakespeare at this time: it is just this bold synthesis of major
tropes which makes the play so vast, a many-colored tapestry
of titanic actions and gorgeous language. Shakespeare is at the

6. In *Ideas of Good and Evil* (New York: Macmillan, 1903), p. 341.
7. Ibid., p. 340.

top of his powers here, and the broad canvas of *Antony and Cleopatra* gives him scope to incorporate much of what he has previously learned.

Perhaps the most obvious and yet important change from the sequence of *Hamlet, Macbeth, Othello,* and *King Lear* is that this play's title links *two* characters, in the pattern of *Romeo and Juliet* and *Troilus and Cressida.* Our attention is thereby drawn to the linking "and," the connection between the two, rather than to either specific consciousness without the other. We are not concerned only with love, even with the titanic love of Antony and Cleopatra, which in its imagery as well as in its oscillation from Rome to Egypt bids fair to encompass the world. Instead we may perhaps conjecture that the entity "Antony-and-Cleopatra" in itself has meaning—essentially, that these two majestic figures, towering over the play which bears their names, are aspects of a single conscience, a single—and outmoded—way of looking at the world. Theirs is an ancient world of heroic values, not unlike that of old Hamlet, or, indeed, of Hector. They are, we might say, older than the thrones upon which they sit; their view of the world, and the extent to which it is controllable and manipulable by their own private actions, is a view which must give way to the practical, colorless reason and "high order" of Octavius Caesar. "Conscience" connotes awareness of self, and of all characters in Shakespeare perhaps none are more intrinsically self-aware than Antony and Cleopatra. "The nobleness of life / Is to do thus;" says Antony,

> When such a mutual pair
> And such a twain can do't, in which I bind,
> On pain of punishment, the world to weet
> We stand up peerless.
>
> [I.i.38–40]

The fact that there are two of them means, in dramatic terms, that they are more often than not characterizing one another; even more significantly, characterizations of them are extremely alike. "She makes hungry / Where most she satisfies," (II.ii.239–40) says Enobarbus, Antony's closest companion, of

Cleopatra; and Cleopatra in her great dream vision of Antony
says of his bounty, "an autumn 'twas / That grew the more by
reaping" (V.ii.87–88). Their relationship to the world of dream
as we have described it is an extremely close one: they, like
Othello, are votaries of dream, believers in prophecy and the
supernatural. Antony's exchange with the soothsayer is paralleled by the augurers in Cleopatra's retinue. Dreaming is
looked upon by the practical Romans as superstitious delusion: "he dreams," scoffs Pompey, dismissing a false report
(II.i.19). The dichotomy we have previously observed, between
the scoffers who try to control dream and the believers who
are controlled by it, is softened here because of the concen-
tration on character, or what we have been calling "conscience." Antony's encounter with the soothsayer is a good example, because it simultaneously sets a thematic tone and gives us
a rapid insight into Antony's overwhelming strengths and
weaknesses.

The soothsayer appears at a pivotal moment in Antony's
thought. We have met him before at Cleopatra's palace, where
in the play's second scene he performed the oracular dramatic
function of forecasting in riddle the course of the drama, predicting to Cleopatra's attendants that they will outlive their
mistress. Characteristically, the attendants misinterpret this as
an omen of long life; yet it is literally true in another sense,
since they will die within a few moments of one another and,
indeed, within moments of their mistress. In this first encounter the soothsayer is thus parallel to the soothsayer of *Julius
Caesar* or to the earlier monitory dreams. "In Nature's infinite
book of secrecy," he says, "A little I can read" (I.ii.10–11); and
the fact that it is "Nature's book" will assume a growing thematic importance as the play proceeds. His second appearance,
however, is markedly different in tone. We have by now accepted the official place of soothsayers and augurers in the
Egyptian court as a major distinguishing factor between the
worlds of Egypt and Rome. When the soothsayer appears
again, however, he is in Rome; and this subtly but completely
alters the comfortable climate of belief. Antony has just accepted the hand of Octavia in a political marriage calculated

to bring peace between him and Caesar. With her good-night to him the soothsayer enters and is catechized by Antony on the prospects of the future.

Antony: Now sirrah: you do wish yourself in Egypt?

Soothsayer: Would I had never come from thence, nor you thither.

Antony: If you can, your reason?

Soothsayer: I see it in my motion, have it not in my tongue, but yet hie you to Egypt again.

Antony: Whose fortunes shall rise higher, say to me, Caesar's, or mine?

Soothsayer: Caesar's.

Therefore, O Antony, stay not by his side.

Thy daemon, that thy spirit which keeps thee, is

Noble, courageous, high, unmatchable,

Where Caesar's is not. But near him thy angel

Becomes afeard, as being o'erpow'red: therefore

Make space enough between you.

[II.iii.10–22]

Plainly, this is in part an internal monologue of the sort we examined in *Macbeth*. The soothsayer has a corporeal existence and even a dramatic history in the play; he is not imaginary within the play's terms. But the voice of warning we hear through him is Antony's own voice, projecting a brooding internal premonition of disaster. The soothsayer, like the witches, is here simultaneously an internal and an external character. Maynard Mack, in "The Jacobean Shakespeare," points out that when the soothsayer says, "I see it in my motion," he means "intuitively," and that this is also true of Antony. Mack acutely calls this prediction a "visual surrogate for Antony's own personal intuition." [8] As such it follows the patterns of many similar supernatural or irrational happen-

8. In *Jacobean Theater*, Stratford-upon Avon Studies, No. 1 (New York: St. Martin's Press, 1960), p. 27.

ings we have already noted in the tragedies: to put it in its simplest form, the personae and the loci of the drama are themselves consistently surrogate, or complementary, to the operations of conscience in the main characters themselves. We should also note the incorporation of an older theatrical device—the good and bad angels, familiar from the moralities and *Doctor Faustus*—into the soothsayer's language of metaphor. Once more the irrational is, so to speak, domesticated, made plausible. When later we hear that the "god Hercules, whom Antony loved" (IV.iii.15) leaves him, the effect is the same: a set of character traits—courage, boldness, integrity—have been concretized into a character with a name, though that character's appearance, like that of the "daemon" above, is entirely allusive in the drama itself.

We have touched upon the fact that Antony and Cleopatra are associated with old heroic values which their world can no longer support. In its tacit relationship to myth-making, this tendency is clearly related to the concept of the dream state. Nowhere is the confrontation between this world of heroic gesture and the real, tactical, and unromantic political present made more evident than in Antony's desire to meet Caesar in single combat. He has lost the battle of Actium, and, desperate to regain his honor, he sends a challenge back to Rome for Caesar to meet him "sword against sword, / Ourselves alone" (III.xiii.27–28). The mode of the challenge recalls the world of old Hamlet, who "the ambitious Norway combated" (*Ham.* I.i.61), and that of Hector, who seeks to settle the seven years' Trojan conflict by meeting singly with a champion of the Greeks. Both in *Hamlet* and in *Troilus and Cressida* these heroic moments are relics of a past age; old Hamlet falls victim to the wily and politic Claudius, and, despite the dreams of his wife and the warnings of Cassandra, Hector is slaughtered by the terrifyingly modern-seeming Myrmidons of Achilles. Antony's challenge is no less doomed to failure. Enobarbus murmurs aside on hearing it:

> Yes, like enough: high-battled Caesar will
> Unstate his happiness and be staged to th' show

> Against a sworder! I see men's judgments are
> A parcel of their fortunes, and things outward
> Do draw the inward quality after them
> To suffer all alike. That he should dream,
> Knowing all measures, the full Caesar will
> Answer his emptiness! Caesar, thou has subdued
> His judgment too.
>
> [III.xiii.29–37]

Enobarbus is another of those interpreter figures we have found so frequently in the tragedies, who perceives and reports the facts uncolored by imagination. He knows that Antony's behavior is wholly unrealistic; that, unlike Hector, he will not even receive the satisfaction of an affirmative reply. For Antony's mind dwells with the heroism of an earlier age. "Things outward / Do draw the inward quality after them"— this is precisely the movement toward subjectivity we have been recording. Fittingly Enobarbus calls it "dream," and although for him, as for so many, this means "delusion," it is a strength in Antony as well as a mortal weakness. His "judgment," that omnipresent marked boundary of reason, is perhaps his least reliable attribute.

However, it is not for his judgment that we seek to admire Antony, but rather for his superb imagination, which turns all things to dream. His imagination is incommensurate with the exigencies of reality, and what is real to Antony is properly dream to Enobarbus. Yet Antony's self-awareness, his conscience, is by and large adequate to apprehend these shifting realities. His remarkable capacity lies in a kind of negative capability, what in the Antony of *Julius Caesar* was a strong impulse toward chaos; he is not afraid of metamorphosis. Consider his self-analysis to an only partially comprehending Eros, after the second defeat of his forces:

> *Antony:*   Sometime we see a cloud that's dragonish,
> A vapor sometime like a bear or lion,
> A towered citadel, a pendant rock
> A forkèd mountain, or blue promontory
> With trees upon 't that nod unto the world

> And mock our eyes with air. Thou hast seen
>   these signs:
> They are black vesper's pageants.
>
> *Eros:*   Ay, my lord.
> *Antony:* That which is now a horse, even with a thought
>   The rack dislimns, and makes it indistinct
>   As water is in water.
>
> *Eros:*   It does, my lord.
> *Antony:* My good knave Eros, now thy captain is
>   Even such a body: here I am Antony,
>   Yet cannot hold this visible shape, my knave.
>   [IV.xiv.2–14]

Antony's metaphor is clearly related to Hamlet's teasing of
Polonius, as well as to Theseus's speech on "airy nothing" and
imagination. The play metaphor ("black vesper's pageants")
suggests the fictive quality of the visual metamorphosis he is
describing; the effect is once more that of a reversal of categories, the "air" here as in *A Midsummer Night's Dream* a
mockery of reality, which imitates and simulates the real objects of nature. The apparitions of tree and horse shift under
the scrutiny of the imagination "even with a thought"—a temporal notation which recalls Lysander's "short as any dream."
Antony is acutely aware of his own role-playing existence; the
"real" Antony is as indistinguishable from the many momentary shapes as the "real" cloud from rock or dragon. He looks
upon himself as a quicksilver entity in a real world—as protean as Puck, but burdened with the mortal substance of Hamlet. He is torn between conflicting sets of values, neither of
which he can wholly embrace, and both of which are by this
point largely corrupt. When, only moments later, he receives
the false message of Cleopatra's death, his personal pattern of
reversal becomes complete. Reduced to a sense of total subjectivity in the cloud passage above, he is now moved to action once more, but an action which is still conditioned by
the dream of an older age. Convinced by this crowning illusion—that Cleopatra is dead—he makes it come true by kill-

ing himself in response. His method of suicide, the ancient
Roman custom of running on his sword, is like the earlier impulse to single combat, a heroic gesture which belongs to another time. For Antony's personal dream is a kind of myth-
making, the translation of the mortal to the immortal. It is
what T. S. Eliot has called "the point of intersection of the
timeless with time." And the defeat of time, as we have seen,
is a major achievement of the world of dream.

Antony's death comes at the close of act IV, and the whole
of the fifth act is therefore Cleopatra's. Cleopatra's sense of
self is very acute; she is a constant manipulator of illusion and
reality, herself the embodiment of the irrational, the ultimate
exception to all rules:

> she makes hungry
> Where most she satisfies; for vilest things
> Become themselves in her, that the holy priests
> Bless her when she is riggish.
>
> [II.ii.239–42]

She, too, shows an intuitive understanding of the workings of
dream, the degree to which reality is only a partial truth.
When the clown brings her the "pretty worm of Nilus" in a
basket, he warns her not to touch it, "for his biting is immortal" (V.ii.246–47). The malapropism, "immortal" for
"mortal," is precisely the impulse we have been tracing in
both Antony and Cleopatra; as in so many similar cases, subjective truth comes to the audience in the guise of error, and
the clown speaks better than he knows.

Cleopatra's choice of a death is the heroic alternative to a
demeaning captivity, a captivity which she particularizes for
her attendants by means of the play image:

> The quick comedians
> Extemporally will stage us, and present
> Our Alexandrian revels: Antony
> Shall be brought drunken forth, and I shall see

> Some squeaking Cleopatra boy my greatness
> I' th' posture of a whore.
>
> [V.ii.216–21]

The image is that of a downward metamorphosis, a rude translation back from the splendid world of Egypt to the shallow
imitations of the stage. A version of the play-within-the-play
incorporated into natural allusive speech, Cleopatra's verbal
picture is a mirror of what has actually been happening upon
the stage, but a mirror with a basic distortion. In a sense the
reversal is reversed. Sigurd Burckhardt, in *Shakespearean
Meanings,* puts the matter clearly: "What happens here is
that we are compelled, against common sense and the everyday certitudes about truth and falsehood, to accept illusion *as*
illusion, trickery *as* trickery, and in this acceptance find
truth." [9]

But while *dramatic* reality is boldly exposed for itself, magically without destroying the spell of the play, there is another
kind of reality which is deliberately undercut. If there is a
truth about Cleopatra, it lies in the "serpent of old Nile" and
not in the squeaking boy. For Cleopatra, like Antony, projects
what is in a sense a myth of herself, which is incompatible
with political fact and yet transcends it. She is too large for
the world which tries to contain her. And *Antony and Cleopatra,* like the chronicle plays of the second *Henriad* with
which it has so much in common, is compelled to suggest the
impossibility of a coexistence between dream and "reason" in
its limiting sense of "order." "The air," says Enobarbus

> but for vacancy,
> Had gone to gaze on Cleopatra too,
> And made a gap in nature.
>
> [II.ii.218–20]

The air would have—if it could have. But it could not. Order
in nature must be maintained. The "airy nothings" of Theseus, the "air . . . thin air" of Prospero and even the "piece

9. "The King's Language" (Princeton: Princeton University Press, 1968),
pp. 281–82.

of tender air" of Posthumus's riddle must give place in this play to natural law, just as the dream world of Antony and Cleopatra themselves is forced to give way to civil law. Reality, as exemplified by the coming of the sober order of Caesar, is in itself a significant limitation. And yet Cleopatra, conscious of so much, is conscious of this too. In her last magnificent dream vision of Antony she confronts the problem of art and nature, vision and reality; her answer, which is both a tortured and a transcendent one, is our direct and proper portal into the dream world of the romances.

Dolabella is Cleopatra's confidant here, as Eros and Enobarbus have been Antony's; significantly, a great deal of the play's character analysis is verbalized through the device of a major character speaking to a subordinate. It is a more sophisticated dramatic device than that of soliloquy, and in effect it externalizes the interior dialogues of earlier protagonists with themselves. As concrete evidence we may note the comparative simplicity of syntax, as compared, for instance, with an extreme example like Hamlet's "rogue and peasant slave" soliloquy, which contains eleven rhetorical questions, nine exclamations, and twelve sentences in direct discourse. By contrast Cleopatra, though her words are mostly for her own ears, is fairly straightforward.

Cleopatra: You laugh when boys or women tell their
        dreams,
    Is 't not your trick?
Dolabella: I understand not, madam.
Cleopatra: I dreamt there was an Emperor Antony.
    O, such another sleep, that I might see
    But such another man.
Dolabella: If it might please ye—
Cleopatra: His face was as the heav'ns, and therein stuck
    A sun and moon, which kept their course
        and lighted
    The little O, th' earth.
Dolabella: Most sovereign creature—

Cleopatra: His legs bestrid the ocean: his reared arm
                 Crested the world: his voice was propertied
                 As all the tunèd spheres, and that to friends;
                 But when he meant to quail and shake the
                   orb,
                 He was as rattling thunder. For his bounty,
                 There was no winter in 't: an autumn 'twas
                 That grew the more by reaping. His delights
                 Were dolphinlike, they showed his back above
                 The element they lived in. In his livery
                 Walked crowns and crownets: realms and is-
                   lands were
                 As plates dropped from his pocket.
Dolabella: Cleopatra—
Cleopatra: Think you there was or might be such a man
                 As this I dreamt of?
Dolabella: Gentle madam, no.
Cleopatra: You lie, up to the hearing of the gods.
                 But if there be nor ever were one such,
                 It's past the size of dreaming; nature wants
                   stuff
                 To vie strange forms with fancy, yet t' imag-
                   ine
                 An Antony were nature's piece 'gainst fancy,
                 Condemning shadows quite.

                                              [V.ii.74–100]

Cleopatra's dream is a waking dream, but it is a true one—
true, at least, within her own "conscience" and communicating
itself to us. She acknowledges the generally low reputation of
dream among the forthright Romans; "boys or women" are
the dreamers there. Her description of Antony, however, is no
weakling's delusion, but rather virtually a theogony in little.
In her eyes he becomes a figure like Mars or Thor—related
indeed to the Julius Caesar of Cassius's disgruntled description, who "doth bestride the world like a colossus." When we
look closer, however, we can notice that a great deal of her

description is actually natural imagery: the "sun and moon" in his eyes, his anger like "rattling thunder," his generosity of spirit a constant harvest, with "no winter in't." He is a relative of Adam Kadmon, the sum of the world's inheritance rather than a beneficiary. "Realms and islands were / As plates dropped from his pocket." The structural principle of this description is of considerable interest, for it is actually the reverse of what we have been calling "internal landscape." Where in *King Lear,* for example, the heath mirrored an aspect of Lear's state of soul, here Antony's soul is the subject, and the world of nature the applied metaphor. This is the creative function of dream again, the dream work producing a verbal artifact. The literal man is indeed, as Dolabella gently implies, not wholly recognizable here; but the dream has an independent verisimilitude of its own. It is the last and greatest production of Cleopatra's conscience. Derek Traversi has remarked, apropos of this subject, that "Cleopatra is living in a world which is the projection of her own feelings. That world, while it lasts, is splendidly valid, vital in its projection; only death, which is the end of vitality, can prevent her awakening from it." [10] The connection we have been striving to demonstrate between conscience and dream is here made manifest.

Even the pacing of this remarkable scene is nothing short of brilliant; just at the point when Dolabella's exasperation begins to communicate itself to us, in the middle of a breathtaking virtuosity of creative description, Cleopatra finely turns the dialogue back to her listener for a moment, before drawing the lesson of her own vision. She is dreamer and augurer in one, expounder and interpreter, and her hyperbole is so instinct with vitality and conviction that she carries us with her through an extraordinary train of reasoning: if there had ever been anyone like the dream-Antony she has described—and there has been and is from the moment she describes him—he would be "past the size of dreaming," since the process of

10. *An Approach to Shakespeare,* 2d ed. (Garden Cty, N.Y.: Doubleday, 1956), p. 258.

dream itself is not capable of such a creation. Things of nature are not as wonderful as things created by the fancy, she continues; yet to imagine an Antony—as she has, and as Shakespeare has—gives nature for once a creature more extraordinary than those of fancy, defeating the fictive, the "shadows," by means of the real. The circle is complete, the exchange of the dream for the reality translated back into a new form of reality which includes and transcends "shadows." At this level of the imagination the two categories at last flow into one another unimpeded. We have had a hint of the same transcendence in Enobarbus's earlier description of Cleopatra, "O'erpicturing that Venus where we see / The fancy outwork nature" (II.ii.202–03). And it is most fitting that in their ultimate enshrinement they should be again equal, as they have been throughout.

The new concept of nature here beginning to make its appearance is one which includes both dream and reality. It is characteristic of the language of *Antony and Cleopatra*, and indeed of all the tragedies, that Cleopatra should state the concept in terms of argument: "Nature's piece 'gainst fancy." To Perdita and Polixenes it will become "great creating Nature," incorporating without strain the one pole into the other. For in the romances a renewed and expanded nature will in a sense become equivalent to the world of dream, a temporary but transcendent stage of regenerative awareness; the "art" which "itself is Nature" will encompass for a significant moment the antinomies of illusion and reality.

4

The Truth of Your Own Seeming: Romance and the Uses of Dream

> The freshness of transformation is
>
> The freshness of a world. It is our own,
> It is ourselves, the freshness of ourselves,
> And that necessity and that presentation
>
> Are rubbings of a glass in which we peer.

> Wallace Stevens, *Notes toward a Supreme Fiction*

The close relationship between the romances and the dream world has been often noted by critics. Northrop Frye, for example, points out that "the green world has analogies, not only to the fertile world of ritual, but to the dream world that we create out of our own desires." [1] G. Wilson Knight, in a study of Ariel's songs, calls attention to "the triumphant mysticism of the dream of love's perfected fruit in eternity stilling the tumultuous waves of time." [2] And Derek Traversi, speaking specifically of *Pericles* but with clear intent to generalize, writes that "plot, in short, exists . . . as a function of imagery, and imagery, in turn, is directed to the elaboration of a kind of dream in the course of which normal human qualities, detached from their customary attributes and elevated above their usual status, undergo a process of poetic sublimation to become symbols of a moral rebirth." [3] All of these insights are

---

1. *Anatomy of Criticism: Four Essays* (Princeton: Princeton University Press, 1957), p. 183.

2. "Myth and Miracle," in *The Crown of Life* (London: Oxford University Press, 1947), p. 26.

3. *Shakespeare: The Last Phase* (Stanford, Calif.: Stanford University Press, 1965), p. 35.

suggestive and reflect trends of thought which might be considered characteristic of the authors in question. But in each of these cases "dream" has been introduced as a descriptive term supportive of the author's thesis, while its concrete meaning or meanings remain largely impressionistic. "Dream" in these cases is subject to the same overextensions as the word "romantic" in its broadest sense; both suggest a general aura of the mystical, the faraway, the fairy-tale. Yet the uses of dream in the romances are specific as well as general, local as well as transcendent. It is possible, and perhaps imperative, to examine these specific uses, in order that we may better understand the remarkable range of meanings "dream" has come to have in the plays. For the issue Shakespeare places before us here is no less than the entire question of value: What is the proper place of dream and the irrational in the life of man? And it is this question, more than any other, that we seek to answer.

Dream and its attributes appear in the romances in three general forms: (1) actual dreams and related forms like omens, riddles, and oracles (e.g. Antigonus's dream of Hermione, the conundrum in *Cymbeline,* the oracle of Apollo); (2) the dream state of subjectivity, which blurs the distinction between waking and sleeping, reality and illusion (e.g. Gonzalo after the shipwreck, Imogen when awakening from the potion); (3) specific dream elements and motifs which are related to the actual behavior of the unconscious when dreaming, and thus to the kindred areas of fable and archetype. This last category includes a number of significant subtopics, which we should set forth in brief before examining their application in the plays. The first of these, and the one which metaphorically at least may be said to be almost synonymous with dream itself, is the process of metamorphosis.

We have considered metamorphosis and transformation before, most particularly as they appeared in *A Midsummer Night's Dream.* There, as in the romances, they were related to change of scene, to seasonal and temporal change, to disguise and somatic translation, and ultimately to poetry itself, the creative energy of metaphor and fiction. In *A Midsummer Night's Dream* these elements, while manifest, were still crescent: the play's resolution made clear the fact that the transformations achieved in the forest were limited by lack of self-knowledge on the part of the participants; the literal art object within the play, the "Pyramus and Thisby" interlude, is marred and disordered to reflect the confusion which has gone before. We receive from it the impression of great energy and an indulgence of human folly, at the same time that we are reminded of the dangers of the irrational, the lion in the forest. By contrast, metamorphosis in the romances achieves a serenity, a sense of peace, which seems compounded at once of wisdom and of resignation. The poet is confronting his own craft. The most direct expression of this confrontation in terms of metamorphosis is probably Ariel's second song:

> Full fathom five thy father lies;
>   Of his bones are coral made;
> Those are pearls that were his eyes;
>   Nothing of him that doth fade
> But doth suffer a sea change
>   Into something rich and strange.
>
>   [*Tmp.* I.ii.399–404]

The transformation described here is that of living matter into timeless jewels, the movement we recorded in *Antony and Cleopatra* as the consolidation of the mortal and the immortal. There is no horror in this scene; it should by its subject matter frighten, and yet it reassures. The bones *are* coral, the eyes *are* pearls; we have moved into the timeless present of eternity. The mutability of the mortal frame is arrested at last in a thing of beauty, a created object. (We may note that both coral and pearls are produced in the sea by living organisms; they are not minerals but rather animal concretions, themselves engendered through "sea change" and death.) Ariel's song is entirely fictive; in point of fact Alonso is not dead, but merely separated from his son. Yet as a trope for the activity of artistic creation, and its analogy for human life, the moral truth of the song exceeds its local purpose.

All transformations in Shakespeare are of course in some ways transformations into art, because of the created nature of the plays themselves. The romances, however, place a renewed emphasis upon particular art objects within them: not only upon disguise and discovery, which are kinds of metamorphosis, but also upon the play-within-a-play and the created artifact. Consider, for example, the description given by Gower of Marina and her needlework:

> She sings like one immortal, and she dances
> As goddesslike to her admired lays;
> Deep clerks she dumbs, and with her neele composes
> Nature's own shape of bud, bird, branch, or berry,
> That even her art sisters the natural roses.
>
> [*Per.* V.i.3–7]

The attribution of divinity is a recurrent one in the romances; compare Ferdinand's "Most sure the goddess / On whom these airs attend" (*Tmp.* I.ii.424–25) and Florizel's "no shepherdess, but Flora" (*WT* IV.iv.2). It is itself a kind of translation by analogy into the realm of the "immortal," the transformation occurring here by language rather than by magic. But Marina's needlework is even more interesting: by means of it she creates "Nature's own shape," "her art sisters the natural roses." We may recall a strikingly similar passage from *A Midsummer Night's Dream,* in which Helena describes her childhood:

> We, Hermia, like two artificial gods,
> Have with our needles created both one flower,
> Both on one sampler, sitting on one cushion,
> Both warbling of one song, both in one key.
>
> [III.ii.203–06]

But where "artificial" there hinted at disaster, and the whole passage was an idealized reminiscence from the point of view of a disillusioned present, the picture of Marina, also like a goddess, sewing and singing, carries no such reservations. Marina is not a child but a grown woman, herself Nature's flower, and it is entirely fitting that she should "sister" Nature. She is the instrument of transformation, the poet figure in little, whose art redeems. Again we may note the context of this observation; having escaped the brothel, she performs the poetical task so praised by Shelley: she turns all things to loveliness.

Marina's needlework is an object of visual art, and there is one other significant visual artifact in the romances, the "statue" of Hermione supposedly created by "Julio Romano." But in general the art objects in these plays tend to be verbal rather than visual: songs, plays-within-plays, and, in the case of *The Winter's Tale*, a tale within a tale. We will consider some of these in more detail below, but for the moment it will suffice us to consider them in general as reflexive mirrors of the ongoing action and as expanded metaphors for the plays themselves, transformations of theme and action into redemptive moments of crystallized insight. For metamorphosis is really another name for the imagination: in the subconscious mind, the manifest energy of poetry.

Related to metamorphosis and transmutation into art is the distinct propensity toward the artificial in the romances. In its most reductive sense "artificial" means contrived, unnatural; and certainly this is true of both plot and certain aspects of character in these plays. Character, in fact, has almost ceased to exist in the naturalistic sense of coherent psychological personalities. There are possible exceptions in Leontes and Polixenes, even perhaps in Prospero; but in general the characters in the last plays are constructed along the lines of the typical and universal. This is achieved almost completely without the feeling of contrivance which we experience in reading so structurally artificial a play as *Much Ado about Nothing* or *All's Well That Ends Well*. In these earlier plays there is an imperfect balance between the fantastic and coincidental (the "resurrection" of Hero, the strange fulfillment of Bertram's conditions) and the naturalistic, that which imitates life. The same inequity is occasionally found in *Pericles* and *Cymbeline*, for example in the scenes of Marina in the brothel, where the "low" and insistently real brothel atmosphere conflicts with the allegorical tendencies implicit in Marina's name and character. The diminution of emphasis upon psychologically real, individual characters and their replacement by types is an instance of the symbol-making tendency, in which the concept "the queen" becomes "all queens" and by simple extension "all women," or "womankind." That Shakespeare has long been moving in this direction in the plays is manifest; we noted in Hamlet an inclination to turn dreaming into a kind of private myth-making, and with the romances the creation of private symbols gives way to an identification with the broader and more universal symbols of the human mind.

Freud, writing on symbology in dreams, elucidates some of the more common of these symbols, cautioning that of course they can mean many different things simultaneously and should not be arbitrarily interpreted. His extensive list includes the following entries of particular interest in regard to the romances: "The Emperor and Empress (or the King and Queen) as a rule really represent the dreamer's parents; and a Prince or Princess represents the dreamer himself or herself. . . . Boxes, cases, chests, cupboards and ovens represent the uterus, and also hollow objects, ships, and vessels of all kinds. . . . To represent castration symbolically, the dream-work makes use of baldness, hair-cutting, falling out of teeth, and decapitation." [4] We may—despite Freud's caveat—briefly note the frequency with which these symbols appear in the romances in contexts suggestive of just such meanings. All four of the plays are concerned with kings, queens, and their offspring, usually with some concept of redemption through the second generation; many of the royal and titled children, and especially those with specifically symbolic names (Imogen, Perdita, Miranda) refer to their own dreams and to being in a dreamlike state. Boxes and chests appear prominently in both *Pericles* and *Cymbeline*: in *Pericles* both the "satin coffin" (III.i.68) of the newborn Marina and the "chest . . . caulked and bitumed" (III.i.71–72) which contains the body

4. *Interpretation of Dreams*, pp. 389–92.

of Thaisa are closely connected with birth images; in the scene
which follows their first mention Thaisa will be "reborn" and
lifted from the chest. Likewise in *Cymbeline*, Iachimo refers
to a "trunk" containing "plate of rare device, and jewels / Of
rich and exquisite form" (I.vi.189–90), which he arranges to
have safeguarded in Imogen's chamber. It is reasonable to associate such a coffer with a symbolic representation of her
chastity, which Iachimo has verbally tested and attempted to
violate in the preceding scene. This is a typical structural ar-
rangement for the romances: the alternation of visual (symbolic) and verbal methods of treating a single theme. The
train of imagery is completed when Iachimo, emerging from
the trunk in which he has concealed himself, observes that
his duplicity will force Posthumus to think that

> I have picked the lock and ta'en
> The treasure of her honor.
>
> [II.ii.41–42]

The ship, another of Freud's birth- and sex-associated symbols,
is even more frequently represented in the romances than is
the chest or coffer. The arrival of a newborn infant in the
plots of these plays is inevitably paired with an account of a
sea voyage: Marina receives her name from this circumstance,
but it is also true of Perdita and Miranda. More metaphorical
births, births of awareness and revelation, are also associated
with ships and voyages, for example the Neapolitan ship which
founders through Prospero's intervention, and the ship which
carries shepherd, clown, and Polixenes to Sicilia with news of
Perdita's identity. To Freud's list we might add the symbol of
the storm or tempest, which according to his system is a pre-
dominant feature of the birth dream. In *Pericles, The Winter's Tale,* and *The Tempest* itself a storm accompanies the
birth or early childhood voyage of the heroine. Finally, at the
opposite pole, castration and consequent infertility are associated with the cutting of hair, and the protagonist of *Pericles*
vows never to cut his hair until his daughter is married
(III.iii.28–30).

All of these associations are suggestive rather than conclusive, and merely point toward a special use of language and imagery. Without losing their literal identity, the ships and chests as well as the character types of the romances have acquired a multiple significance which sets them apart from the mundane and incidental and moves them toward the universal and eternal. In fact, the very universality of both character and symbol contributes to the development of what Erich Auerbach calls "figural interpretation": "the here and now is no longer a mere link in an earthly chain of events, it is simultaneously something which has always been, and which will be fulfilled in the future; and strictly . . . it is something eternal, something omni-temporal, something already consummated in the realm of fragmentary earthly event." [5] Timelessness, the achievement of Spenser's "eterne in Mutabilitie," is a major preoccupation of the romances, precisely because of this quality of fable or archetype. Most simply stated, it is the sudden access of "grace," or redemption, in a world governed by seasonal and temporal change. *The Winter's Tale* and *The Tempest* provide opposite solutions to the problem of time, the one containing a gap of sixteen years at its midpoint and taking its internal structure from the succession of the seasons, the other rigidly limited in time to a four-hour span which is frequently and pointedly alluded to by its characters. Freud, citing the psychologist Paul Haffner, draws a direct line between this impulse to timelessness and the world of dream. "The first mark of a dream," he writes, "is its independence of space and time. . . . The second basic feature of dreams is connected with this—namely, the fact that hallucinations, phantasies, and imaginary combinations are confused with external perceptions." [6] This second feature is the subjectivity of the dream state, which we have already mentioned and to which we will return.

The peculiar management of time in the romances is thus another defining element which is simultaneously an integral part of the process of dream. We may properly place it under

5. *Mimesis* (Princeton: Princeton University Press, 1953), pp. 64–65.
6. *Interpretation of Dreams*, p. 84n.

the large rubric of "artifice" in a structural sense, because time in these plays becomes an active and protean instrument, yet another material malleable to the poet's hand. "Artifice" is used here in the dual senses of "contrived" and "crafted," as a controlling metaphor for structural elements within the plays; equally, it is a word descriptive of the activity of the unconscious mind in dream. Some artificial elements closely resemble the structural devices of the earliest plays; for example, there is a renewed emphasis upon the use of oracles, riddles, and prophecies. The tragedies strove to incorporate these monitory devices into the mind of the protagonist; the romances, as if liberated from verisimilitude, restore them. It is as if the morning spirits of Oberon's half-light had suddenly and brazenly decided to show themselves at noon. Each of the romances contains an Olympian god, whose presence is accepted without question in plays which are also overtly Christian and place a strong emphasis on the quality of grace. Not even in the earliest plays did such abrupt authority figures emerge: Diana in *Pericles;* Jupiter in *Cymbeline;* the oracle of Apollo in *The Winter's Tale;* and the masque-figures of Juno and Ceres, as well as the non-Olympian genius loci spirits under Ariel and the various incarnations of Ariel himself, in *The Tempest.* The gods function in much the same way as the prophecies: they unite strands of plot and imagery in brief but often dense poetic statements. Poetry here has indeed taken pride of place over plot; in fact it might be more just to say that plot and poetry are coterminous in the romances. The linguistic virtuosity of the poet extends itself to become astonishing creative license in structure as well.

All of these devices are to some degree reflexive; they mirror in little the larger movement of the play which surrounds them. Perhaps the most fully developed of the reflexive forms is the play-within-a-play, the progress of which we have been following since Christopher Sly's induction. *The Winter's Tale* contains a self-enclosed playlet in the great pastoral scene, in which Perdita describes herself as playing "as I have seen them do / In Whitsun pastorals" (IV.iv.133–34). The real question here, as in most similar situations, is whether the mask assumed will turn out to be more real than the "reality" it replaces, a fundamental question of the world of dream. The play-within-a-play in *The Tempest* has a different though equally familiar function, that of externalizing a trend of thought implicit in the mind of one of the characters. Prospero's strictures on chastity and lawful fertility are embodied in the forms of Juno and Ceres, goddesses of marriage and harvest, at the same time that the triple awareness of roles—actors playing spirits playing goddesses—most concretely poses problems of illusion and reality. But *The Tempest*, like the other romances, also contains fragmentary versions of the play-within-a-play which are equally tied in with the overriding theme of metamorphosis. Problems of disguise, dissimulation, the exchange of clothing (as in act IV of *Cymbeline*) are all metaphorical gestures analogous to the activities of dream condensation and dream displacement, in which the mind alters or consolidates its symbolic images. As always in Shakespeare, certain thematic concerns parallel these structural and imagistic developments: the mythic or fictive pattern which most closely resembles this kind of metamorphosis-through-disguise is the omnipresent theme of losing and finding, one of the most common and typical of dreams.

In our treatment of *A Midsummer Night's Dream* and also in briefer notes on *The Taming of the Shrew* and *Othello,* we mentioned the stage-manager figure who acts as a kind of poet-playwright within the play, defining and organizing its levels of reality and fiction. Such a creative consciousness acts as a kind of link between the audience and the internal worlds of the play, manipulating handy-dandy with a gentle expertise. Neither in *Pericles* nor in *Cymbeline* does such a figure appear, and the result is a certain dramatic confusion: the recognition scenes of Pericles with his daughter and his wife follow too closely upon one another without a fluctuation in intensity. In *Cymbeline* an extraordinary number of recognitions, unmaskings, and reversals, including the unscrambling of a gnomic prophecy, are all crowded into the last scene, produc-

ing resultant confusion and necessitating a certain narrative
flatness in the verse. By contrast, stage-manager figures appear
in both *The Tempest* (Prospero) and *The Winter's Tale*
(Autolycus and, in another sense, Time, the Chorus). All three
are masters of metamorphosis, controllers of dream.

One of the most compelling instruments of this control over
dream is the art of music, whether embodied in the droll and
pertinent ballads of Autolycus, the "rich and strange" songs of
Ariel, or the numerous strange musical moments which sur-
round awarenesses, awakenings, and resurrections in the romances. Elizabethan England retained a largely Neoplatonic
theory about the place and value of music, which might be
thought of as analogous to the patterns of dance in a poem
like Davies's *Orchestra*. According to this theory music was a
sign of heavenly harmony, indeed the heavens continually re-
sounded with song; man, in playing and singing music, thus
attempted to bridge the spiritual gap created by the fall—
fundamentally, to transpose himself for a moment to the condition of the heavens. This is very like the other devices of
momentary transference from one world to another which we
have discussed in relation to dream. In the romances music
will become the principal sign of this change of worlds, a barrier erected between the denizens of dream and its recusants.
Susanne K. Langer speaks of "a twilight zone of musical enjoyment when tonal appreciation is woven into daydreaming." [7]
Here is the twilight world again, often in the romances as in
A Midsummer Night's Dream populated by spirits, and this
time the spirits find their natural medium in song. For as
Shakespeare uses it, music, like dream, is a sphere of the imagination, appropriated and implemented by the subconscious
mind. When Ariel sings to Ferdinand on the shore, he is manifesting his own nature, for song is his natural element; but he
is also articulating in symbolic form thematic ideas which will
later become part of Ferdinand's conscious knowledge: "Come
unto these yellow sands, / And then take hands," as the actors
will do at the close of the play. "The wild waves whist," as

7. *Feeling and Form* (New York: Scribner, 1953), pp. 64–65.

the internal tempest is quelled like the external one. "Sweet sprites bear / The burthen." He knows these things and he does not know that he knows them, for Ariel speaks to us in the language of symbol, and the sign of that directness of communication is the form of song.

W. H. Auden has pointed out that the music in *Cymbeline* at the moment of Posthumus's vision functions to depersonalize the speaker, making his words seem "not *his* statement but a message, a statement that has to be made." [8] This suggestion is of considerable significance, because it links music with the important question of timelessness discussed above. When music sounds in these last plays, time is for a moment arrested. It is not that the flow of the action is disturbed, as is sometimes the case with song in the early comedies. Songs here comment upon the dramatic action at the same time that they are part of it. But almost inevitably in these plays music heralds a mystical moment of communication with a supernatural and nonrational world, and these moments are indeed out of time. This is even true of the songs of Autolycus, though at first glance they would appear to be "low" and "natural," because of the protean character of Autolycus-the-poet; his daemon is chthonic, rather than Olympian, but it abides. We should note in passing that situations often arise when some characters present cannot hear the music to which others respond. This is a dramatic assertion of the same barrier between dream and reality with the tacit addition, in these plays, of a spiritual element in the power of music; we may perhaps say that it is an agency of redemption. For more and more, music in the last plays becomes identified with a regenerative and re-creative force which is the pattern of creation itself, the model of poetry and dream.

In setting forth some of the major structural themes and devices of the romances in light of their relation to dream, we have continually if glancingly touched upon the under-

8. "Music in Shakespeare," in *The Dyer's Hand and Other Essays* (New York: Random House, 1948), p. 508.

lying assumption that the plays are to a very large extent concerned with the nature of poetry. Magic, transformation, resurrection, song—all these are metaphors for poetry and its
power. They are not summed up in that equation, nor are
they limited by it, but surely those many critics who write of
The Tempest as the poet's vision of his own art are correct.
And the world of dream, as we have described it here, may be
said in a sense to *be* that vision. Dream by the time of these
last plays is imagination of the highest order, imagination
fleetingly captured in moments of transcendence as Ariel is
fleetingly captured by Prospero. The services it performs are
for the enlightenment of the dreamers, though none are ever
wholly enlightened. In its ultimate form the concept of dream
becomes as elusive as that of poetry itself. But within the aura
of the dream state, which seems to envelop the entire world of
the romances, all these concrete and specific usages continue
to function. In *Pericles* and *Cymbeline,* which for all their
moments of richness and insight are in a way still experiments
in the romance form, the dream tropes possess a luminous
intensity greater than that of the plays which contain them.

The problems implicit in an examination of *Pericles* are
compounded by serious textual questions about the division
of authorship. Without entering into these, we may note with
interest the fact that neither the word "dream" nor any of the
major motifs we have cited appear in the sector usually
ascribed to a non-Shakespearean hand. The one possible exception, the incest riddle of act I, scene i, does support the
pervasive theme of perversion in nature. But the tone of the
play shifts radically in the third act, when Pericles, in accents
reminiscent of Clarence's dream, mourns the supposed fate
of Thaisa:

>   nor have I time
> To give thee hallowed to thy grave, but straight
> Must cast thee, scarcely coffined, in the ooze;

> Where, for a monument upon thy bones,
> And e'er-remaining lamps, the belching whale
> And humming water must o'erwhelm thy corpse,
> Lying with simple shells.

[III.i.59–65]

His vision is one of decay where there should be immortality;
"for" here means "in place of." "Belching" and "humming"
are relatively colloquial terms for great activity: the implication is that she will have no rest. But the facts of the case are
quite different, and the pattern of transmutation into art will
parallel, as thematically it must, the human pattern of resurrection.

Cerimon: The music there! I pray you give her air.
            Gentlemen,
            This queen will live: nature awakes; a
               warmth
            Breathes out of her. She hath not been
               entranced
            Above five hours. See how she 'gins to
               blow
            Into life's flower again!

First gentleman: The heavens
            Through you increase our wonder, and
               sets up
            Your fame forever.

Cerimon: She is alive! Behold
            Her eyelids, cases to those heavenly
               jewels
            Which Pericles hath lost, begin to part
            Their fringes of bright gold; the dia-
               monds
            Of a most praisèd water doth appear
            To make the world twice rich. Live,
            And make us weep to hear your fate,
               fair creature,
            Rare as you seem to be.

> *Thaisa:*   O dear Diana,
>   Where am I? Where's my lord? What
>   world is this?
>
> [III.ii.92–107]

Thaisa has just been discovered upon the shore in the chest which was to be her coffin, a chest filled with gold, royal clothes, and spices. Cerimon the physician, who refers to his profession as a "secret art" and who in many ways resembles the later figure of Prospero, succeeds—with the help of "still and woeful music" (89)—in reviving her from what is apparently merely a deep swoon or sleep. It is noteworthy that his first metaphors are natural ones: "nature awakes"; "she 'gins to blow / Into life's flower again." The image here is of seasonal renewal, a natural progression from sleeping to waking as from dormancy to life. In his next remarks, however, Cerimon turns to the language of treasure and jewel, a language the power of which we have already examined in Ariel's second song. Her eyelids are "cases," a comparison familiar from *Lear*, but here the image is tender rather than grotesque. Eyes are "heavenly jewels"—the metaphor is commonplace, and yet the meaning here precise. She too has in her way suffered a "sea change," even if only in a renewed awareness of the value and precariousness of life. Similarly the "fringes of bright gold" carry a sense of value and permanency; "diamonds," for eyes, suggest both riches and tears, with a presumed pun in "praised water" (luster, wetness). These metaphorical jewels match the "literal" jewels of the treasure chest, and we are meant to feel the ambiguity: which are more real? Thaisa's waking cries are thematically pertinent: the instinctive appeal to Diana foreshadows the later role that goddess will play in preserving her and reuniting her with her husband; Diana is also the goddess of chastity, a central theme running through *Pericles* as a whole. But the most interesting question from our point of view is the last one—"What world is this?" It is the romantic counterpart of Lear's awakening, and it calls to mind as well the equivocal inquiry of Christopher Sly: "Or do

I dream? Or have I dreamed till now?" It is a new world into which Thaisa has passed, the Ephesus world in which resurrection and regeneration are possible.

Pericles, however, is unaware of his wife's revival, and as the play progresses he also learns of his daughter's apparent death. This gap in knowledge, the belief by two or more characters in conflicting realities which govern their actions, is characteristic of the romances, and leads directly to the unmasking or recognition scene which is the meeting of the worlds of fiction and reality. In a way such an unmasking is like the dream interpreted, shadowy figures in fictive garb finally reconciled with their usual identities. The technique of reversal of categories is integral to this process, and "dream" once more becomes a word equivalent to fiction. Thus in the moving recognition scene between Pericles and Marina he halts her in the middle of her tale:

> O, stop there a little!
> This is the rarest dream that e'er dulled sleep
> Did mock sad fools withal. This cannot be:
> My daughter's buried.
>
> [V.i.164–67]

The "dream" is the fact of her survival; a few lines earlier he asks unbelievingly "But are you flesh and blood? / Have you a working pulse, and are no fairy?" (155–56). At the same time, of course, the dream is the play as a whole, the plot of which Marina has just told in brief; again we have a covert hint of the near-identity of dream and poetry. Pericles' reaction continues to be reminiscent of the awakening scene in *Lear;* turning to a friend he implores

> O Helicanus, strike me, honored sir!
> Give me a gash, put me to present pain
>
> [194–95]

recalling Lear's

> let's see;
> I feel this pin prick.
>
> [*Lr.* IV. vii.55–56]

Then, assured of his condition, he calls Marina to him, addressing her as "Thou that beget'st him that did thee beget" (199). The surfacing of the metaphor is unlike *Lear* and is characteristic of the dream world of the romances; Pericles speaks openly of rebirth, and by his very mention of it he confirms the fable, and softens the sense of "improbability" in the facts of the plot.

The two recognition scenes in *Pericles* are bridged by a vision, which is the play's only actual dream. The scene (V.i.) begins with music, the sign of dream, and although other characters (Helicanus, Lysimachus, Marina) are present, they do not hear it. Like the ghost of old Hamlet, the goddess Diana who now appears will speak to one hearer alone.

> *Pericles:*   I hear most heavenly music.
> It nips me unto list'ning, and thick slumber
> Hangs upon mine eyes. Let me rest. (*He sleeps*).
>
> *Lysimachus:*   A pillow for his head. So leave him all.
> Well, my companion friends,
> If this but answer to my just belief,
> I'll well remember you.
>
> *Diana (appears to Pericles in a vision):*
> My temple stands in Ephesus. Hie thee thither,
> And do upon mine altar sacrifice.
> There, when my maiden priests are met together,
> Before the people all,
> Reveal how thou at sea didst lose thy wife.
> To mourn thy crosses, with thy daughter's, call
> And give them repetition to the life.
> Perform my bidding, or thou liv'st in woe;
> Do't, and happy, by my silver bow!
> Awake, and tell thy dream.
>
> [V.i.236–52]

The sleep of Pericles enables the world of dream to take over, as it did during the sleep of the Athenian lovers in *A Midsummer Night's Dream;* the emphasis, once more, is on the symbolic rather than the naturalistic. The heavenly music, however, reminds us that this is no ordinary slumber; later Ariel will use the same musical means to enchant characters in *The Tempest.* That Pericles alone hears the music sets him apart; there now ensues one of those timeless moments, in which the others seem to fade from the stage and from the progressing plot, as Diana instructs him. He is in the state of subjectivity, the dream state. Diana's words are straightforward, and on the whole less distinguished as verse than some other parts of the play. It is interesting, however, that she uses the cumbrous phrase "repetition to the life" to mean "lifelike recital." The phrase suggests the possibility of a hidden ambiguity, "repetition, so that their lives might repeat or revive." We should also note the emphasis on telling, on the repetition of the tale itself. Marina has already recapitulated it in abbreviated, mythic form. Diana here urges Pericles to "tell" his dream to the onlookers, and to "repeat" his story at her shrine. He will in fact do so, in the final scene which brings about the restoration of Thaisa. When we add to this the fact that the entire play is told to us in advance by Gower (and once again in act III by a dumb show), it becomes evident that the act of telling, the created fiction of the tale, is of considerable significance. The fictive quality is calling attention to itself, as the poet reflexively examines the nature of his art.

As a play *Pericles* has a number of shortcomings, both structural and poetic. Its fragmentary nature is distracting, and it seldom rises to the heights of language reached in the tragedies or in *The Tempest* or *The Winter's Tale.* There are, however, moments of linguistic clarity which all at once seem to focus the entire play in a line or phrase, phrases which themselves seem to shift the level of discourse from the ongoing plot to the realm of the timeless and symbolic. One such phrase is Marina's gnomic explanation of her birthplace; she is not of these shores, she says, "nor of any shores" (V.i.106), a riddling answer which seems to recall the prophecy in *Mac-*

beth of the man "not of woman born." That she so calmly and straightforwardly relates her life in terms of seeming paradox affords us a sudden insight into the whole ground-quality of the play. The most striking of these "window" lines, however, is Thaisa's question to Pericles, after he has once more repeated his tale:

> Did you not name a tempest,
> A birth and death?
>
> [V.iii.33–34]

This is in its way yet another telling of the tale, now reduced to its mythic outlines—a pattern we have seen in many of Shakespeare's plays. Yet this mode of expressing the whole redemptive cycle does not really reduce but rather expands the significance of the drama. The whole play, viewed in this radical moment of insight, becomes a universal myth, the model of a dream. In *Pericles* such moments are few; in the plays that follow they will become more frequent and more dominant. Yet the pivotal statement of the shepherd in *The Winter's Tale,* "thou met'st with things dying, I with things new born," is here anticipated in tone and meaning by Thaisa's solitary question.

None of the four romances has a plot which could be described as plausible; in fact, this very implausibility is what we have been referring to as the mode of the sublime artificial that moves toward myth and reflexivity. For sheer improbability, however, *Cymbeline* far exceeds the others. It contains an example of almost every one of the dream devices we have reviewed, and its final scene presents five literal unmaskings (Posthumus as the peasant soldier, Imogen-Fidele, the two sons, and Belarius) and two revelations of duplicity or figurative unmasking (the queen's, Iachimo's). The uses of dream as we examine them seem to be largely counterparts of this theme of unmasking, which is a variation of metamorphosis, and the play again becomes almost coterminous with the protean dream world. The geographical dream world within the play is Milford Haven, following the established Shakespearean pattern of "rational world of responsibilities—strange world of irrational happening—renewed and enlightened return to order and reason." But the actual working out of metamorphosis in *Cymbeline* is complicated by a plot which, though largely symbolic in form, returns sporadically to a somewhat discordant realism. Nonetheless, the dream passages are interesting in themselves, and particularly interesting for what they tell us about the final two plays.

We have already discussed the bedchamber scene, in which Imogen sleeps as Iachimo inventories her possessions. It is interesting that he strikes the note of "conscience," familiar to us from the tragedies, linking it with the outward question of subjective versus objective truth; taking Posthumus's bracelet from her arm, he says

> 'Tis mine, and this will witness outwardly,
> As strongly as the conscience does within.
>
> [II.ii.35–36]

Equally interesting is the fact that his inventory lights upon an artifact: "She hath been reading late / The tale of Tereus" (44–45). The tale of Tereus, of course, appears in Ovid's *Metamorphoses;* even so seemingly insignificant a detail is designed to conform to the play's major themes. Later, when Pisanio confronts Imogen with the apparent fact that Posthumus believes her "false to his bed," she cries,

> False to his bed? What is it to be false?
> To lie in watch there and to think on him?
> To weep 'twixt clock and clock? If sleep charge nature,
> To break it with a fearful dream of him,
> And cry myself awake?
>
> [III.iv.40–44]

Iachimo belongs to the pattern of the would-be controllers of dream. He knows the facts, and his concern is to obscure and confuse them. He is not a strong character, and after the initial duplicity of the bedchamber he drops out of the play until the final scene. His role, fundamentally, is to place the two lovers in the dream state of subjectivity, where each is forced to confront and accept the irrational they do not understand. Imogen, on the other hand, is of all the play's characters the one most comfortable with dream. In this passage she refers to a "fearful dream" of Posthumus, and it seems likely that she has an initial respect for dream. We may contrast her with Cymbeline himself, who is trapped in the court "realities" of an equally fictive world made by his queen, in a way most reminiscent of *Macbeth*. Belarius, in an early soliloquy (III.iii.79–86), exclaims

> How hard it is to hide the sparks of nature!
> These boys know little they are sons to th' king,
> Nor Cymbeline dreams that they are alive.
>
> [79–81]

Part of the lesson of the play is that Cymbeline must learn to dream, and a possible interpretation of the final recognition scene is that he has begun to learn to do so, accepting the multiple revelations which restore his children and denounce his queen. For in *Cymbeline,* as in all the plays, the state of the king is the state of his realm.

Imogen's principal experience with the world of dream occurs in the cave at Milford Haven, when disguised as the page Fidele (another Spenserian allegorical name) she tastes the drug the queen had given to Pisanio. Immediately she falls into a deathlike trance, as did Juliet, and is discovered by Belarius and the two boys. They bury her sorrowfully next to the trunk of the dead Cloten, who remains dressed in Posthumus's clothes, and when they depart, she wakes. "I hope I dream," she says,

> For so I thought I was a cave-keeper
> And cook to honest creatures. But 'tis not so;
> 'Twas but a bolt of nothing, shot at nothing,
> Which the brain makes of fumes. Our very eyes
> Are sometimes like our judgments, blind. Good faith,

I tremble still with fear, but if there be
Yet left in heaven as small a drop of pity
As a wren's eye, feared gods, a part of it!
The dream's here still. Even when I wake, it is
Without me, as within me; not imagined, felt.

[IV.ii.298–307]

Imogen is now in the dream state, unable to distinguish the apparently real from the fictive or illusory. The dream is "without her as within her," the scene reflecting her thoughts, the boundary between sleeping and waking diminished or removed. That she should call this insight "not imagined, felt," testifies to the degree to which she has given herself to the experience of dream. Her use of the always significant word "nothing" recalls Theseus's "airy nothing" rendered into dream shapes by the creative imagination. Like Posthumus and Cymbeline, Imogen must learn to submit herself to the dream world, to accept its more vibrant realities. As another of the now frequent resurrection figures in the plays she points toward a cycle of nature. Her dream is structurally a reversal, reality seen as dream, yet once again the facts of the play as they have occurred much more closely resemble dream happenings than real or plausible ones. As evidence we might particularly cite the moment when Imogen-Fidele, encountered by Guiderius and Arviragus, is immediately told that they will be her "brothers." This instantaneous and subconscious penetration of disguise is an event fittingly placed in the dream world of Milford Haven; that the metaphor ("brothers") will become literal reality in the court world accords with the sense of redemptive dream we have been developing.

The old machinery of omen and prophecy is more evident in *Cymbeline* than in the other romances. As Diana appeared in *Pericles,* so Jupiter will make his appearance here, and that appearance is heralded by a conversation between the Roman general Lucius and his soothsayer (IV.ii.346–53). There may be significance in the fact that the Romans, rationalists in

Antony and Cleopatra, have put their faith in dreams of the gods. But the soothsayer's vision of the Roman eagle and the British sun is a curiously sterile incident, without either poetry or symbolism to redeem it from mere linear plot prediction. The soothsayer himself is atmospherically useful, because he reinforces the sense of mystery and disguise which obtains throughout, but his existence is on balance more cumbersome than enlightening. Only the mention of "Jove's bird," which in Posthumus's dream vision will become "the holy eagle" on "immortal wing" (V.iv.85, 88) hints at the direction in which his symbolic function might have been expanded and enriched.

Posthumus's dream vision itself is similarly flawed, its verse, in undistinguished fourteeners, less dense and rewarding than we have come to expect from the language of the visionary moment. Posthumus, in prison and despairing of reunion with Imogen, falls asleep upon the stage, just as Pericles had done, and like Pericles he is then visited by an apparition. To the accompaniment, once more, of mysterious heavenly music, there appears to him a vision of his parents and brothers, none of whom—as his name implies—he had known in life. They castigate Jupiter for unfairly trying him, after which Jupiter himself appears, informs them that he has caused Posthumus to suffer "to make my gift, / The more delayed, delighted" (V.iv.71–72), and ascends to the heavens once more. At this point the ghosts vanish, and Posthumus awakes. And here the verse regains some of its richness, becomes once more the ambiguous and rewarding language of the world of dream.

> Sleep, thou hast been a grandsire and begot
> A father to me, and thou hast created
> A mother and two brothers; but O scorn,
> Gone! They went hence so soon as they were born.
> And so I am awake. Poor wretches that depend
> On greatness' favor, dream as I have done,
> Wake, and find nothing. But, alas, I swerve.
> Many dream not to find, neither deserve,

> And yet are steeped in favors. So am I,
> That have this golden chance and know not why.
>
> [V.iv.93–102]

Again we should note the emphasis on metaphors of birth, particularly strange birth and rebirth. Sleep is addressed as a progenitor because of the creative power of the imagination, producing a compact metaphor which supports the recurrent Shakespearean theme of simultaneous fertility in nature and in art. There is an interesting ambiguity, also, in Posthumus's lament that "they went hence as soon as they were born." The loss of the mother and two brothers in dream is a recapitulation of their loss in life, as soon as *he* was born, and this echo helps to set the worlds of fiction and actuality again in equipoise. The ruminations on dreams that follow, which first condemn the vision as illusory, then alter to express a faith in what may come, are rewarded by the discovery of the book containing the gnomic prophecy of the lion's whelp and the stately cedar. As Paulina will admonish in *The Winter's Tale*, "It is required / You do awake your faith," in order that the visionary and improbable may come to pass.

The prophecy, like so much of *Cymbeline*, is gnomic and involuted, difficult to unravel and anticlimactic when the soothsayer explains it at the play's close. The *"mollis aer–mulier"* equation is symptomatic of the difficulties of the play as a whole; it fails to ring true and consequently appears contrived and unconvincing. But once more Posthumus's own reaction is of interest;

> 'Tis still a dream, or else such stuff as madmen
> Tongue, and brain not; either both, or nothing;
> Or senseless speaking, or a speaking such
> As sense cannot untie. Be what it is,
> The action of my life is like it, which
> I'll keep, if but for sympathy.
>
> [115–20]

Dream or madness—Theseus's choice, in either case an illusion. But Posthumus, unlike Theseus, does not take refuge in the rational, but rather deliberately moves forward toward acceptance of dream: "Be what it is, / The action of my life is like it." The action of his life, of course, *is* the prophecy, as both are the plot of *Cymbeline*. Language here again is as dense as meaning; "Tongue, and brain not" boldly compresses the metaphor of the madman till it springs yet another meaning, the primacy—once more—of speech and poetry over reason. Posthumus does not understand the riddle, but he accepts it. It is Imogen's "not imagined, felt" again; and these very moments of transcendent faith in the world of dream are what render the interlocutory figure of the soothsayer a jarring intrusion into the play's world. Yet for all its improbabilities, this world, like the world of *Pericles*, contains many of the same essential elements which produced the great masterpieces of the late period, *The Winter's Tale* and *The Tempest*. The success of these two plays consists in part of the very acceptance of dream with which Imogen and Posthumus have struggled. For the subject of *The Winter's Tale* and *The Tempest* is man's confrontation with the irrational, the complex and subtle role of the dream world in the life of poet and man.

The Winter's Tale, as we have already indicated, centers much of its attention on problems of timelessness and time. Metamorphosis is everywhere in its plot and imagery. The large structural units of the play are the four seasons of the year: winter in the opening "jealousy" scene at Leontes' court; spring with the finding of the child in Bohemia; summer in the great pastoral scene of the sheepshearing; and autumn or harvest in the return to Sicilia and the restoration of the king's wife and child, assuring order and fertility. This cyclical movement is occasionally cut, or halted, by moments of the sort we have been calling timeless, when the world of dream and the irrational intersects with the ongoing world which surrounds it. We are now purposely using "dream" in a double sense, for the entire world of *The Winter's Tale* is indeed a dream world as we have described it, and the fundamental element of dream, metamorphosis or transformation, will continue to

inform it throughout. The other kind of dream is frequently
accompanied by an artifact—a tale, play, or statue. This is
the redemptive element, the moment beyond time, often at-
tended by music, which suggests that the cyclical action may
not after all have to repeat itself endlessly. T. S. Eliot, writing
of these moments of the "intersection of the timeless with
time," calls them "only hints and guesses," and so they are in
The Winter's Tale. But it may be that the play is suggesting
that hints and guesses are all that man is given, that always
underneath these startling moments of transcendence and insight there must be cycle and change, metamorphosis, life and
death. Just as the young Mamilius dies and is not revived, so
mortality, the moment of Hamlet in the graveyard, is ultimately the radical condition of man.

The metamorphosis of seasonal change in the play is, of
course, matched by appropriate human actions in each season.
Contained within this broad structure, however, there are
many little cycles; and these too are enlightening on the question of metamorphosis and dream. For example, in the opening moments of the play, Polixenes, recalling his childhood
with Leontes, describes them as

> Two lads that thought there was no more behind
> But such a day tomorrow as today,
> And to be boy eternal.

[I.ii.63–65]

Had they remained in that state, he suggests, they would have
avoided the taint of original sin. He is thus evoking a kind of
golden age, an almost Wordsworthian innocence which is
simultaneously Christian and pagan. But in longing to be
"boy eternal" he is protesting against the very cycle which
gives life, against the necessity of experience before eternity.
The "Ode: Intimations of Immortality from Recollections of
Early Childhood," is perhaps the best commentary on his
wish; the children on the shore in Wordsworth's poem are
very like the "boy eternal," but the "sober colouring" of mortality is essential to Polixenes, to Shakespeare, and to any per-

manency which is to come out of *The Winter's Tale*. Just as
in the Intimations Ode the man of imagination succeeds the
child of nature, so in *The Winter's Tale* the essential experiences of nature and time alone produce imagination and art.
The critical turning point at which Wordsworth praises

> Those obstinate questionings
> Of sense and outward things,
> Fallings from us, vanishings

is very like Paulina's crucial call to "awake your faith." Geoff-
rey Hartman writes that

> the strength which [the child's] imagination exhibits in
> going out of itself and blending with a lesser nature is the
> source of all future strength: it is for Wordsworth *the* act
> of regeneration. . . . The mature man . . . bases his
> faith in self-transcendence on the ease or unconsciousness
> with which the apocalyptic imagination turned in child-
> hood toward life. Then the crisis was to go from self-love
> (unconscious) to love of nature, and now it is to go from
> self-love (conscious) to love of man.[9]

A very similar psychological process seems to be animating the
transcendent activity of dream in the romances.

Polixenes' assertion is therefore a clue to lack of self-knowledge, manifested in a resistance to the normal flow of the
seasons. His deficiency is at the outset much less evident than
Leontes', although they are actually very similar figures, because much of the first act is occupied by Leontes' internal
monologue of jealous suspicion. And the substance of Leontes'
remarks testifies to a limited understanding of dream which
is also an aversion to change:

> Affection! Thy intention stabs the center.
> Thou dost make possible things not so held,
> Communicat'st with dreams—how can this be?—

9. *Wordsworth's Poetry 1787–1814* (New Haven: Yale University Press,
1964), p. 277.

With what's unreal thou coactive art,
And fellow'st nothing. Then 'tis very credent
Thou mayst co-join with something, and thou dost,
And that beyond commission, and I find it,
And that to the infection of my brains,
And hardening of my brows.

[I.ii.138–46]

According to this reasoning "affection," or passionate emotion,
since it is known to ally itself with dreams and "what's unreal," is even more likely to be provoked by a real stimulus,
such as sexual infidelity. The logic is extremely dubious, itself affected by "affection." Once more Shakespeare shows remarkable insight into the operations of the dream work, for
Leontes' problem is precisely that he has subconsciously displaced and substituted the fictive for the real in order to give
vent to a latent "affection," a propensity for sexual jealousy.
As a synonym for dream he uses the significant "nothing,"
which anticipates his Tourneurian interrogation of Camillo:

                    Is whispering nothing?
Is leaning cheek to cheek? Is meeting noses?
Kissing with inside lip? . . .
                    . . . Is this nothing?
Why then the world and all that's in't is nothing,
The covering sky is nothing, Bohemia nothing,
My wife is nothing, nor nothing have these nothings,
If this be nothing.

[I.ii.284–86; 292–96]

The manifest irony here is of course that these things *are*
nothing in the sense of Leontes' question—they do not exist
and are therefore not evidence of suspicious conduct between
Hermione and Polixenes. As always, however, "nothing" is a
richly ambiguous word, and here particularly so, since Leontes
himself has equated it with dream, and since it so clearly
draws attention to itself in the lines just quoted. All the
grievances he catalogues are indeed Leontes' dreams and delusions, though he means to assert the contrary. What is more

interesting, however, is the reading of the last four lines we produce if we answer the preceding question ("Is this nothing?") with its proper answer, yes. Then, following Leontes' logic, "the world," "the covering sky," "Bohemia," and his wife are all nothing, dreams, as well. But what are these elements but the primary components of the drama itself—the fictive world, the stage, the scene, the characters? In its way Leontes' hyperbole is an anticipation of Prospero's great speech at the close of the masque in *The Tempest:*

> like the baseless fabric of this vision,
> The cloud-capped towers, the gorgeous palaces,
> The solemn temples, the great globe itself,
> Yea, all which it inherit, shall dissolve,
> And, like this insubstantial pageant faded,
> Leave not a rack behind.
>
> [*Tmp.* IV.i.151–56]

With consummate skill the poet suggests an underlying sense of reflexivity, even in Leontes' most self-delusive moments. Leontes himself is, so to speak, confounded by his own logic. From the first he confuses reality and illusion in the court world of Sicilia, and his illusion is nightmare, malign fiction: "I have drunk, and seen the spider" (II.i.45). In the trial scene in act III his dialogue with Hermione further bares his confusion, which is not a transcendent reversal but rather an error of fact.

Hermione: Sir,
You speak a language that I understand not.
My life stands in the level of your dreams,
Which I'll lay down.
Leontes: Your actions are my dreams.
You had a bastard by Polixenes,
And I but dreamed it.

[III.ii.77–82]

Again he speaks truth in the guise of irony; he *has* "but dreamed it." Hermione asserts that her life is totally at the mercy of his delusions. His reply, that her actions "are his dreams," has been true in many dream situations in past plays but is wholly untrue here. One of the many effects of this symmetrical and devastating exchange is to warn us about the negative power of dreams, a facet hinted at in *A Midsummer Night's Dream*. The world of dream possesses the power it does because its creative energy produces poetry and art. But the essence of dream is the irrational, and the irrational contains the seeds of danger and destruction. Leontes' progression from this point to the awakened faith of the unveiling scene is in part a progress from bad dream to good, from daemonic nightmare to creative imagination. Here is metamorphosis of yet another kind, coupled with a serious and sober appraisal of the doctrine of dream.

The immediate effect of these unwholesome "dreams" upon Leontes is to produce sleeplessness, a malady which is by now familiar to us from the cases of Macbeth and Richard III. Leontes' delusory daydreams have crowded out the possibility of normal sleeping dreams; and he, like Macbeth, is forced to live in a waking world governed by his own fictions. Leontes himself is aware of this, though characteristically he disregards facts for impressions;

> Dost think I am so muddy, so unsettled,
> To appoint myself in this vexation? Sully
> The purity and whiteness of my sheets—
> Which to preserve is sleep; which being spotted,
> Is goads, thorns, nettles, tails of wasps—
>
> [I.ii.326–30]

"Goads, thorns, nettles"—Leontes uses these words as metaphors for a psychological state. His world is all "in the mind." When the same images appear in *The Tempest,* they will be part of an externalized dream world, the "Toothed briers, sharp furzes, pricking goss, and thorns" (*Tmp.* IV.i.180) with which Ariel abuses the shins of Stephano, Trinculo, and Caliban. But Leontes is the fabricator of his own delusions and the cause of his own inability to sleep. Paulina acknowledges this fact in her reply to the servant who tries to keep her from entering the court with the newborn Perdita:

> I come to bring him sleep. 'Tis such as you
> That creep like shadows by him, and do sigh
> At each his needless heavings—such as you
> Nourish the cause of his awaking.

[II.iii.33–36]

Again we have the verbal contrast between "his awaking," which is a barren state, and the awakened faith at the close of the play. Leontes' state of mind is frozen and sterile, and he denies evidence of his own fertility, the child who is "the whole matter / And copy of the father" (II.iii.98–99). Images of physical dream, sleeping and waking, are thus early integrated into the larger pattern of change and growth.

The seasonal metaphor of reawakening has as its counterpart in the plot the "death" and resurrection of Hermione. It is the knowledgeable Paulina, again, who suggests the possibility of such a revival as early as the third act. Like all her most significant utterances, however, this one is slightly gnomic, because it is deliberately phrased as a condition contrary to fact.

> if you can bring
> Tincture or luster in her lip, her eye,
> Heat outwardly or breath within, I'll serve you
> As I would do the gods.

[III.ii.202–05]

There is some possibility that when Shakespeare wrote this scene and the one that follows, Antigonus's dream, he had not yet conceived the idea of reviving Hermione. It is difficult to think, however, that he would have let this passage stand, after altering the play's ending, if it conflicted with his dramatic or symbolic purposes. The net effect of Paulina's avowal, in any case, is to put into the minds of the audience the very possibility she denies. The scene thus becomes a dramatic anticipation of the denouement, an emphatic statement of the impossibility and irrationality of something which will turn out to be true. It is the pattern of dream in little again, a cycle within the cycle.

We have discussed the large structure of metamorphosis in terms of time. That structure can also be analyzed spatially, in the geographical fluctuation from Sicilia to Bohemia and back again. Sicilia here is initially the "real" world of the court, Bohemia and its inhabitants the dream world and its spirits; and the return to Sicilia brings with it a faith in dream by which what was previously impossible, Hermione's regeneration, becomes possible and true. Again and again in this play large movements of this sort are anticipated by smaller ones, and thus in the lyric "window" passage at the opening of the third act we catch a glimpse of redemption. Cleomenes and Dion have been sent by Leontes to the oracle of Apollo, which Shakespeare mistakenly places on the isle of Delos. The mistake serves him well, however; Delphi, the actual site of the oracle, is inland, while Delos, an island, provides opportunity for a symbolic sea journey and itself becomes proleptic to the Bohemian dream world of the main plot. Cleomenes' report of the island is indicative:

> The climate's delicate, the air most sweet,
> Fertile the isle, the temple much surpassing
> The common praise it bears.
>
> [III.i.1–3]

It might almost be a description of Prospero's isle. We may especially take note of the emphasis on fertility, associating that trait with poetic inspiration (Apollo) and again anticipating the pastoral abundance of the Bohemia scenes. This short scene functions like a metaphor in the play as a whole; the two messengers are for a moment in that state of "grace" which is so central to the language of *The Winter's Tale*. When Cleomenes says the oracle "so surprised [his] sense / That I was nothing" (III.i.10–11), we see the other side of the question of "nothingness," a transcendent subjectivity which leads to insight. The breathing space is short-lived, however; Leontes denies the oracle, the deaths of Mamilius and Hermione are reported, and Perdita is doomed to exile. At this point the scene shifts to Bohemia, a tempest, and a dream.

Antigonus's dream vision of the dead Hermione is the only literal dream in the play, and like the dream visions of Pericles and Posthumus this one lacks the real energy and imagination of Shakespeare's maturest writing. Its tone is discursive and its images somewhat underdeveloped, hints of symbols rather than symbols themselves. Antigonus makes a number of observations about dream and the dream state of a kind which have become wholly familiar to us by now: "ne'er was dream / So like waking"; "I . . . thought / This was so, and not slumber"; "Dreams are toys; / Yet for this once, yea superstitiously, / I will be squared by this. I do believe . . ." (III.iii.14–45). He defines himself as a person who ordinarily scoffs at dreams, implying that there is something unusual about this particular dream which sets it apart. In outline the dream itself is an old-style monitory dream, the return of a spirit from the dead to warn the living: the figure of Hermione, "in pure white robes / Like very sanctity" (21–22), requests him to take Perdita to the shores of Bohemia and informs him that he will never see his wife again. This last circumstance, one of the two irreversible tragedies of the play (the death of Mamilius is the other), is partially responsible for a sense of sobriety that obtains even at the play's close, when Paulina points out that all are revived and reunited but he. Yet there is internal justification for Antigonus's death more than for Mamilius's: when he says of the infant Perdita "this being indeed the issue / Of King Polixenes" (42–43), he demonstrates his own lack of faith. The apparent fact of Hermione's death in the dream is at first more puzzling, since she is later demonstrated to be alive. Yet in a metaphorical sense she is properly imaged as dead, since in the imaginative worlds of poetry and dream "death" is a failure of belief, another instance of unawakened faith. What is most interesting, however, is the language of imagery with which he chooses to describe her, in a long passage relatively devoid of images. "Her eyes," he says, "became

two spouts" as she began to speak. The picture calls to mind
the figure of Niobe from the *Metamorphoses* of Ovid (VI.146ff.),
who turns into a fountain and weeps for the loss of her children. Like the "pure white robes / Like very sanctity" this is
in part an allegorizing tendency, but it is also a hint of transformation. When Perdita, at the close of the passage, is addressed as "Blossom," the covert growth and transformation
imagery is once more supported.

If the dream of Antigonus is in some ways the least successful
symbolic incident in the play, it is followed by what might be
called the most successful: the unexpected entry of the bear
and the extraordinarily rich and vivid dialogue between the
shepherd and the clown. Greene's *Pandosto,* the direct source
of *The Winter's Tale,* makes no mention of the bear who pursues Antigonus and is later so placidly described by the clown.
But the bear is an important symbol for the play as a whole;
though it exemplifies the wild and irrational character of the
land of Bohemia, it seems unanticipated by anything in the
previous action. Yet in folklore the bear is one of the most
common symbols of immortality and resurrection, because of its
habit of winter hibernation.[10] Adherents of the cult of the
Thracian Salmaxis, the bear-god, believed that the bear first
feasted, then slept in an underground chamber as though dead,
returning to the world of the living with the spring thaw. The
bear was thus the symbol of a cult of immortality, his own
cycle coinciding with the pattern of the *sacre du printemps,*
the spring resurrection festival. The related legend of Kallisto,
the Great Bear, includes the fact that the bear child, her son
Arkas, the ancestor of the Arcadians, was sacrificed at a feast of
the clan. Mimetically in his memory a human child was an-
nually offered at the shrine of Zeus Lykaios, in a gesture not
unlike the abandonment of Perdita. It is also interesting to
note that the house of Odysseus was traditionally associated
with the bear, and that the heroes Melikertes ("honey-cutter"),
Sisyphos, and Autolykos are closely related to one another and

10. Rhys Carpenter, *Folk Tale, Fiction, and Saga in the Homeric Epics*
(Berkeley: University of California Press, 1946), pp. 112–56.

to Odysseus.[11] Autolykos, the maternal grandfather of Odysseus, is the father of Sisyphos; and Sisyphos, the Master Thief
of Greek folktale, is the hero of a story about the outwitting
of death which takes the same general pattern (apparent death,
descent to Hades, release and revival) as the bear cult and the
fertility myths. The episode of the bear is thus symbolically
related to the appearance of Autolycus at the same time that it
reinforces the cyclical framework of regeneration with which
we have been concerned.

With the exit of the bear there arrive onstage the shepherd
and the clown, the native inhabitants of Bohemia, possessed
of much of the uncalculated insight we have come to expect
from the denizens of a dream world. A great deal of what they
say in this pivotal scene has an arresting simplicity, a vividness
of image which strikes the ear. The old shepherd's first remark
is a recapitulation of the hibernation motif:

> I would there were no age between ten and three-and-
> twenty, or that youth would sleep out the rest; for there is
> nothing in the between but getting wenches with child,
> wronging the ancientry, stealing, fighting.
>
> [III.iii.58 ff.]

The tone of this, as of many of the shepherd's observations, is
detached, removed from the difficult human passions which
trouble the other characters. His son's account of the destruction of the ship and the death of Antigonus has the same curious and striking fictive distance; it is much more like the
telling of a dream than was Antigonus's tale:

> O, the most piteous cry of the poor souls! Sometimes to
> see 'em, and not to see 'em; now the ship boring the moon
> with her mainmast, and anon swallowed with yeast and
> froth, as you'd thrust a cork into a hogshead. And then for
> the land-service, to see how the bear tore out his shoulder

11. H. J. Rose, *A Handbook of Greek Mythology* (New York: E. P. Dut-
ton, 1959), p. 294.

bone, how he cried to me for help, and said his name was
Antigonus, a nobleman! But to make an end of the ship, to
see how the sea flapdragoned it; but first, how the poor
souls roared, and the sea mocked them; and how the poor
gentleman roared, and the bear mocked him, both roaring
louder than the sea or weather.

[III.iii.88 ff.]

The immediacy of images, the lack of logical development,
and the way in which no background is supplied for events
narrated are all characteristics of the process of dream. The
clown's world is indeed one in which dream enters the waking
consciousness, as the world of Bohemia is illustrative of that
consciousness. And just when we are caught by the haunting
power of his prose, Shakespeare has the same clown break
the spell, saying without transition "the men are not yet cold
under water, nor the bear half dined on the gentlemen; he's at
it now" (102–03). The spurious elegance of "dined," together
with the sudden insistence of "now," removes the previous narration some distance from the quality of fable, without invest-
ing it with human horror. The shepherd and the clown are ob-
servers for us; they translate us into the realm of Bohemia, by
talking of tragedy as if it were romance—as, indeed, Shakespeare is to do in *The Winter's Tale* as a whole. It is at this
point, ascribing the development to "fairies" in whom he most
fittingly believes, that the old shepherd makes his crucial observation: "thou met'st with things dying, I with things new
born" (110–11). Again such a stark and pivotal assessment of
the play's purposes, in which myth for a moment rises to the
surface of language, is placed at the midpoint of the action.
From this moment *The Winter's Tale* moves toward renewal
and redemption. The pattern of natural metamorphosis is
again affirmed.

We touched briefly upon Antigonus's evocation of Niobe in
the vision of Hermione with eyes which "became two spouts."

Specific uses of Ovid's *Metamorphoses*, whether allusively, as here, or more directly, as in the tale of Tereus in *Cymbeline*, are highly significant in the larger context of metamorphosis and the dream world. In the great pastoral scene we now approach (IV.iv.), the internal pattern of seasonal growth and decay is once more recapitulated. In its opening lines Florizel describes Perdita as "no shepherdess but Flora, / Peering in April's front" (IV.iv.2–3). Flora is described in Ovid *(Fasti* V.231ff.) as possessing a magical flower which, given to Juno, makes her pregnant; later in the scene Perdita will herself enact this role, giving flowers to the assemblage at the sheep-shearing and both directly and symbolically encouraging fertility and fruition. "April's front" is of course an image of the shyness of early spring flowers; it is succeeded in act IV, scene iv, by the full blossoming of summer: "the year growing ancient, / Not yet on summer's death, nor on the birth / Of trembling winter" (79–81). This is a literal description of the time in which the sheepshearing is taking place, but it is also a figurative way of expressing the temper of the moment of flower-giving. With the announcement of the love of Perdita and Doricles and the plighting of troth, the idea of maturation and harvest is introduced, and this in turn quickly gives way to a new repressive and authoritarian regime with the unmasking of the irate Polixenes. Within this framework the idea of metamorphosis is continuously suggested. Florizel, explaining the appropriateness of his disguise as a shepherd and hers as a queen, cites Ovid for a precedent:

> The gods themselves,
> Humbling their deities to love, have taken
> The shapes of beasts upon them. Jupiter
> Became a bull and bellowed; the green Neptune
> A ram, and bleated; and the fire-robed god,
> Golden Apollo, a poor humble swain,
> As I seem now. Their transformations
> Were never for a piece of beauty rarer,

> Nor in a way so chaste, since my desires
> Run not before mine honor, nor my lusts
> Burn hotter than my faith.

>   [IV.iv.25–34]

Florizel's classical examples, characteristically, have both a local and a broader significance; they are not randomly chosen. Jupiter the king, Neptune the sea-god, and Apollo the poet and giver of inspiration are the three gods regnant in the play as a whole. The same relevance characterizes Perdita's later invocation of Proserpina:

>   O Proserpina,
> For the flow'rs now, that, frighted, thou let'st fall
> From Dis's wagon!

>   [116–18]

The story of Proserpina and Ceres is of course the pattern of the story of Perdita and Hermione, the cycle of death and re-birth. These small grace notes from the mythological past add dimension and timelessness to the play as it proceeds. So naturally are they introduced into the action that they do not jar or obtrude, yet their presence in itself contributes to the quality of myth or fable the poet has carefully been develop-ing. Each such moment is yet another "window," opening on the inexhaustible past on which the present action draws.

The espousal of the process of metamorphosis by Perdita and Florizel is closely related to the problem of disguise, which in turn is part of the larger problem of illusion and reality. Florizel is a prince disguised as a shepherd; Perdita is a prin-cess who thinks she is a shepherdess disguised as a queen. Thus unmaskings in Perdita's case are really maskings of a sort, since they reveal a partial truth and hide a full one. Even the sheepshearing itself is a symbol of the shedding of disguise. Given this complexity of fact, the uses of the concept of dream in the pastoral scene acquire an additional significance. For example, early in the scene the old shepherd speaks with pride

to Polixenes about his daughter's virtues. "If young Doricles /
Do light upon her," he says,

> she shall bring him that
> Which he not dreams of.
>
> [IV.iv.179–80]

The context of this observation is praise of her dancing, and
by "that / Which he not dreams of" the shepherd refers overtly
to her personal graces and accomplishments. Yet there is a
covert meaning to his words as well, since he knows of the
gold left by her side as an infant, and the "bearing-cloth for
a squire's child" (III.iii.112–13) in which she was wrapped. His
phrase is thus also an aside to himself, a reminder that he
knows more than the others about the true situation. And the
audience, of course, knows more still; for them "that / Which
he not dreams of" encompasses as well the fact of her royal
birth and the expectation that this will affect the relationship
between Leontes and Polixenes. Similarly, later in the same
scene, the shepherd and Florizel discuss the question of the
marriage portion, and the shepherd, thinking of the gold, announces to the assemblage:

> I give my daughter to him, and will make
> Her portion equal his.
>
> [388–89]

Florizel, believing her a shepherdess and knowing the truth
of his own condition, replies in words very like the shepherd's:

> O, that must be
> I' th' virtue of your daughter. One being dead,
> I shall have more than you can dream of yet,
> Enough then for your wonder.
>
> [389–92]

"Dream" in both these cases is used to mean "imagine." But
in each case the speaker's point is that what his audience
"dreams of" (or "not dreams of," which carries an even fur-

ther implication of impossibility) will in fact turn out to be true. This is the reversal of categories yet again, its application complicated and enriched here by the concrete fact of disguise and the entire atmosphere of dream.

Perdita herself has throughout the scene been particularly conscious of the fictive aspect of her role and her disguise. She has continual recourse to the play metaphor, which brings together the themes of change (role playing, metamorphosis) and timelessness (transmutation into art). "Methinks," she says,

> I play as I have seen them do
> In Whitsun pastorals; sure this robe of mine
> Does change my disposition.

[133–35]

She herself makes the implicit equation between the play and the dream, as fictive constructs which—from her point of view —perpetrate illusion. Thus when Polixenes finally reveals his identity, Perdita speaks to Florizel in the metaphor of dream:

> Will't please you, sir, be gone?
> I told you what would come of this. Beseech you,
> Of your own state take care: this dream of mine
> Being now awake, I'll queen it no inch farther
> But milk my ewes, and weep.

[IV.iv.449–53]

Here is the same reversal yet again. The "dream" of being a queen is more true than the apparent "reality" of being a shepherdess. Further, it is from this point, and the subsequent flight of the lovers, that there is precipitated the true awakening or unmasking. Florizel unconsciously emphasizes the exchange that has taken place between the true and the fictive by a reply to the cautious Camillo which recalls the language of Theseus's speech on imagination. "Be advised," says Camillo, and Florizel responds

> I am, and by my fancy; if my reason
> Will thereto be obedient, I have reason;

> If not, my senses better pleased with madness,
> Do bid it welcome.
>
> [485–88]

A variation on the theme of "we lose our oaths to find ourselves," his reply is a sign that he has accepted the world of
dream. When Camillo advises Perdita to disguise herself for
flight, urging her to

> disliken
> The truth of your own seeming
>
> [655–56]

the vocabularies of seeming and being, disguise and revelation
are once more joined in an act of transformation. Yet at the
same time the note of reflexivity, the out-of-time recognition
of the play as an artifact, is struck again. Camillo assures Florizel that "it shall be so my care / To have you royally ap-
pointed, as if / The scene you play were mine" (594–96), and
Perdita's reply to his suggestion about disguise is

> I see the play so lies
> That I must bear a part.
>
> [658–59]

The play metaphor, thus integrated into the ongoing action,
is a hint of what will come. If the process is metamorphosis
and transformation, the product is art. With the appearance
of Autolycus in the fourth act, the two realms are fused in a
single character.

Of all the agents and objects of metamorphosis in *The Winter's Tale*, Autolycus is the master. He belongs to the category
of quicksilver characters which also includes Puck and Ariel.
To a certain extent he *is* transformation itself and not merely
a practitioner of it. His lightning facility with disguise and his
almost aesthetic pleasure in gulling others with a pretended
identity places him thematically near the center of the play,
though his dramatic role of poet-observer precludes true par-
ticipation in the society of the play's world. When we first

meet him, alone, he is himself, a thief by choice and an enjoyer
of the goods of the world. Under our gaze he rapidly transforms himself into a "robbed man" who robs the clown, a
peddler of ballads and furbelows at the sheepshearing, and a
"courtier" purportedly in the service of King Polixenes. In a
way he is like the fox and ape of Spenser's *Mother Hubberd's
Tale,* satirizing the pretensions of society by pretending to
have those pretensions. But his fictive and symbolic role is
clearly even more complex than this. He is the play's artist
and poet and thus its master of imagination and manipulator
of dream. When he enters the house of the shepherd in his
guise as peddler, an impressed servant reports his prowess to
the company:

> Why, he sings 'em over, as they were gods or goddesses;
> you would think a smock were a she-angel, he so chants to
> the sleevehand, and the work about the square on't.
>
> [IV.iv.207 ff.]

The servant's report, the more believable for its naïveté, is
essentially an account of transformation. The image is amus-
ing to the audience, especially because we are familiar with the
"peddler's" other activities, but plainly the audience that
Autolycus has set out to please is already under his spell.
Moreover, Autolycus is a seller and singer of music; his entrance in the fourth act is the first appearance of music in the
play. In all he sings six songs and snatches of two others; calling himself a "snapper-up of unconsidered trifles" (IV.iii.26),
he makes of those trifles, whether song or costume, another
version of Wallace Stevens's "fictive covering." His first song,
"When daffodils begin to peer" (IV.iii.1–12) is a song of the
seasons and the passions, which rejoices in the arrival of spring
and summer, making yet another small cycle within the larger
one; and the witty image of melting snow as sheets pulled off
hedges seems to suggest that Autolycus himself is in a way

responsible for the coming of the spring. Two of the subsequent songs, sung in his guise as peddler, are about the peddler's wares, considered as fictions or affectations, "masks for faces and for noses" (IV.iv.222). Language is designedly his medium, and he is a dream figure of the most direct sort, assuming whatever guise his situation and companions demand; at the close of the fourth act, encountering the terrified shepherd and his son, he articulates their basest fears and inner thoughts. Like other quicksilver figures of the Shakespearean dream world, he finds himself ultimately outside the charmed circle of resolution, and is not included in the summing-up.

Autolycus's language is the language of metamorphosis by reason of his command of craft. By contrast, the clown, the old shepherd's son, is for *The Winter's Tale* a figure parallel to the *Hamlet* gravedigger, the *Macbeth* porter, or the clown in *Antony and Cleopatra*. His malapropisms carry multiple meanings, the more effective for his total unawareness of them. Thus after the offstage recognition scene at Leontes' court (V.ii.) he confronts Autolycus (still in his role of courtier) with his new position: "See you these clothes?" he crows,

> Say you see them not and think me still no gentleman born; you were best say these robes are not gentlemen born. Give me the lie, do; and try whether I am now a gentleman born.
>
> [V.ii.132 ff.]

To which Autolycus amusedly replies, "I know you are now, sir, a gentleman born" (137–38). Clothing and high birth are here images deliberately related to an absolute belief in transformation. The episode is a comic diminution of an idea which has been of the utmost seriousness throughout. Perhaps the best example, however, is the clown's venture into the special world of music, as reported to us by Autolycus. "No hearing, no feeling, but my sir's song, and admiring the nothing of it" (IV.iv.615–16). "My sir" is of course the clown;

and "nothing" is simultaneously "poor quality," "fictiveness," and "noting," or singing.[12] To Autolycus this is merely an opportunity to cut purses; the sense that the rustics are spell-bound, however, is important to the play's major themes, here once more presented in comic reduction. Music in all its forms has a particular significance in *The Winter's Tale,* and the clown's attempt to emulate Autolycus, like the dances of shepherds and satyrs at the feast, is positioned in part to prepare us for the very different music of the final scene.

The great accomplishment of this scene is its reconciliation of the fictive and the real, the metaphoric and the literal. The reawakening of Hermione is a transcendent event, made possible by "faith" and art, but it is at the same time carefully made explicable in natural terms. Hermione is not dead; her rebirth is subjective, in the minds of the onlookers, and not objective or magical. This "naturalizing" of the supernatural is startling in its effect; once again it is the "art that Nature makes" which leads to new insight, and the world of dream which demonstrates its primacy over the merely "real." There is an interesting anticipation of this moment earlier in the act, during the discussion between Paulina and Leontes on the subject of remarriage. It is useless for him to remarry, she contends; the oracle has plainly said that he will have no heir "till his lost child be found" (V.i.40). Moreover, no woman could match the dead queen. Leontes concurs, and in doing so he creates a rhetorical ghost, a fictive shade of Hermione:

> One worse,
> And better used, would make her sainted spirit
> Again possess her corpse, and on this stage,
> Where we offenders now appear, soul-vexed,
> And begin, "Why to me?"
>
> [56–59]

12. The quibble on *noting* is suggested by J. Dover Wilson in the New Cambridge edition of *The Winter's Tale* (ed. Arthur Quiller-Couch and J. Dover Wilson [London: Cambridge University Press, 1931]), who compares *Much Ado About Nothing* II.iii.56: "Note notes, forsooth, and nothing."

The spirit here is entirely subjective, a figure of speech, and yet in his imagination it walks and speaks. Paulina, quick to catch his mood, reinforces the image with embellishments of her own:

> Were I the ghost that walked, I'd bid you mark
> Her eye, and tell me for what dull part in 't
> You chose her; then I'd shriek, that even your ears
> Should rift to hear me, and the words that followed
> Should be, "Remember mine."
>
> [63–67]

The resemblance to the ghost in *Hamlet* is striking. Revenge for a moment hovers in their air and then is put aside in favor of grace. Relenting of her sternness, Paulina now begins to blend the fictive ghost with the real one, the mental image with the living statue. If Leontes must marry again, she says,

> she shall not be so young
> As was your former, but she shall be such
> As walked your first queen's ghost, it should take joy
> To see her in your arms.
>
> [78–81]

The double meaning here is perceptible only to Paulina; neither Leontes nor the audience know that Hermione is still alive. At this point the arrival of Perdita and Florizel is announced, and Leontes greets them "Welcome hither, / As is the spring to th' earth!" (V.i.151–52). The underlying natural cycle again reinforces the larger pattern of regeneration.

The actual "resurrection" of Hermione takes place, significantly, in a part of Paulina's house variously described as a "chapel" and a "gallery." The contents of the gallery are works of art, artifacts of the sort we have described as being removed from the round of time. The statue of Hermione, however, is insistently linked with time and life, even while it partakes of the stillness of eternity: "Prepare," says Paulina,

> To see the life as lively mocked, as ever
> Still sleep mocked death
>
> [V.iii.19–20]

reminding us of Juliet and Imogen, and later Leontes, "transported" (69), will exclaim "we are mocked with art" (68). Just as Perdita was a princess who thought she was a shepherdess masquerading as a queen, so the "statue" of Hermione is a living woman who is thought to be a statue but described as looking "alive." These are dream equivalences too, the subjective dream state rendering the onlookers unable to distinguish between art and life. Even the visible contribution of "great creating Nature," the wrinkles on Hermione's face, are described by Paulina as evidence of the "carver's excellence" (30), showing her as she would be if she were still alive. The process of reawakening is deliberately a slow one, as Leontes begins to become aware of reality; "no longer shall you gaze on't," says Paulina, "lest your fancy / May think anon it moves" (60–61), yet in fact his fancy is once again more accurate than reason. The final breaking of the boundary, the flowing together of dream and reality, is preceded by Paulina's crucial pronouncement:

> It is required
> You do awake your faith.
>
> [94–95]

The sleeping-waking metaphor is no accident here, but rather the culmination of a figure which has been highly significant throughout; faith is to be awakened by an acceptance of the possibility of dream. And once the faith is awakened, so too is the "statue":

> Music, awake her: strike.
> 'Tis time; descend; be stone no more; approach;
> Strike all that look upon with marvel; come;
> I'll fill your grave up.
>
> [98–101]

Music is the sign of metamorphosis and redemption, the union of the myths of Proserpina and Galatea. Time and timelessness, the art object and the process of mortal growth and change, are brought together for a moment in a symbol of regeneration.

It is important that the condition of art is here transitional, rather than terminal and eternal; Hermione returns to life, returns moreover with the wrinkles of time upon her, and the final emphasis is on mortality. Even in the last glad moments of reconciliation we are reminded of the death of Antigonus. For in *The Winter's Tale* Shakespeare has measured art and nature, the dream world and the real world, and resolved them into the "art that Nature makes." The stage of art is essential to the play's resolution: the play itself contains a number of internal artifacts—the "winter's tale" itself, the songs of Autolycus, the play-within-a-play in the pastoral scene. But fundamentally the play moves through art to life again, the statue descends and becomes flesh. Without the transcendent insight of the dream state this movement could not have occurred, but just as the return to Sicilia is necessary, so too is the return to mortality. The very perfection of the reanimated statue as a symbol is its blending of the two states into one. In the "winter" section of the play the boy Mamilius, asked for a tale, replied

> A sad tale's best for winter; I have one
> Of sprites and goblins.
>
> [II.i.25–26]

"Sprites and goblins"—the traditional denizens of dream, the spirits of *A Midsummer Night's Dream*. By the time of the last scene Paulina will declare

> that she is living,
> Were it but told you, should be hooted at
> Like an old tale; but it appears she lives.
>
> [V.iii.115–17]

The "sprites and goblins" have been replaced by kings and shepherds, the tale, though it seems fictive, is real. The imperative word of the last scene is "awake," and the progress through dream to a renewed and heightened reality, the symbolic fulfillment of dream, is achieved through a coming together of symbols which express and contain it.

The Winter's Tale is fundamentally a play of metamorphosis in which the stage of "becoming" is central to the action. Time and change, "things dying" and "things new born," underlie each of its essential symbols and processes; the space of sixteen years between the third and fourth acts, a violation of the "unities" which Shakespeare deliberately elects to make, is indicative of a tendency to render credible the most improbable events through a mature integration of poetry and action. With The Tempest, which immediately succeeds it in chronology, Shakespeare's attention turns to yet another way of treating the same major themes. Where The Winter's Tale was designedly cyclical, analogous patterns repeating themselves as redemption and reconciliation emerged from the union of the temporal and eternal, in The Tempest events are even more directly transcendent. Essentially, things happen in The Winter's Tale against a background of their having happened before and with the possibility that they may happen again; in The Tempest, the most remarkable of all Shakespeare's dream worlds, things happen on the island in order that they need never happen again. Our attention is drawn from the first to the moment of revelation and discovery, the dream that unveils truths and self-truths. At the very close of the play, Gonzalo puts this redemptive discovery into words which once more recall Berowne:

> in one voyage
> Did Claribel her husband find at Tunis,
> And Ferdinand her brother found a wife
> Where he himself was lost; Prospero his dukedom
> In a poor isle, *and all of us ourselves*
> *When no man was his own.*

> [V.i.208–13]

The theme of losing and finding here attains its ultimate expression, the journey to the enchanted isle which is the dream world, the conversion of loss into new and transcendent awareness. For *The Tempest* is a play which takes the dream state for its subject, deliberately and directly exploring the poles of sleeping and waking, vision and reality, art and the human condition.

Both the spatial and the temporal worlds of the play are tightly circumscribed, as compactly constructed as *The Winter's Tale* was deliberately broad. In his first interview with Ariel, Prospero stipulates that they have only four hours to do their work, and Ariel confirms the success of this design at the beginning of the denouement (V.i.4). The entire action takes place on Prospero's island, although behind it we can see the political world of Milan, from which the travelers have come and to which they will return, and beyond even that the limitless scope of Tunis and "the great globe itself." Prospero's island is both subjective and objective, a state of mind as well as a location; his neglect of political affairs in Milan, as he explains to Miranda, came about because he inclined instead to the private study of the "liberal Arts."

> Those being all my study,
> The government I cast upon my brother
> And to my state grew stranger, being transported
> And rapt in secret studies.
>
> [I.ii.74–77]

The dream world of the island is simultaneously the world of these "secret studies," which Prospero will not abjure until the play's close. From the examples of *Richard III* and *Antony and Cleopatra* we know that such neglect of political responsibility is dangerous: the experience of the island is therefore redemptive for him as well, persuading him to "discase" himself and appear "as [he] was sometime Milan." (V.i.85–86). But within the dream work of the play itself he stands apart, as the stage direction fittingly says "at a distance, unseen," the

final and greatest of Shakespeare's poet and stage-manager
figures, whose world is the creative world of the imagination.

The play begins with the tempest of its title, which resembles in symbolic purpose the similar storms of *Pericles* and
The Winter's Tale. The uproar of the storm and the anguished
cries of the mariners are in deliberate contrast to the calm of
the island, and are significantly associated with the strife and
confusion of the external Milan world, dominated by usurpation and greed. The characters of the Milanese company—the
surly, cynical Sebastian, the arrogant Antonio, the good-
hearted but abstracted Gonzalo—are all for a moment adumbrated against the background of crisis and fear. The scene is
itself a nightmare of sorts, a dark scene cut through with thunder and lightning, the symbolic equivalent of the more psychologically conceived opening scene of *Othello*. With Gonzalo's
despairing cry for "an acre of barren ground, long heath,
broom, furze, anything" (I.i.64–65), the scene rapidly shifts
to the island itself, a lush and romantic haven in marked contrast to the harshness of this description. We are immediately
transported into a world of dream and dreams, as unlike the
assumptions and expectations of the new arrivals as is Gonzalo's word picture from fact.

Prospero and his daughter Miranda have watched the
storm from the island; and Miranda, whose name implies that
she is both "wondered at" and "wondering," begs him to in-
tervene:

> If by your art, my dearest father, you have
> Put the wild waters in this roar, allay them.
>
> [I.ii.1–2]

Were she "any god of power" (10), she says, she would have
acted to save the "brave vessel" (6) and its crew. "Brave" is a
word which recurs frequently in her language; it is later used
to describe both Ferdinand and the "brave new world" of men
she has discovered, and it carries, always, an innocent hope
which is very like the Shakespearean "grace." As the storm

abates, Prospero reassures her that no harm has been done to
the passengers, and in what is really a long, broken monologue,
narrates for her the story of their arrival on the island. Significantly, he first lays aside the magic robe in which he has
been dressed, saying "Lie there, my art" (I.ii.25), in the first
of what will be many direct associations of his magical powers
with the related transforming power of poetry. The robe is a
costume, and thus an agent of willed metamorphosis. Throughout the play there will occur similar garment images, all having to do with illusion, transformation, or self-deception: the
"sustaining garments" of the ship's survivors (I.ii.218), the
"glistering apparel" which seduces Stephano and Trinculo
(IV.i.SD), and the costume of Prospero as "sometime Milan"
(V.i.86). Disguise is thus from the first integrated into the radical symbolism of the play, supporting an allegorizing tendency which is yet not sufficient to disturb the delicate balance
of the play's poetry.

Prospero prefaces his tale by asking if Miranda remembers
her life before they came to the island. " 'Tis far off," she
replies,

> And rather like a dream than an assurance
> That my remembrance warrants.
>
> [I.ii.44–46]

This is the first explicit reference to dream in the play.
Miranda, whose only reality is the world of the island, significantly refers to life beyond it as "like a dream," while all those
who come from without will find the island itself dreamlike
and inexplicable. The "dark backward and abysm of time"
(50) to which Prospero alludes is a temporal frame, like the
spatial frame of the Tunis-world, against which the figural
and timeless present action is performed; the phrase is both
specific and symbolic. He now proceeds with his narrative,
pausing every few moments to make sure she is attending: his
role is now that of storyteller, and he is anxious to affect his

audience properly. His description of the usurper Antonio is
a diagram of self-delusion:

> like one
> Who having into truth—by telling of it—
> Made such a sinner of his memory
> To credit his own lie, he did believe
> He was indeed the duke.
>
> [99–103]

This is the pattern of falsehood to self, self-disguise, which
the play will seek to unravel; the exchange of "lie" and "truth"
is a familiar one, and the characteristic task of the dream
world will be to restore "truth" to its proper place. There is
another familiar pattern in the account of the expulsion of
Prospero and the infant Miranda from Milan; the tempest in
which they are set adrift, though it is mentioned after the
present storm, temporally foreshadows it, again in a mythic
or figural manner. Gonzalo's bounty, in placing upon the ship
"rich garments, linens, stuffs and necessaries" (164). recalls
the launching of the richly laden coffin of Thaisa or the cloth
and gold which accompanied the infant Perdita. The recapitulated narrative of the "dark backward and abysm of time"
is thus deliberately evocative and echoic, a collection of symbolic actions as well as a tale of past events. We might say that
this kind of multiple referent, at once factual and mythic, is
metaphorically in the imperfect tense, the tense of recurrent
action, as opposed to the simple past. It is a mode which will
be frequently used in *The Tempest,* as it has been to a certain
extent in *The Winter's Tale,* and it makes the luminous dream
of the narrow four-hour span expand to fill up all of time.

Having finished his tale, Prospero now induces Miranda to
drowsiness, a drowsiness which has in part been abetted by the
rhythmic periodicity of his narrative:

> Thou art inclined to sleep. 'Tis a good dullness,
> And give it way. I know thou canst not choose.
>
> [I.ii.185–86]

The readiness with which Miranda falls asleep is a sign of virtue, as has been true in other plays we have examined. Her sleep here is coterminous with the arrival of Ariel, the dominant spirit of the play's dream world, and she is therefore to be associated with innocence rather than with art. For Ariel's nature, which is central to the play as a whole, is supremely that of art and the imagination; he is at once the agent, the instrument, and the substance of transformation.

In the course of the play Ariel undergoes a number of metamorphoses: during the tempest he is himself the fire in the riggings of the ship, which, in a lovely transference of epithet, is said to have "flamed amazement" (198); at the end of his conversation with Prospero he is told to make himself "like a nymph o' the sea" (302), recalling and extending into the supernatural Florizel's image of natural metamorphosis, "When you do dance, I wish you / A wave o' th' sea" (*WT* IV.iv.140–41); through much of the play he is invisible to all except Prospero, thus approximating the condition of the air to which he is so closely related; and in the climactic speech of the play, the remarkable address to the "three men of sin" (III.iii.53ff.) he appears as a harpy, and calls himself and his fellows "ministers of Fate" (III.iii.61). But somatic transformation is rather the beginning than the end of his powers. As we have mentioned above, it is difficult to avoid looking at *The Tempest* in partly allegorical terms, associating Prospero with mankind and the poet, Ariel with the imagination, and Caliban with the body and with natural or instinctive man. Plainly these are only beginnings, and approximate ones, but it seems clear that Ariel's association with the imaginative part of man is a very close one; he anticipates the thoughts of others, and his language is "poetic" in the most extended sense of that term. It is Ariel who both plays and sings throughout the play, and his songs are themselves transformations in little. His music, which can be as light as a pipe or as common as a tabor, is the accompaniment of the acts of "magic" or vision which recur throughout the play, and which are the operative dreams within the dream world. He is at once an elemental spirit, compact of water, air, and fire, an English fairy of the type of Puck, and the embodiment of poetry as a transforming power; of all the quicksilver characters we have discussed, he is the most consummate. Yet his bondage to Prospero is enforced though good-tempered, and his progress to freedom first necessitates imprisonment by the chthonic natural forces of Sycorax. His definition, like his appearance, must elude us, for he is a mood and a quality; and like dream itself he appears and sings only in moments of transcendence which shed light on more ordinary experience. Here in his first appearance we learn of his part in the tempest and of the effect the experience has had upon the travelers:

> *Prospero:*   My brave spirit!
>   Who was so firm, so constant, that this coil
>   Would not infect his reason?
> *Ariel:*   Not a soul
>   But felt a fever of the mad and played
>   Some tricks of desperation.
>
> [I.ii.206–10]

Once again, the rejection of "reason" appears as a necessary prelude to the dream experience. The "madness" which seizes the voyagers is not unlike the much more psychologically determined madness of Hamlet or Lear, a first essential step into subjectivity which is likewise basic to dream. The mariners, we may notice, are excluded from this translation; when they awaken in the first act at Ariel's bidding, they serve as the ground of common experience, the frame within which the action and reconciliation have occurred. Ariel reports that he has left them asleep "'with a charm join'd to their suffer'd labor" (231), their ship safely in harbor. The noble passengers have made their way to shore, and Ariel describes their condition in terms of clothing imagery:

> On their sustaining garments not a blemish,
> But fresher than before.
>
> [I.ii.218–19]

The transforming power of the island is already at work upon
them, freshening their external as it will their internal selves.

Ariel's truest language, however, is song, and it is through
song that he is able to cross the boundary between the internal
and the external, the thought and the heard; his music
throughout, but most particularly the two haunting songs
sung to Ferdinand, approach the condition which T. S. Eliot
has described as

> music heard so deeply
> That it is not heard at all, but you are the music
> While the music lasts.
>
> ["The Dry Salvages," V]

This is the dream state again, the intrusion of the fictive and
the irrational into the known. We have discussed these two
songs elsewhere, and here need only emphasize the extraordinary multiplicity of meaning and thematic relevance contained in so simple and controlled a form. The first song,
"Come unto these yellow sands," is an invitation to reconciliation, in which the storm image ("the wild waves") refers
simultaneously to the physical tempest and the spiritual tur-
moil within. The phrase "sweet sprites bear / The burthen"
carries the primary sense of "sing the refrain," as indeed they
do in the voices of dog and cock, the night watch and the
morning of reawakening and rebirth. But "burthen" also retains its nonmusical meaning of "responsibility" or "obliga-
tion," and it is to some degree true that the responsibility of
carrying out the reconciliation is entrusted by Prospero to
Ariel and his attendant spirits. The first song is thus a song
of hope, and Ferdinand associates it with "some god o' th'
island" (392). "This music," he says,

> crept by me upon the waters,
> Allaying both their fury and my passion
> With its sweet air.
>
> [394–96]

This "allaying" is the beginning of the fulfillment of the song's prophecy, the "wild waves whist"; "sweet air" is at the same time "music" and "atmosphere," a rich ambiguity which *The Tempest* will continue to develop. Both interpretations, and most especially the blending of the two, suggest the elusive condition of Ariel.

The remarkable beauty and relevance of the second song have been discussed at some length at the beginning of this chapter: the themes of transformation, transmutation into art, and the concept of the "sea change" are articulated, and the effect is such that Ferdinand concludes

> This is no mortal business, nor no sound
> That the earth owes.

[409–10]

The imputation of divinity or divine inspiration is important to all of the romances, but most particularly to *The Tempest;* later in the same scene Ferdinand will exclaim at the sight of Miranda

> Most sure the goddess
> On whom these airs attend!

[424–25]

and Miranda, seeing the "brave form" of Ferdinand, is moved to call him "a spirit" (414) but finds herself refuted by Prospero: "No, wench; it eats and sleeps and hath such senses / As we have, such" (415–16). Caliban's encounter with Stephano and Trinculo leads to a parodic conception of the drunken butler as a "brave" god, and in the final reconciliation scene Alonso asks of Miranda

> Is she the goddess that hath severed us
> And brought us thus together?

[V.i.187–88]

We may be reminded of Hamlet's observation, though it is cast in a different key:

What a piece of work is a man, how noble in reason, how infinite in faculties, in form and moving how express and

admirable, in action how like an angel, in apprehension
how like a god: the beauty of the world, the paragon of
animals; and yet to me, what is this quintessence of dust?

[*Ham.* II.ii.311 ff.]

The illusion of godhead and the subsequent acknowledgment
of mortality are equally valuable and important; the island's
occupants are the more wonderful for their human condition.
For the pattern of *The Tempest,* as of *The Winter's Tale,* is
to take man through dream to a renewed appreciation of his
mortal state, bringing him through dream to a transfigured
reality.

This sharpening of experience is part of Prospero's purpose
in affecting to discourage the attraction of the lovers; echoing
the god Jupiter in Cymbeline, he fears "lest too light win-
ning / Make the prize light" (I.ii.454–55). Moreover, Ferdinand's response to this pretended sternness is, fittingly, a willing acknowledgment of the strong subjective power of dream:

My spirits, as in a dream, are all bound up.
My father's loss, the weakness which I feel,
The wrack of all my friends, nor this man's threats
To whom I am subdued, are but light to me,
Might I but through my prison once a day
Behold this maid. All corners else o' th'earth
Let liberty make use of. Space enough
Have I in such a prison.

[I.ii.490–97]

It is interesting that heightened emotional experience converts
itself for Ferdinand, as it does for the play as a whole, into
spatial terms. Like the lover of Lovelace's Althea, he paradoxically finds liberty in bondage, just as his fellows will find
enlightenment in privation. It is the theme of Gonzalo's summation again: "Ferdinand, her brother, found a wife / Where
he himself was lost"; "and all of us ourselves, / When no man
was his own."

The arrival of the shipwreck victims has a similarly paradoxical effect upon Prospero's island. Before their advent it is
tranquil, harmonious, virtually uninhabited—a dream in the
sense of an idyll, atemporal and ruled by magic. With the intrusion of political and personal strife in the persons of the
voyagers, this dream world is disrupted and replaced by internal dream episodes, levels of conscious and subconscious
discovery which will lead to a greater and more far-reaching
synthesis. Hints of this are sharply adumbrated in the conversation of the survivors at the beginning of the second act, as
the wordy Gonzalo, aided by Adrian, tallies the charms of the
island:

Adrian:	The air breathes upon us here most sweetly.
Sebastian:	As if it had lungs, and rotten ones.
Antonio:	Or as 'twere perfumed by a fen.
Gonzalo:	Here is everything advantageous to life.
Antonio:	True, save means to live.
Sebastian:	Of that there's none, or little.
Gonzalo:	How lush and lusty the grass looks! How green!
Antonio:	The ground indeed is tawny.
Sebastian:	With an eye of green in 't.
Antonio:	He misses not much.
Sebastian:	No; he doth but mistake the truth totally.

[II.i.49–60]

This stichomythic dialogue is a demonstration of the subjectivity of the dream state, which is essential to transformation.
Gonzalo and Adrian see the island as a fertile and aromatic
paradise; its fertility is thematically significant and is substan-
tiated by the words "lush and lusty," which are hotly contested
by the others. Sebastian's jest about the air possessing "lungs,"
since Adrian has poetically said that it "breathes," demonstrates a literalism of spirit which is opposed to imagination.
Truth on the island is clearly subjective, as protean as the
denizens of dream themselves, and the allegation that it is
Gonzalo who is mistaken is usefully countered by a remark he

himself makes to Sebastian earlier in the scene: "you have spoken truer than you purposed" (21–22). We have frequently come upon this circumstance in the world of dream, the partial truth of the speaker superseded by the greater truth communicated to the audience, and an acknowledgment of it this early in the play hints at a willingness on the part of the speaker to accept the irrational and the inexplicable. But Gonzalo, though more amiable than the others, is nonetheless in need of the transfiguring power of the dream world. His vision of the island as an innocent Arcady is reminiscent of Polixenes' vision of eternal innocence and suffers from the same misconception about the necessity of time and change:

> I' th' commonwealth I would by contraries
> Execute all things. For no kind of traffic
> Would I admit; no name of magistrate;
> Letters should not be known; riches, poverty,
> And use of service, none; contract, succession,
> Bourn, bound of land, tilth, vineyard, none;
> No use of metal, corn, or wine, or oil;
> No occupation; all men idle, all;
> And women too, but innocent and pure:
> No sovereignty.
> . . . .
> All things in common nature should produce
> Without sweat or endeavor. Treason, felony,
> Sword, pike, knife, gun, or need of any engine
> Would I not have; but nature should bring forth,
> Of it own kind, all foison, all abundance,
> To feed my innocent people.
>
> [II.i.152–61; 164–69]

The determining element here is timelessness, a disregard of the processes of natural growth and experience which are necessary for redemption. Gonzalo's vision is a dream of sorts, but a delusory one, and the truth it reveals is a misconception on its speaker's part. The need for a radical transformation of this attitude is symbolically demonstrated during the next episode by Ariel, the embodiment of subconscious action, who must forcibly awaken the sleeping Gonzalo with song in order to warn him of the plot against the king.

The entrance of Ariel at this point in the action, as Gonzalo quibbles on the sign word "nothing" (181–83), produces the third literal "sleep" of the play, following those of Miranda and the mariners. Though visible to the audience, he is unseen by the courtiers, and the "solemn music" he plays is likewise apparently below the level of consciousness, for it is not remarked. Sleep here, as ever in Shakespeare, is a mark of spiritual innocence; it comes instantly to all but those who are guilty of past misdeeds or contemplating present ones. Gonzalo finds himself "very heavy" (193) and sleeps at once, as do all but Alonso, Antonio, and Sebastian. Alonso, whose guilt (in arranging with Antonio for tribute from Milan) is at least partially balanced by his sorrow at the supposed loss of his son, is the next to succumb:

> What, all so soon asleep? I wish mine eyes
> Would, with themselves, shut up my thoughts. I find
> They are inclined to do so.
>
> [II.i.195–97]

He is preparing, by a consideration of his own state, for the moment of redemption which will transform him finally from guilt to grace.

Antonio and Sebastian remain awake, and are indeed both amazed and slightly contemptuous of the slumber of their fellows:

> *Sebastian:* What a strange drowsiness possesses them!
> *Antonio:* It is the quality o' th' climate.
> *Sebastian:*   Why
> Doth it not then our eyelids sink? I find not
> Myself dispos'd to sleep.
> *Antonio:*   Nor I: my spirits are
>   nimble.
> They fell together all, as by consent.
> They dropped as by a thunderstroke.
>
> [203–08]

Here again they "speak truer than they have purposed"; the climate does induce the slumber of the courtiers, but out of its dream function rather than for merely meteorological reasons. Antonio's assertion of "nimble" spirits seems to imply that sleep is weakness, and the apolcalyptic note in the lines which follow suggests a subconscious awareness of supernatural powers at work and a derogation of their objects. But though both remain awake, there is a decided difference in the tone of their conversation. For Sebastian the period that follows is itself like a dream: "it is a sleepy language," he says, "and thou speak'st / Out of thy sleep" (215–16). Antonio's attempt to persuade him to kill the king and inherit the crown is couched in images of the dream world; in a passage which bears a strong resemblance to the witches' scene in *Macbeth* (I.iii),[13] he begins with a seductive image phrased like a vision:

> My strong imagination sees a crown
> Dropping upon thy head.
>
> [212–13]

This is the malignant imagination of the conscious mind, Iago's sphere, the dream enforced and thrust upon the latent ambition of Sebastian.

Sebastian:	What? Art thou waking?
Antonio:	Do you not hear me speak?
Sebastian:	I do; and surely
	It is a sleepy language, and thou speak'st
	Out of thy sleep. What is it thou didst say?
	This is a strange repose, to be asleep
	With eyes wide open; standing, speaking, moving
	And yet so fast asleep.
Antonio:	Noble Sebastian,
	Thou let'st thy fortune sleep—die, rather; wink'st
	Whiles thou art waking.

13. For other echoes of *Macbeth* in this play, see G. Wilson Knight, "The Shakespearian Superman," in *The Crown of Life* (London: Oxford University Press, 1947), pp. 212–13.

Sebastian: Thou dost snore dis-
                                                tinctly;
There's meaning in thy snores.

                                                        [213–22]

Sebastian is yet again speaking truer than he has purposed; the "strange repose" he speaks of is indeed much more like dream as we have observed it than like waking. Antonio, sensing his advantage, pursues the metaphor with more directness; in a reference to the distant Claribel, the rightful heir after Alonso and Ferdinand, he apostrophizes

>   "Keep in Tunis,
> And let Sebastian wake!" Say this were death
> That now hath seized them, why, they were no worse
> Than now they are. There be that can rule Naples
> As well as he that sleeps; lords that can prate
> As amply and unnecessarily
> As this Gonzalo; I myself could make
> A chough of as deep chat. O, that you bore
> The mind that I do! What a sleep were this
> For your advancement!

                                                        [263–72]

And Sebastian's reponse is itself like an awakening, deliberate, halting, with a note of the dazed and the tentative:

Antonio: Do you understand me?
Sebastian: Methinks I do.
Antonio: And how does your content
Tender your own good fortune?
Sebastian: I remember
You did supplant your brother Prospero.

                                                        [272–75]

The startling effect of this last is itself an indication of the vestiges of dream; its apparent irrelevancy speaks to the subject covertly behind Antonio's remarks, rather than to the less significant remarks themselves. The effect of this entire episode is not unlike the "jealousy" passages at the beginning of *The*

Winter's Tale. We are here presented with the dangers of dream, although dream is related in this case to ambition rather than to sexual jealousy, to *Macbeth* rather than to *Othello*. But the creative and benevolent actions of Ariel are deliberately counterpointed by incidences of irrational destructivness. When, swords drawn, they are frustrated in their attempt at assassination by the watchful machinations of Ariel, they produce a fictive account of their intentions which fittingly mirrors the truth: they have heard, they say, a "hollow burst of bellowing / Like bulls, or rather lions" (315–16). The implications of "hollow" and the created and "untrue" image of discordant sound are symbolic translations of the dream scene which has gone before. Gonzalo, by contrast, has heard "a humming, / And a strange one" (321–22), the harmonious and almost undetectable dream actions of Ariel in defense of the king. The two realms, symbolic and dramatic, are fused in Gonzalo's pious hope for Ferdinand: "Heavens keep him from these beasts!" (328). And with this note the scene shifts to the literal beasts of the play, Caliban and the drunken butler and jester, whose seriocomic conspiracy is a symbolic counterpart of the sophisticated political plots of the courtiers.

The nature of Caliban, like that of Ariel, is a crux for the play as a whole. He is the only true native of the island, the son of "the foul witch Sycorax, who with age and envy / Was grown into a hoop" (I.ii.258–59), an earth magician of black and chthonic sorceries who is the unredeemed counterpart of Prospero and his theurgic arts. Prospero has supplanted Sycorax, taking over the rule and management of the island, but he has retained Caliban in bondage to serve him. This retention has a dual significance in light of our association of the island with the dream world. Prospero keeps Caliban because he is necessary to life:

> But, as 'tis,
> We cannot miss him. He does make our fire,
> Fetch in our wood, and serves in offices
> That profit us.
>
> [I.ii.312–15]

Yet he also keeps him because he cannot let him go: "this thing of darkness," he says at the close, "I acknowledge mine" (V.i.275–76). Caliban is, like Ariel, a denizen of the dream world of the irrational, but his is the dark side of dream. His attempt on Miranda, his foulness of language, his desire to usurp the power of the island are all manifestations of an impulse toward destruction which is centered in the subconscious mind. Like Prospero, we must have Caliban if we are to have Ariel; further, we must keep Caliban, even when, as we must, we let Ariel go.

The dramatic world which surrounds Caliban is an effective analogue to this spiritual condition. The comic scene in which he is discovered by Stephano and Trinculo has many of the aspects of dream or nightmare: Stephano, fearing devils, observes a strange shape and takes it for a monster, when actually it is the combined form of Caliban and Trinculo half-hidden beneath a cloak. Moreover, the "monster" inexplicably speaks the language of the Neapolitans, further startling Stephano with its incongruities. This is a visible enactment of metamorphosis, the "monster of the isle, with four legs" (II.ii.65–66) turning into a pair of people, one of whom is himself seen as a "monster." In the momentary union of Caliban and Trinculo there is a direct manifestation of the aspect of the dream work described by Freud as "condensation": Trinculo, a man with many of the malign qualities which Caliban symbolizes, is conflated with Caliban, the metaphorical embodiment of those qualities. Stephano's mistake, in thinking the two to be one, and "monstrous," is presented as a symbolic truth.

But just as we were able to perceive something of the quicksilver nature of Ariel through his language, we may also profit from a study of the language of Caliban. We know from Caliban himself that his speech is something with which he has been endowed by Prospero:

> You taught me language, and my profit on't
> Is, I know how to curse.
>
> [I.ii.365–66]

Even the medium of language, then, can be misshapen and transformed. But often in this play Caliban's language seems to contain, not coarseness, but a strange and transforming lyricism. His naïve vision of the early days on the island recalls the omnipresent time theme, presenting a brief glimpse of lost innocence:

> When thou cam'st first,
> Thou strok'st me and made much of me; wouldst give me
> Water with berries in 't; and teach me how
> To name the bigger light, and how the less,
> That burn by day and night, and then I loved thee
> And showed thee all the qualities o' th' isle,
> The fresh springs, brine pits, barren place and fertile.
>
> [334–40]

Just as Miranda, familiar only with the island world, finds wonder in the shape of man, so Caliban, the island's sole native inhabitant, sees a paradise in the teachings of civilization; the enchantment of transformation, wrought by the island upon its recent visitors, is produced in them by the visit itself.

The most striking instance of Caliban's transforming use of language, however, is his enchanting address to his fellow conspirators on the subject of music:

> Be not afeard; the isle is full of noises,
> Sounds and sweet airs that give delight and hurt not.
> Sometimes a thousand twangling instruments
> Will hum about mine ears; and sometime voices
> That, if I then had waked after long sleep,
> Will make me sleep again; and then, in dreaming,
> The clouds methought would open and show riches
> Ready to drop upon me, that, when I waked,
> I cried to dream again.
>
> [III.ii.138–46]

His pleasure in music it itself musical. The dream he here describes is a recurrent one, the only such dream which we have encountered with the exception of Lady Macbeth's. And while Lady Macbeth's dream was a recapitulation of past action in the world of fact, Caliban's dream is clearly a fantasy or wish fulfillment. Music, which we have seen to be the sign and instrument of transfiguration, lulls him to sleep; and he dreams of riches dropping from heaven, a dream so seductive that he "cries" to dream again. It is in part an enlightenment dream, a dream of missed or only partially realized opportunity; the "hum" of voices like Ariel's intimates to him, though only in the actual state of dream, the transcendent possibilities of the world they inhabit. The aspect of recurrence is a particularly interesting one, since in psychoanalytic theory recurrent dreams are considered regressions to an anxiety of childhood; such a dream, says Freud, "was first dreamt in childhood and then constantly reappears from time to time during adult sleep." [14] Caliban is conceived as a character uniquely child and man at once, as the wonderful simplicity and purity of his diction in this dream passage bears witness: the sheer imitative enjoyment of "twangling," the concern for those things that "hurt not," the readiness with which he "cries," both vocally and, perhaps, through tears. As a childlike figure he is more than ever indissolubly bound to Prospero in a compact which neither can escape. Shakespeare's intuitive understanding of the dream process is once more demonstrated in a dream form which precisely mirrors the thematic and symbolic identity of the dreamer.

In a wider sense the conspirators' scene has a dream form of its own. The existence of two bands of conspirators, the "high" (Antonio, Sebastian, Alonso) and the "low" (Stephano, Trinculo, Caliban) is similar to the process of "doubling" in the dream work, where more than one image is called up by the mind to express a certain idea or theme. Ariel's incidental appearances in the scene enhance the dream feeling as well: the echo incident, in which, while invisible, he intermittently "gives the lie" to the conspirators, causes them to turn upon one another in confusion; later, when Stephano and Trinculo

14. *Interpretation of Dreams*, pp. 222–23.

begin to sing a song to the wrong tune, he corrects them by playing the tune accurately on a tabor and pipe, prompting them to call him—with the usual dimension of hidden meaning—"the picture of Nobody" (130). But the designs of the low conspirators, though too uncompromising to be comic, are only antecedent to the pivotal scene which exposes and confronts the nobles with their greater iniquity. In this scene Ariel plays a critical role, and through the agency of metamorphosis the subconscious world of dream becomes again vivid and visible upon the stage.

The dumb show of the "several strange Shapes" which precedes the appearance of Ariel is accompanied by "solemn music" of the kind that recurs throughout the play. The king and his company are astonished at their "excellent dumb discourse" (III.iii.39), but when the shapes vanish, the royal party abandons speculation:

Francisco: They vanished strangely.
Sebastian: No matter, since
They have left their viands behind; for we
    have stomachs.

[40–41]

Before they are able to reach the banquet, however, it disappears in thunder and lightning and is replaced by the vision of Ariel as a harpy. Structurally the harpy's sudden appearance is a refinement of the descents of Diana and Jupiter in *Pericles* and *Cymbeline:* here it is not an external deity appearing for the first time, but rather a significant metamorphosis of a familiar and central character which precipitates the sudden access of self-knowledge. Ariel's successive transformations have reflected both Prospero's and Shakespeare's purposes; from the invisible singer of subconscious thoughts he has become a visible and frightening judgmental figure who allies himself with destiny. When he addresses the "three men of sin" (Antonio, Sebastian, and Alonso), he descants upon the theme of retribution as a stern prelude to the play's ultimate objective, reconciliation.

> You are three men of sin, whom destiny—
> That hath to instrument this lower world
> And what is in't—the never-surfeited sea
> Hath caused to belch up you and on this island,
> Where man doth not inhabit, you 'mongst men
> Being most unfit to live. I have made you mad;
> And even with suchlike valor men hang and drown
> Their proper selves.

> [III.iii.53–60]

Madness as a preface to renewed vision is the culminating image of a series of thematic summations: the world, and most particularly the familiar symbol of the cleansing and devouring sea, is a purposeful "instrument" of their arrival; the island, heretofore regarded as fair, is seen as the proper isolation of the less-than-human, as well as the found haven of the exemplary. "I and my fellows / Are ministers of Fate" (60–61); thus the natural and the supernatural are joined in an overwhelming search for redemption.

The appearance of the harpy is yet another dream within the larger dream of *The Tempest* itself, directed by the unseen stage-manager figure of Prospero and invisible except to those to whom it has relevance. Like Macbeth's guests at the banquet, Gonzalo is baffled by behavior of the others: "Why stand you," he asks, "in this strange stare?" (III.iii.94–95). Those who do hear are caught in a solemn "ecstasy" (108), "all knit up / In their distractions" (89–90)—they are in the dream state, attentive only to the vision of conscience. Their interpretation of the event includes yet another factor of the dream work, "secondary revision," which tries to make waking sense out of the irrational and inexplicable happenings of the moment of dream. Thus Alonso attributes the message to some concatenation of natural forces;

> Methought the billows spoke and told me of it;
> The winds did sing it to me; and the thunder,
> That deep and dreadful organ pipe, pronounc'd
> The name of Prosper; it did bass my trespass.

> [96–99]

Ariel is indeed a spirit of wind and water; in Alonso's rational-
izing view, it is these externals only which remain in the conscious mind. But the process of awakening his begun; the
"ecstasy" to which Gonzalo refers is the liberating madness of
dream, a madness which will, in Alonso's case at least, lead to
self-knowledge. For Sebastian and Antonio the vision provokes
anger rather than sadness, moral blindness rather than acceptance. Unlike Alonso they adhere stubbornly to the objective
state of consciousness, and so the harmony of nature, even in
reproach, is a radical awareness denied them.

This harmonious relationship of human life to the natural
world and the round of the seasons is the subject of the scene
which follows, the performance of the masque and the con-
tract between the lovers. The dialogue which begins this scene
is reminiscent of the conversation between Florizel and the
old shepherd in *The Winter's Tale*. Again the father and the
young lover recount the praises of the beloved:

> *Prospero:*   O Ferdinand,
> Do not smile at me that I boast her off,
> For thou shalt find she will outstrip all
>   praise
> And make it halt behind her.
> *Ferdinand:*   I do believe it
> Against an oracle.
>   [IV.i.8–12]

The image of the oracle takes the rhetorical place of "that/
Which he not dreams of" in *The Winter's Tale*—the meaning
in both is that the beloved's quality is such that it surpasses
the ability of the supernatural world to define it, a superlative
mode which recalls in turn Cleopatra's "past the size of dreaming." Both are "nature's piece 'gainst fancy, / Condemning
shadows quite," and thus they move toward the reconciliation
of the illusory and the real which is part of the play's purpose.

The masque itself reinforces a number of themes we have
associated with dream and its transforming power: the structural unit of the play-within-a-play and the recurrent images

of metamorphosis and transformation. The mention of the myth of Proserpina functions as a reminder both of natural fertility and of the danger of unlawful love. Fundamentally, however, the role of the masque is secondary to that of the play which surrounds it; Ferdinand's remarks before and after the performance carry more weight than the performance itself. Thus he engages Prospero in a significant dialogue after the marriage song of Juno:

> Ferdinand: This is a most majestic vision, and
> Harmonious charmingly. May I be bold
> To think these spirits?
> Prospero: Spirits, which by mine art
> I have from their confines called to enact
> My present fancies.
>   Let me live here ever!
> So rare a wond'red father and a wise
> Makes this place Paradise.
>
> [IV.i.118–24]

"Vision" and "harmonious" substantiate the symbolic integrity of the masque as it relates to the ongoing action. The enactment of "present fancies," on the other hand, is a note of warning, which is soon to be validated by Prospero's remembrance of Caliban and the conspirators. And Ferdinand's plea for eternity on the island makes clear the fact that a further transformation is required. Eternity in the dream world, as we have before discovered, is an illusory concept, one which fails to take into account the imperatives of the human condition. Ferdinand will have to acknowledge the serpent in the paradisal garden, or, in Leontes' figure, the spider in the cup, in order that his renewed awareness may be fused with purpose in the Milan world to which he must return. It is to this end that the "harmonious" masque is disrupted by Prospero's sudden memory of treason. His exclamation, "the minute of their plot / Is almost come" (141–42), touches again on the time theme, bringing the precision of specific time to interrupt and terminate the dream of eternity. The celebrated speech with which he ends the episode is yet another such reminder of mortality:

> Our revels now are ended. These our actors,
> As I foretold you, were all spirits and
> Are melted into air, into thin air;
> And, like the baseless fabric of this vision,
> The cloud-capped towers, the gorgeous palaces,
> The solemn temples, the great globe itself,
> Yea, all which it inherit, shall dissolve,
> And, like this insubstantial pageant faded,
> Leave not a rack behind. We are such stuff
> As dreams are made on, and our little life
> Is rounded with a sleep.
>
> [IV.i.148–58]

The reflexive quality of the image has already been noted: the actors upon the stage are spirits playing actors who in turn play gods and nymphs. So too the physical world is at once illusory and real; the two framing phrases, "like the baseless fabric of this vision," and "like this insubstantial pageant faded," reinforce one another and contain between them three lines which, though fictive and "poetic" in tone, are descriptions of that which is real. Prospero's tone is at once regretful and proud, a glorification of man and an acknowledgment of his radical limitations. With the phrase "our little life / Is rounded with a sleep," he recapitulates in language the structural organization of the play, in which sleep becomes the boundary between one kind of life and another. This calm resolution—that "we are such stuff / As dreams are made on" —is curiously reminiscent of Hamlet's tortured imaginings, though it differs wholly in tone:

> To die, to sleep—
> No more—and by a sleep to say we end
> The heartache, and the thousand natural shocks
> That flesh is heir to! 'Tis a consummation

Devoutly to be wished. To die, to sleep—
To sleep—perchance to dream.

[*Ham*. III.i.60–65]

Again, as in the transmutation of the skull image from Clarence's dream to Ariel's second song, the vision presented by
The Tempest is purified of passion, sublime in its acceptance
of the real. For Prospero's whole great speech is in fact an
exploration of the relationship between the dream world and
the world we know as real, in which the analogy is finally resolved into identity, and metaphor becomes metamorphosis.
His speech suggests on the level of language what *The Tempest* in its entirety will accomplish in dramatic terms: the
merging of the worlds of dream and reality in the creative
mind of man.

As has happened so many times, a rhetorical evocation of
the dream world passes into a vision of that world itself; Ariel
in his "shape invisible" (IV.i.185) reveals the bewitched Caliban and his confederates. Having lured them with music, he
now tempts them with "glistering apparel," which continues
the prevailing clothing imagery and introduces the question
of the fictive and the real. Stephano and Trinculo, more "mon-
trous" than the "monster" himself, are captivated by the display; Caliban, fruitlessly insisting "it is but trash" (224) pleads
without success that they perform the murder first, or else

We shall lose our time
And all be turned to barnacles, or to apes
With foreheads villainous low.

[247–49]

Once again the time theme is closely linked with metamorphosis; even the choice of "barnacles" alludes to the widely
held notion that the sea animal transformed itself into a bar-
nacle goose. With the entry of "divers spirits" shaped like dogs
and hounds, the nightmare quality of the scene is completed,
balancing the idyll of the masque with an equally persuasive
vision of the dangerous and passionate irrational.

Reconciliation and revelation, the deciphering of dream, are the tasks which remain to Prospero; having created a world of illusion, in which each man perceives in the dream state truths he does not know in the external world, he now prepares to restore them to "reason" transfigured by self-knowledge. Significantly, this final turn in the pattern of the play is prefaced by a change in Prospero himself: "The rarer action," he confirms, "is / In virtue than in vengeance" (V.i.27–28), love and grace taking the place of anger and revenge. This is in itself a returning to the real world of men, an accommodation toward grace which takes note of human frailty. Dispatching Ariel for the "spell-stopped" courtiers, he sounds once more the tonic note of new reality found through illusion:

> My charms I'll break, their senses I'll restore,
> And they shall be themselves.
>
> [V.i.31–32]

Like Gonzalo's later echo, "all of us ourselves / When no man was his own," this declaration asserts at once the primacy of dream as an agency of transformation and the necessity of a return to "senses," to "themselves," as participants in the ongoing round of time. His abdication of his art ("but this rough magic I here abjure") is accompanied by yet another evocation of metamorphosis, an address to the spirits of the island which closely follows Golding's Ovid (33 ff.).[15]

But these spirits, like the spirits of a *A Midsummer Night's Dream,* are part of the special dream world they inhabit, and cannot function in the full daylight world of reality. Music, ever the harbinger of transformation, accompanies the entrance of the courtiers; and Prospero's description of the lifting of the spell recalls Oberon's "spirits of another sort," transforming citizens of the dawn:

> the charm dissolves apace;
> And as the morning steals upon the night,
> Melting the darkness, so their rising senses

15. Ovid *Met.* VII.197–209.

Begin to chase the ignorant fumes that mantle
Their clearer reason.

[64–68]

Here too imagination and the dream world give way in the
half-light of morning to "clearer reason," both clearer than the
"fumes" which cloud them and clearer than before their
transformation. The image of the "rising senses," like the sun
rising through morning mist, is an image of awakening and of
new birth, binding the idea of transcendence once more to the
round of nature. From this point there begin the series of
awakenings which will culminate in reconciliation. Prospero
"discases" himself and appears to the courtiers "as I was sometime Milan" (86), fusing the idea of identity with that of locality in a usage which, though common, nonetheless echoes a
major symbolic theme. With conscious double meaning, he
discusses the "loss" he shares with the grieving Alonso, who
has not yet learned that his son is alive:

Prospero: I
            Have lost my daughter.
    Alonso: A daughter?
            O heavens, that they were living both in
                Naples,
            The king and queen there! That they were, I
                wish
            Myself were mudded in that oozy bed
            Where my son lies. When did you lose your
                daughter?
Prospero: In this last tempest.

[V.i.147–53]

The subsequent "discovery" of Ferdinand and Miranda playing chess is yet another naturalized rebirth, like the awakening of Hermione in *The Winter's Tale*. Miranda underscores
the sense of renewal in her delighted exclamation, "O brave
new world / That has such people in't! (183–84), which is immediately undercut by Prospero's customary warning note of

realism, " 'Tis new to thee" (184); Alonso's expressed fear lest
"this prove / A vision of the island" (175–76) becomes yet another proof of the identity of the visionary and the real. The
master and boatswain of the ship now appear, reporting that
their ship is "tight and yare and bravely rigged as when / We
first put out to sea" (223–24); and the boatswain recounts the
mariners' dream:

> If I did think, sir, I were well awake,
> I'd strive to tell you. We were dead of sleep
> And (how we know not) all clapped under hatches;
> Where, but even now, with strange and several noises
> Of roaring, shrieking, howling, jingling chains,
> And moe diversity of sounds, all horrible,
> We were awak'd; straightway at liberty;
> Where we, in all our trim, freshly beheld
> Our royal, good, and gallant ship, our master
> Cap'ring to eye her. On a trice, so please you,
> Even in a dream, were we divided from them
> And were brought moping hither.
>
> [229–40]

Like so many others, they, too, have had the experience and
missed the meaning. Finally, the trio of low conspirators is
driven in by Ariel, and their treacheries exposed. Caliban with-
draws after anatomizing his own fictive transmutation:

> What a thrice-double ass
> Was I to take this drunkard for a god
> And worship this dull fool!
>
> [296–98]

Yet Prospero's great phrase of acceptance, "this thing of darkness I / Acknowledge mine" (275–76) advises us that Caliban's
withdrawal is only temporary and that his anarchic energies,
though they can be restrained, can never be wholly forgotten.
By contrast Ariel and the whole sphere of the creative imagination which he represents are by necessity released from service; the utility of the dream world has been to regenerate the

company, and that transformation accomplished, the worlds of
art and nature once more diverge. Their intersection has been
momentary but transcendent.

In the superb octasyllabic couplets of the Epilogue, Prospero
once again expresses the identity of reality and vision, the
transforming uses of the world of dream:

> Now my charms are all o'erthrown,
> And what strength I have's mine own,
> Which is most faint. Now 'tis true
> I must be here confined by you,
> Or sent to Naples. . . .
>
>   . . . Now I want
> Spirits to enforce, art to enchant;
> And my ending is despair
> Unless I be relieved by prayer.

[1–5, 13–16]

The speaker is a magician bereft of his magic; he is also, manifestly, an actor who has finished with his part. In the traditional appeal to the audience for applause, there is implicit
the deeper appeal of Paulina's admonition: "It is required /
you do awake your faith." The life of the play is the condition of the dream state, that subjective state in which reason
gives place to imagination. Its existence is momentary and yet
for all time, as the play itself exists in time and beyond it. The
poet in this moment speaks through his character, asserting
the identity of art and dream. His affirmation here, and in the
last plays as a whole, is an acknowledgment of the central role
of the creative imagination, the vital transforming power of
the world of dream in the life of man.

Afterword

> Will it please you to see the epilogue, or to hear a
> Bergomask dance. . . ?
>
> *MND* V.i.351–52

The fantastical Spaniard Don Armado of *Love's Labor's Lost*
explains the poetical form of "the l'envoy" to Moth as "an
epilogue or discourse to make plain / Some obscure precedence" (III.i.81–82). Just as Theseus hastily chose the Ber-
gomask when threatened with an epilogue, so the reader may at
this point wish that I would leave the "obscure precedence" to
history, rather than worrying it further toward a conclusion.
The preceding chapters have attempted to make clear what I
view as the radical significance of dream in Shakespeare's concept of theater, and its crucial relationship to the imaginative
life of man. *The Tempest* itself is so perfect a summation of the
transforming world of dream, its art, its creatures, and its
language, that any further elaboration may seem surely to have
been rendered superfluous. But the language in which we talk
of dream is by its very nature so evanescent, and, like Antony's
clouds, so shifting, that it must sometimes appear like them
"indistinct / As water is in water" (*Ant.* IV.xiv.10–11). It is
therefore with a desire to pin down these wandering shapes,
and not, I hope, to suggest that they may as easily be seen for
camels or weasels as for whales, that I attempt here to sum-
marize what has been said in the foregoing chapters.

When Shakespeare first began to work with concepts of
dream in the plays, he adapted dream conventions to his dramatic needs as well as to his poetic and imagistic design. *Richard III*, which contains by far the largest number of dream references (24) of any Shakespearean play, utilized dreams, omens,
and apparitions as part of a monitory system, so that the play's
structure was forecast by its dream events, and its protagonist's

psychology explored through a series of glimpses into the workings of his mind. This was a fundamentally manipulative use of the dream trope, and one well suited to plays concerned with adumbrating history and character; its predictive component was to be used, in a more polished form, in all the great tragedies of character, from *Romeo and Juliet* to *Antony and Cleopatra*. During his early period of experimentation and development, however, Shakespeare found other uses for dream which led in different, though related, directions. *The Taming of the Shrew*, which wedded the idea of dream to the already extant dramatic device of the induction, suggested the possibility of dream as a kind of play-within-a-play, an interior world of imagination, and further raised the serious question of how we tell dream from reality. *Romeo and Juliet*, through the voice of Mercutio, explored the poetic question of the language of dream, a language of association and image rather than of reason and logic. In *Romeo*, too, we can see the beginnings of Shakespeare's visionary association of dream with *ekphrasis*, transformation into art—an association which was to be further examined and developed in *A Midsummer Night's Dream* and, with special emphasis, in the late romances, where the naturalized or animate artifact—like the shifting clouds observed by Antony—embodies for a moment the creative energy of imagination. *Julius Caesar*, here considered with the early plays because it exemplifies a decided new trend in dream presentation, followed the line of *Richard III* in closely linking predictive dreams with plot, but added a crucial further element, that of interpretation. As dreams moved formally away from the single monitory dream figure and became more fictive and more gnomic, they required interpretation and insight. Here, too, they began to come closer to the form of art: the dream interpreter emerged as a critic, and sometimes a deliberately misleading one. *Julius Caesar* thus introduced the idea of a controller or fabricator of dreams, a concept which would reappear in enriched form later, notably in *Othello*. Dream, in all of these comparatively early plays, was closely related to the elucidation of plot and, at the same time, to the reflexive nature of dramatic structure: the retold dreams predicted future action and also mirrored, in their form and imagery, the larger design of the play around them.

A Midsummer Night's Dream, Shakespeare's first direct examination of the transforming *world* of dream, marks an important new stage in his use of the metaphor of dreaming. In it the worlds of court, faerie, and comic "art" are deliberately interwoven, and the act of dreaming is presented as emphatically creative, though not without its intrinsic dangers. The spirits of this world are very unlike the ghosts which visit Hamlet or Richard III; they are clearly counterparts, not of the "prophetic soul" or the guilty conscience, but rather of the imagination—and, by a slight but secure extension, of poetry itself. The fact that the structures of the court world and the fairy world so clearly mirror one another—so that productions of the play often "double" the roles of Theseus and Oberon, Hippolyta and Titania—is yet another indication that the fairies represent an interior mode of consciousness, concerned with love, madness, and the necessary limits of reason. Transformation in the world of *A Midsummer Night's Dream* becomes a literal reality, as Bottom undergoes a visible metamorphosis, manifesting in outward form his metaphorical conclusion: "man is but an ass, if he go about to expound this dream." It is significant that in this play we are dealing with a specific and separate world of dream, through which characters will pass on their way to their own transformations. The realm of imagination is thus seen as an omnipresent and necessary part of the life of man; often it may control his actions without his conscious knowledge, and the play presents a spectrum of possibilities for the irrational self, ranging from mischievousness and even malignity to the transforming and educative acts of love, poetry, and art. Literal works of art, like "Bottom's Dream" and the "Pyramus and Thisby" play, appear once again as the product of dream, which thus moves closer to poetry as a mode of creative action involved in the making of a new harmonious order. The quicksilver dream world itself is part of a complex which includes the rejection of reason and the making of art, and serves as a transitional state from which the dreamer will emerge, transformed, into a real world of social interaction.

It is a long way from "a wood near Athens" to the castle at Elsinore, and an equally long way from comedy, however interspersed with hints of danger, to the troubled world of the great tragedies. Dream in the tragedies acquires new powers, while continuing to draw upon the fundamental dream usages of earlier plays—the devices of ghost, omen, and prophecy. The dream state here is a state of mind, a subjectivity of vision in the mind of the protagonist, so that the real and the illusory become difficult to distinguish from one another. The ghost of old Hamlet, the witches, and Banquo's ghost—are they real, or imagined? In dramatic terms they have a palpable reality, since they appear upon the stage. But Gertrude does not see the figure of her dead husband, and Banquo's ghost walks for Macbeth alone. The audience is tacitly included in the consciousness of the principal character—as the titles of these plays imply. The quest in the tragedies is overtly a quest for knowledge of self, consciousness, on the part of the protagonist; and the several aspects of the play's dramatic structure—characters, scene, language, and imagery—are to a large extent conceived as metaphors for aspects of the protagonist's persona. The world of the play thus becomes designedly a counterpart of the interior world of consciousness, a variant of what is often referred to as a "landscape of the mind"—here presented not only as a landscape, but also as a populace and a voice. The values placed upon dream in such a dramatic universe are fundamentally psychological: dream reveals character, permits speculation, insight, and self-delusion, and emerges as a kind of extended mode of wish fulfillment, expressing idealized concepts and desires often at variance with political reality. In the late tragedies, and most particularly in *Antony and Cleopatra*, this level of personal revelation is gradually transformed into an explicit act of myth-making; Cleopatra's great evocation of Antony, a godlike hero "past the size of dreaming," is the creation of a dream figure from the realm of the passionate imagination. Where the specter of old Hamlet came from the memory, the historical past, and the darkness of self-conscious thought, the image of Antony, as Cleopatra draws it, transcends historical time and approaches the condition of timelessness and myth. The idea of *ekphrasis* is here merged with history: the tragedies, as plays of consciousness and character, render mortal historical personages into mythic terms, whether those of personal myth (Hamlet, Othello) or incipient cosmology. The motif of the retelling of the tale, verbalized in the closing lines of each of these plays, is part of the pattern of didactic or instructive dream seen as a pathway to transcendence and redemption.

Antony and Cleopatra is the culmination of the dream trope in chronicle and tragedy, the ultimate realization of dream as a metaphoric transition from history to art. Its poetry, its settings, and its superlative characters all embody that faith in the irrational and imaginative which everywhere in Shakespeare separates the magical from the mundane. Yet in the years following *Antony* the romances, and particularly *The Winter's Tale* and *The Tempest*, were to examine the world of dream from yet another perspective, and to lead toward yet another culmination: a culmination which points inward toward the considering mind of the poet, rather than outward toward the pattern of ongoing history. The emphasis of the romances is directly upon metamorphosis and transformation as redemptive acts, and upon the created artifact as it contains and crystallizes insights into the nature of man. Dream in these last plays is closely related to poetry; their dramatic worlds are also dream worlds, in which the magical becomes commonplace, and the tangible realities of time and space may be compressed or extended as in a dream, to encompass the fables they contain. In *Pericles* and *Cymbeline*, *The Winter's Tale* and *The Tempest*, logic and probability have become secondary qualities, giving way to the "rich and strange": the apparent "rebirths" of Thaisa, Imogen, and Hermione are dreamlike occurrences, literal or figurative awakenings in which not only the waker, but also the spectators, are awakened to truths about themselves. Costume and disguise, likewise significant elements of dream, are here brought even more fully into dramatic use; disguises do not so much mask real identities as they reveal them, and the putting on and off of clothing becomes a visible sign of spiritual transformation. Journeys, and especially sea journeys, become literal ventures into a dream landscape in which the improbable becomes, not only the possible, but the true—the lost child is found, the shepherdess becomes a queen. A bear roams the landscape of Bohemia; Ariel and Caliban, visible images of man's divided nature, do not surprise us as they emerge from the fastnesses of Prospero's island. The figure of Time himself, the literal emblem of metamorphosis, appears in the midst of *The Winter's Tale* to "slide / O'er sixteen years"; while in *The Tempest* the fictive time of the drama is deliberately made identical with the time it takes to play it, so that there is no distinction between play and reality. Works of art, too, appear as interchangeable with life, indivisible from nature: Hermione's statue comes alive; the masque in *The Tempest* dissolves before our eyes.

Shakespeare's use of dream in these last plays has become so all-encompassing that dream and life, art and nature, can hardly be separated from one another, and are seen as part of a continuous cycle. Music, art, and, preeminently, poetry are moments out of time, moments which endow experience with a new richness, making us all, like Ferdinand, votaries of wonder. Just as "our little life / Is rounded with a sleep," and thus becomes equivalent to dream, so the life of Shakespearean drama is inextricably interwoven with dream in both form and language. The Athenian lovers found true loves in the forest, and Hamlet confronted his "prophetic soul" in the visionary figure of the ghost; in the romances, Shakespeare confronts his own "so potent art," an art which is indeed past the size of dreaming. The last plays are in their very nature reflexive, as the figure of Prospero suggests. In them the metaphor of dream achieves its fullest maturation and reveals itself, not as metaphor at all, but rather as metamorphosis—not as comparison, but as identity.

Index